Pascoe, Prince of Gobir

by
Ken Lupton

authorHOUSE®

AuthorHouse™ UK Ltd.
500 Avebury Boulevard
Central Milton Keynes, MK9 2BE
www.authorhouse.co.uk
Phone: 08001974150

© 2009 Ken Lupton. All rights reserved.

No part of this book may be reproduced, stored in a retrieval system, or transmitted by any means without the written permission of the author.

First published by AuthorHouse 10/6/2009

ISBN: 978-1-4389-2946-0 (e)
ISBN: 978-1-4389-2945-3 (sc)

Printed in the United States of America
Bloomington, Indiana

This book is printed on acid-free paper.

Foreword

By: Dr. Rilwanu Lukman CFR, KBE, FIC

Dr Lukman is an internationally known and respected figure in the oil and gas industry and has served as former Secretary General of OPEC (2 terms), President of OPEC several times, Nigerian Minister of Petroleum Resources, Special Adviser to the Nigerian President for Oil and Gas, Nigerian Minister of Foreign Affairs, Nigerian Minister of Mines, and has been honoured in the UK with the KBE, in France with the Legion of Honour and in Venezuela with the Order of the Liberator and, In his native country with the Commander of the Federal Republic CFR.

Dr Lukman had received various honourary awards from prestigious institutions around the World and, among these are the honourary DSc of the Universities of Ahmadu Bello and Maiduguri and Benin in Nigeria and, a PhD from the oldest European University of Bologna in Italy as well as another Doctorate from Moorehouse College in Atlanta, USA. He had also been honoured with Fellowship of the Imperial College, his alma mater.

I am pleased to endorse this book by my friend, and family friend, Ken Lupton OBE, who I have known for over fifty years since I was student and boy scout.

This is a sequel to his book 'Mungo Park', the African Traveler,(OUP 1979), which showed his deep study of the period, and it is flavoured at points by his imagination.

The genesis of the book lay in Ken's personal discovery in the British National Archives of an unknown document written in 1823, giving a detailed description of Hausa land in Northern Nigeria and an assessment of it's informant, Abubakar or William Pascoe, markedly different from a jaundiced account of him already known. Pascoe is not a hero or a paragon but lived his venturesome life through almost endless difficulties in which his character grew including long service in the British Royal Navy and much travelling.

His life began about the time when Britain abandoned it's long standing and remunerative trading in human beings treated as a form of cattle, but the continuation of slavery by many peoples constituted a continuing thread throughout this life, including a probably short period of enslavement and culminating in his witnessing a gruesome by product of the slave trade.

I believe the work presents a credible and balanced account of an Africa long ago, including it's early encounters with Europeans.

Ken Lupton spent 35 years living and working in Nigeria for her governments and universities. I believe that with his deep study of the period he is well qualified to write this book.

As for himself, born 1927, he was a bachelor until at the age of 72 he suddenly married the widowed love of his life, Sheila,(nee Holt,later Taylor). He now boasts a step-daughter Patricia Nunn, the daughter-he-never- had and his Nigerian son he-never-had, Gambo Adamu, raised from childhood.

A readable and intriguing exploratory work by Ken, I commend this book to anyone interest in old Africa.

Table of Contents

Foreword	v
Preface	xi
Introduction	xv
Illustrations	xxiii

Part One

Chapter 1 — Who is Pascoe?	1
Chapter 2 — Abubakar Becomes Pascoe	11
Chapter 3 — Belzoni	25
Chapter 4 — The Niger Expedition Begins	39
Chapter 5 — At Katanga	59
Chapter 6 — Bitter Honey	71
Chapter 7 — Over The Niger and on to Kano	89
Chapter 8 — Bad Spirits	103
Chapter 9 — In the Depths	121
Chapter 10 — Recovering Some Hope	135
Chapter 11 — At Peace Together	159
Chapter 12 — Parting	175

Part Two

Chapter 13 — A New Start   193

Chapter 14 — Farewell to Bussa and Wawa   209

Chapter 15 — Going with the Stream   223

Chapter 16 — Captivity… and Freedom   245

Chapter 17 — On the Niger with Captain Lander   269

    Afterword   287

    Hausa Glossary   301

    Appendix 1 — Unknown Report by John Evans on Hausaland in Nigeria and Pascoe in 1823   305

    Appendix 2 — How the Author Discovered Evans's Report   323

Preface

I thank the National Archives (formerly Public Record Office) for access to much useful information, and permission to quote from their records. The Navy Lists of the period show each ship's station and principal officers, published quarterly in both war and peace. Crews were listed in the detailed Muster Lists for each vessel, written up every two months and unlikely to omit anyone aboard in any capacity, as they were used to account for all wages and other expenses. Pascoe has been found from 1818 onwards. With crews paid off at the end of each voyage, rarely were sailors' previous ships shown, and there were over 700 vessels on the Navy Lists. Few Africans were included in the early lists. Captains' logs sometimes helped with ships' movements, for example on Pascoe's rescue after Belzoni's death. Colonial Office files (CO 2 series) in the National Archives also helped.

I owe a special debt to my late friend Ken Breen, who taught history at St. Mary's College, Twickenham and had a special interest in the navy of the relevant period. His hospitality and advice led me from a reference in The Times of 25th April 1824, praising a Captain Filmore for his help to Belzoni in linking him with 'a native of Houssa' to the file ADM/1/1815 containing Filmore's report to the Admiralty on his duties, in which he mentioned that his vessel had transported 'the famous Belzoni'. Attached to it were the letters exchanged between Belzoni and Filmore and, as a bonus, John Evans's previously unknown 15 page report on African exploration, the Hausa lands and Pascoe. Its sharp divergences from Lander's account of Pascoe in his book prompted this book.

Liza Verity, Information Specialist of the National Maritime Museum, and Eugene Rowe, Librarian of the Royal Geographical Society, have given help. Professor Sambo Junaidu of the Usman Danfodio University, Sokoto, Mrs. Jean Boyd and David Hogarth have helped concerning Nigerian geography. Especially useful have been some books consulted, Hugh Thomas's 'The Atlantic Slave Trade', Janet Macdonald's 'Feeding Nelson's Navy', Brian Lavery's 'Nelson's Navy: the ships, the men and the organisation 1793-1815', Mercedes Mackay's 'The Indomitable Servant', Paul E. Lovejoy's 'Caravans of Kola. The Hausa Kola Trade, 1700-1900', and 'Hugh Clapperton into the Interior of Africa' edited by Jamie Bruce Lockhart and Paul E. Lovejoy. The Journals of Hugh Clapperton (first and second expeditions), Richard Lander, Richard and John Lander, Macgregor Laird and R.A.K. Oldfield and Captains H.D. Trotter R.N. and William Allen R.N and Richard Lander's book 'Records of Captain Clapperton's Last Expedition to Africa' have all been consulted. My thanks to the National Portrait Gallery, Edinburgh for allowing the inclusion of Clapperton's portrait, and to Frank Cass and Co. Limited in respect of Lander's portrait and his 'Ordeal by Poison.'

    I thank my friend John Smith C.B.E. for kindly reading and correcting my script and giving me other advice, my niece Isobel Garlick, Carly Nunn for the map, Jim Jackson for help with computing and others who have helped in preparing this book. Any errors are my own.

Introduction

A man named William Pascoe who had up to fifteen years service in the British Royal Navy, by 1823 and had been promoted from Landsman to Ordinary and finally to Able Bodied Seaman was, surprisingly, an African. Occasionally African coastal families sent sons to England to learn how to run an overseas business. Someone who had been through slavery in the New World but emancipated by a philanthropic master or otherwise might rarely obtain some standing in Britain. Yet at a time when Britain had no prospect of increasing its minute footholds in West Africa, for the Navy to employ someone from inland Africa over a long period with apparent satisfaction at least was something out of the ordinary.

Before entering the Navy he came from an important city in what is now the northern part of Nigeria populated by many Hausa people, their language widespread in West

Africa and known on. the Mediterranean coast at Tripoli, Libya, probably since earlier times. As well as a centre of government it was a major market town where agriculture and trade blended. Each such city had a mud-built wall up to thirty or even forty feet high atop which soldiers could move and if necessary fight across it. It might have a circumference up to ten or fifteen miles, enclosing far more farming than built-up land, but in villages within it sight or smell could detect smaller domestic crops such as spices or gourds. Horses and asses could be seen or heard, goats would be tethered before harvest and chickens scrabbled about. Among the warren of bare earth streets and passages either mud-roofed or thatched houses consisted of one, or more commonly several huts surrounded by high fences or walls, with a large entrance room where the householder at leisure could sit and receive visitors. Dotted among the houses, or frequently part of them, were the workshops of weavers, tailors, carpenters, leather workers and other craftsmen. Somewhat secluded were odorous dye pits and tanneries. The land was well-wooded, even within the city boundaries, and all trees yielding useful fruits or flavours were particularly cared for. Fruits grown included figs, melons, bananas, pomegranates, pawpaws and limes, and vines had been common until the newer Muslim rulers had them cut down. As well as foodstuffs cotton growing was widespread. There were some schools where boys were taught to read and write in Arabic, memorising and chanting the Koran. A minority might also learn to write Hausa in an Arabic-based script called *ajami* . Traditional festivals and ceremonies might easily mix with some formal religion, a sore point with strict Muslims.

Coming from such a background and having taken the momentous step of entering the navy, the fact that such a lowly seaman as Pascoe flickered into British recorded history was due to a series of coincidences. Firstly, while serving that year in HMS *Owen Glendower*, flagship of a small anti-slavery flotilla off Africa, there happened to be an Admiralty Clerk on board called John Evans. Aged 26, he was clearly well-educated, intelligent, interested in the little than known about the African interior and its exploration, and willing to take the trouble to learn about Pascoe, his background and even some elements of his language. Secondly, this happened to be the ship which gave a lift to a man called Giovanni Belzoni, who wanted to be the first European to visit the famed desert city of Timbuktu, having been frustrated in an earlier attempt to go from Morocco. He had previously been a hydrological engineer, actor, and most recently one of the first Egyptologists, well known for exposing from the sand built up over 3,000 years Rameses II's great temples at Abu Simbel, then heard of locally as a legendary Ysambul. Doubtless Evans introduced Pascoe to Belzoni, and the two set off together to start from Benin, but Belzoni's death soon ended his venture and Pascoe found himself back in the navy. Thirdly, when the captain of the *Owen Glendower* included a mention of transporting Belzoni in his report on his official duties and attached a copy of a report on Pascoe by John Evans, this would naturally have gone to John (later Sir John) Barrow, the Second Secretary or civil service head of the Admiralty, who happened to be the chief sponsor of African exploration in that period. Finally, when a naval officer called Lieutenant Hugh Clapperton, immediately on returning home in 1825 after crossing the Sahara Desert from Tripoli into West Africa, wanted to be off again immediately for a new journey from the West African coast, both his naval rank and his exploration keenness would naturally have taken him to Second Secretary Barrow, who would soon edit Clapperton's Journal. In the result Pascoe was engaged as a servant and interpreter to Clapperton's new expedition.

By the time the expedition set off in 1825 Europe's knowledge of West Africa was at a tantalising, inconclusive stage. Mungo Park, sent by the London-based African Association for exploration, had seen the upper River Niger in 1795-7 and reported on it, previously a mystery to Europe. The Journal of his Government-sponsored second attempt in 1805 covered only his journey from the coast to the river. When published in 1812 it had an added report by his guide down the river nearly to his death at Bussa in present-day Nigeria. It inevitably lacked a conclusion and left things open to various theories, especially as the guide's report was misinterpreted by some as covering a distance of only 100 miles from the starting point on the river, instead of the actual over 1,000 miles. Major Rennell, the chief African geographer of the day in Britain, believed that what he called the Kong Mountains stretched right across Africa and prevented the river turning south into the Bight of Benin, part of the Atlantic Ocean: to him the river must end in a large lake or swamp which he placed north of where Lake Chad actually is. Others held that the Niger crossed Africa eastwards to join the Nile, notably John Barrow who clung to this theory, come what may. A third theory which Park possibly accepted was that the Niger, then reported only in its upper portion, ended far to the south as the River Congo, which had a large river mouth but no known river behind it. The fourth –and correct – theory that the Niger *did* turn south into the Bight of Benin received little support. To be fair to Barrow, he did show among several possibilities for the Niger's route in the map printed with Clapperton's Journal the latter's hypothesis that it came out at Benin, but it is unlikely Clapperton argued this with the dogmatic Barrow.

After the conclusion of the Napoleonic War in 1815 the British Government sent expeditions to both the mouth of the Rive r Congo and from Senegal on the western Atlantic coast to the Niger. The Congo expedition was defeated by finding then impassable cataracts and heavy losses from disease. After two commanders had died the Senegal expedition of 1818to

1821 under Major Grey and Staff Surgeon Dochard failed to overcome diplomatic obstruction by the African states, and did not penetrate even as far along the Niger as Mungo Park had done in his first journey. Its report was not published until 1825.

Coming from Tripoli Joseph Ritchie served as British Vice-Consul at Murzuk in southern Libya in 1817-8. Accompanied by Captain George Lyon R.N. but immobilized by a largely self-inflicted lack of resources, they collected some good second-hand information after local explorations, before Ritchie died and Lyon left some time later. What they heard of a river that might be the Niger inaccurately pointed to its heading eastwards, as favoured by Rennell's and Barrow's theories. Lyon also heard that Hausaland in general had been conquered by a Fulani leader Sultan Bello, later learnt to be the outcome of a religiously-inspired rising started by the Sultan's father in 1804.

The German Hornemann, sponsored by the British African Association, had written from Murzuk when he was there in 1798, sending a sketch map showing there were several Hausa states in approximately their correct relative positions, although unfortunately supporting the Niger-Nile junction theory. This should have corrected the mistaken idea in Europe that Hausa was a single kingdom with Katsina as its capital, but it does not seem to have been grasped. Until Pascoe's time Katsina, a name known in England, had been a leading state but not supreme over the others. Lyon could report much later that he had heard that Hornemann had crossed the Sahara to Bornu, a major state adjoining Lake Chad, to Katsina and even beyond, before dying in Nigeria.

Clapperton's cross-Sahara journey was the most productive yet, made with Major Dixon Denham and Dr. Oudney. After some time all together in Bornu he went westwards. Dr. Oudney soon died but Clapperton went alone to the newish Fulani/Hausa capital of Sokoto, where he had been well received by Sultan Bello as an ambassador, and encouraged to come again from the coast to the south. A great advance in knowledge but it still left for someone to settle the two main questions exercising thought in Europe: What was Timbuktu with its reputed riches really like? And how did the River Niger end? Clapperton was in a hurry to start on a new journey mainly to forestall a Major Laing who had just left Tripoli for Timbuktu and then, the latter hoped, the Niger and the answers to both questions.

In this whole period slavery was embedded in African life, and the Atlantic Slave Trade resisted efforts to end it in spite of the British Abolition Act effective from 1808. This story shows that Portuguese slave ships were still active in 1826, and that was not the end. Badagry, where Clapperton's expedition began, had little purpose then apart from a convenient creek in which slaves could be hidden until ready to be shipped to Brazil. As late as 1954 the author had his hair cut in Nigeria by a man born as a slave in Brazil just before the final abolition under 70 years before. Pascoe himself may have been on the way to such a life in Brazil at one time: certainly he was later involved in British efforts to stop the trade, which framed his whole career.

A fortunate person who could announce himself as 'the only surviving member of the (Clapperton's) expedition' on the title page of his subsequent book was called Richard Lander aged 21 when they set off. He was originally appointed as a personal servant, in effect a batman or valet to Clapperton, 16 or 17 years his senior. After spending 2 ½ years with Pascoe, another survivor but not seen as a 'member' of the expedition, Lander was unflattering – perhaps scathing would be a more accurate word – in his book, but he must have had mixed feelings as he re-engaged Pascoe for two later journeys.

Until now Lander's account of Pascoe has stood alone but (again by a series of coincidences) John Evans's independent account has come to view after lying, presumably unseen, in the naval records for 170 years. The differences are startling, as will be shown. To take here just one point: in 1823 the naval records and Evans's account gave Pascoe's age as 34 years. Two years later Lander reckoned he was 60 or more! We shall be looking into this and other divergences and trying to reconstruct Pascoe' actual life and record.

Illustrations

1.   A Palaver. Trotter & Allen book 1848 (copied from Allen of 1840) (Pascoe probably left, rear, facing the artist)

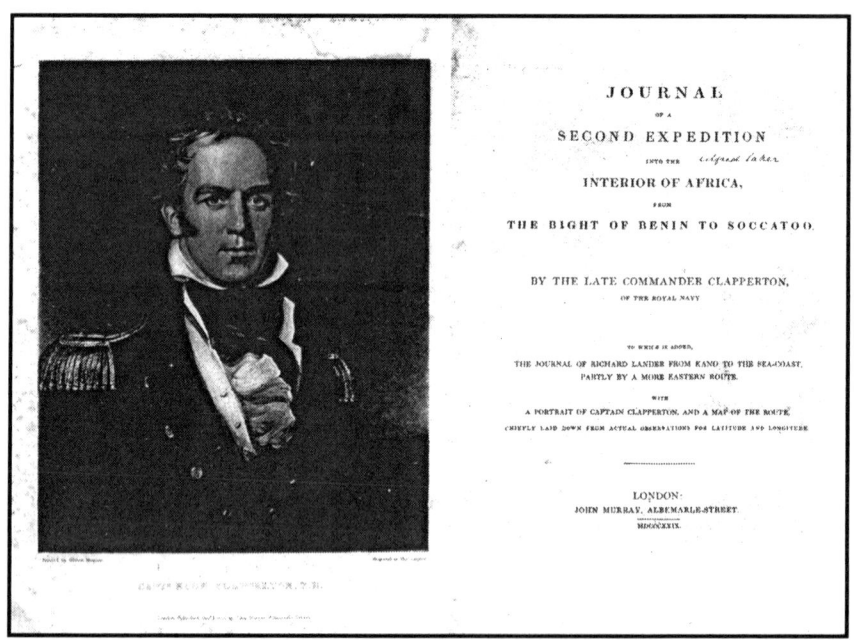

2. Captain Hugh Clapperton R.N. Narrative of Travels 1826 (Original portrait in National Portrait Gallery, Edinburgh)

3. Richard Lander. Richard and John Lander's journal 1832

4. Giovanni Belzoni (from his 'narrative of discoveries in ... Egypt, 1821)

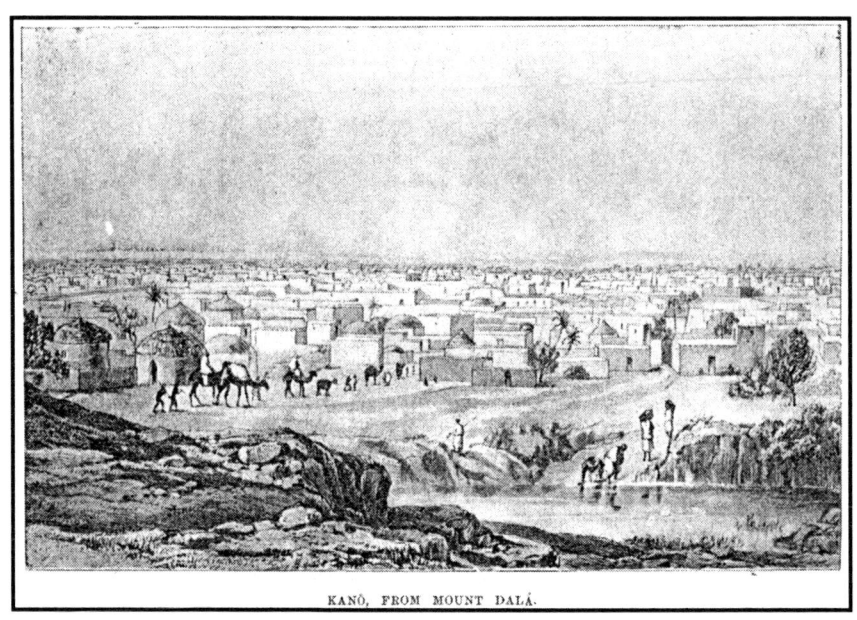

5. Kano from Dala hill Barth's book (1865) "Travels and Discoveries in Central and Northern Africa", Ward Lock edition, (1890.)

6. Market of Sokoto, Barth's book

7. Confluence of Niger and Tshadda (Benue), Trotter & Allen 1848

8.   Crossing the bar Trotter & Allen 1848

9. The Quorra aground below the confluence. Laird & Oldfield 1837

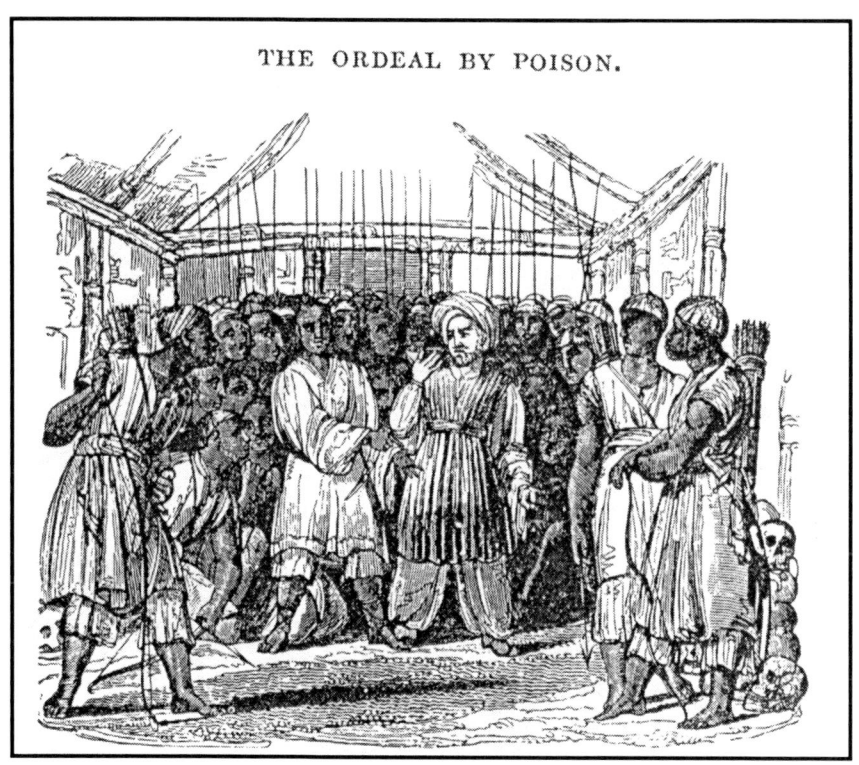

10. The Ordeal by Poison. (from Lander, Clapperton's Last Expedition, 1830, Cass reprint)

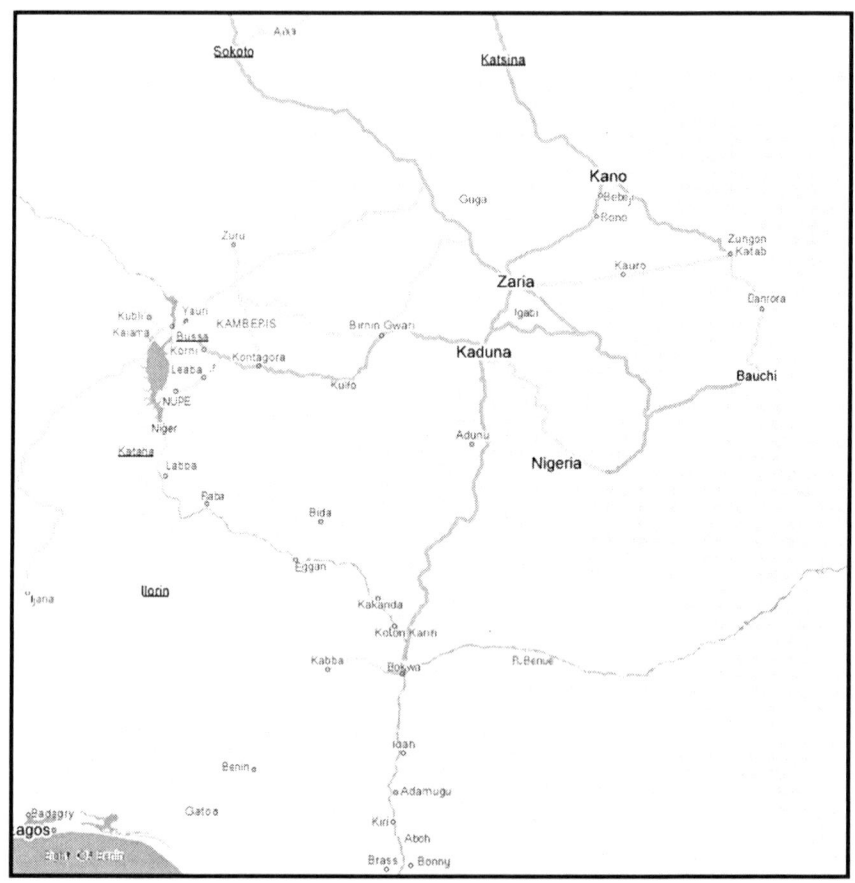

11. Map of the area of present day Nigeria, as known to Pascoe.

xxxii

Part One

Chapter 1 — Who is Pascoe?

John Evans, Admiralty Clerk, aboard HMS *Owen Glendower*, April 1823

At last I have been able to complete a task I have set myself since I joined this ship last November, to learn more about a country far in unknown Africa. I have long been interested in exploration and I had hoped to discover how the famous River Niger, which Mr. Mungo Park saw and told us about, reaches its end somewhere. What Mr. Ritchie, our late Consul in Murzuk, far to the north, wrote a few years ago agrees with what I have learnt, but it leaves us ignorant of the river's end.

What I have now been told does not go far enough, but I hope it may help others to unlock the secret. The source of my information has been an African seaman we know as William Pascoe, although his original name was Abubakar, and it was my good fortune to be on the same vessel as him. I doubt that any of my colleagues as Admiralty Clerk on another ship has had a similar opportunity. He is aged, as far as we can tell, about 34 years, and he came into the Royal Navy as a volunteer up to 15 years ago. By his good service he has risen to become an Able Bodied Seaman. I first questioned him when carrying out my regular two-monthly duty of entering all persons aboard in the Muster List. From there, it was a simple matter to progress gradually to enquire more about himself and his country Katsina. My not being a ship's officer made it easier for me to talk with him.

Pascoe speaks our language sufficiently to enable him to explain his ideas with facility and the veracity of his account cannot be doubted. I have kept careful notes on many matters, including words and phrases in his language. These took me some time to elucidate. There is no dictionary or grammar book I can refer to, and I do not think anyone has yet studied Hausa, as the language is called along with the people who speak it and their whole kingdom. Mr. Ritchie was told that one Bello had in recent years made himself master of the kingdom, being Sultan of a separate people called the Fulani.

Now I believe I have obtained enough information to enable me to prepare a report. I shall present a copy to our Captain, Commodore Sir Robert Mends, and I hope that at some suitable opportunity he may be able to forward this to the Admiralty, where I know that the Second Secretary, Mr. Barrow, is himself desirous of furthering African exploration.

I am confident that, after studying my information, it will be evident that while we remain less informed about Africa than Ptolemy and other ancient geographers, more valuable information may be obtained from natives of Hausa and Bornu than by all the travellers who have attempted to penetrate with bodies of white men from the shores of the Mediterranean. Such natives, carried to Sierra Leone, could be educated when young and given suitable inducements to travel in these regions, which Pascoe's narrative has shown not to be difficult, and then return with fresh information. This would be more effective and less costly.

When talking with Pascoe he showed how anxious he is to return to his hometown and country. Above all, he said his mind kept returning to the one he had loved then but had been unable to marry. In April last year, while serving in HMS *Iphigenia* , also commanded by Sir Robert Mends, he had some converse with slaves released from a Portuguese slaver captured off Lagos, 175 people crammed into the hold of a 100-ton vessel. Some were natives of his hometown Katsina, and they told him that a young woman to whom he was attached in his youth and who had been betrothed to him was still single. She had refused several advantageous offers, firmly believing that the object of her early affections was alive, and would one day return and claim her as his bride.

This is an instance of female constancy to which few parallels can be found in more polished regions. It must be confessed by all those who have the pleasure of his acquaintance that Pascoe, by his good qualities, is fully deserving of such an attachment. I hope that his *Dulcinea* may not be disappointed, though I fear that, with him not knowing Cervantes or Don Quixote, this particular reference would be lost on him!.

Richard Lander, London 1828

Dear Brother John,

I greatly appreciate the help you have given me in preparing my Journal for publication with the account of the travels of the late Captain Clapperton. As you know we went from the west coast of Africa into the interior, as far as the city of Sokoto, which he had visited before,. and where, to my great sorrow, the Captain died and was buried. As the only surviving member of the expedition I was able to get to the coast and then back to England, with the Captain's Journal and belongings. Your help has been particularly great in matters of spelling and punctuation in which, due to my limited schooling, I have always been weak. While I am striving to improve, your continued assistance is important to me.

Pascoe, Prince of Gobir

You have also been aiding me in starting to write my new book on this journey. There is one aspect to which I have given much thought but on which I would like to ask your advice. This concerns Pascoe, our interpreter, who was with me on this entire journey, and who I have now sent back to Africa. I believe he has settled at Cape Coast, by the Castle which is the centre of British Government and trade, where the Governor gave land for him, my two freed slaves Jaudi and Abuda and his final wife from our journey, Miriamu As you are aware, he was often a source of trouble to me. After the Captain had left me in charge at Kano Pascoe disregarded my instructions and ran away twice, taking my belongings. What was most annoying was that he gave no explanation, nor did what little he said make any sense to me. The authorities at Kano were very helpful to me, but on my journey to Sokoto he ran away again with my possessions and provided little sensible reason for his actions. I had to report to the Captain who dismissed him, but he was subsequently reinstated when the Captain was gravely ill and I needed assistance. It is true, however, that he was sometimes a source of amusement to me, lacking all seriousness and responsibility in both his story-telling and his dealings with the fair sex. Here is the gist of what I propose to write about him, but perhaps you can help me express my opinions in more elegant phrases.

Pascoe's original name was Abubakar, without doubt a Muslim name, but he only knew of Islam by name, being in reality a pagan. He came from a country called Gobir and he told me a fanciful tale about his ancestry there. He also told me, with reluctance, about a series of troubles largely of his own making that led to him to be enslaved, freed by a Royal Navy vessel and then inducted into the Navy. He might have been aged about sixty years but looked considerably older.

He was only about five feet tall but with extremely long arms and legs. One leg was in fact shorter then the other but for the most part he could move around without difficulty. His face was open and expressive but not handsome, with a very flat nose, broad lips and a perpetual grin from ear to ear, which exposed pearly white teeth. However, his eye tended to wander, giving him the expression of low cunning and restlessness. I could not help feeling that there was some evil in him, which he tried to hide by appearing stupid and careless, when in reality these did not belong to his disposition.

In spite of Pascoe's plain appearance he had a strange belief that every woman, whoever she was and wherever she came from, must love him on first sight. As a result he did not always conduct himself in relation to them in a civil and agreeable manner, like other gallants, but demanded from them favours that other men entreated and sighed for. In his opinion at least his advances were never repelled from coldness or disdain.

I will write later about other aspects of our travels together and his conduct, but this one has given me great concern about the terms in which I may properly put it in writing. This is why I seek your advice and assistance.

I am, dear Brother, your loving Richard.

Those two statements clearly bring out the wide divergences between John Evans and Richard Lander.

Was Pascoe aged 34 in 1823, as stated by Evans, therefore born about 1789, in *Katsina* kingdom, a long-serving *volunteer* in the British Royal Navy, of good character as shown by his promotion and Evans's report that '*his veracity cannot be doubted*' and that '*all those who have the pleasure of his acquaintance*' could see him '*fully deserving…….by his good qualities*' of a lasting devotion from one he had been unable to marry?.

Or was he, as described by Lander, aged 60 or more in 1825 or 1826, thus born a quarter of a century earlier, around 1765, in *Gobir*, a separate state from Katsina and later only a district in that state and about 100 miles to the west, sometimes hostile, a man who through a self-induced set of troubles *had been enslaved, and who enlisted in the British Navy only after being rescued* by a British ship, showing '*low cunning*' and appearing to have '*some evil*' in him, deliberately concealed by feigning to be '*stupid and careless*' and who was an ardent womaniser?

One thing is certain: both accounts were of the same man, proved by his documented going first with Belzoni and later with Clapperton. There is agreement on one thing at least – at 5 feet tall Pascoe was 'short in stature' Unfortunately the naval record did not comment on Pascoe's grin!

Evans's report on Pascoe and the writings of Clapperton and the Landers have been closely followed but not always in the form they presented them, and their judgments and the correctness of their information have not always been accepted. The 'quoted' contents of Evans's diary, Lander's letter to his brother and Barrows remarks to Clapperton have foundations in fact, even if the actual existence of these documents is conjectural! There are certainly some errors in what Evans wrote, such as there having been many stone-built houses in Katsina, and on the order of crossing the rivers during Pascoe's journey from there to Lagos. It is difficult if not impossible now to identify all the places on the way. However, Evans's taking trouble to get some Hausa expressions right long before the language had been studied or recorded commands confidence in most of his information, even if he was beguiled by Pascoe's little tale about his old beloved!

I have followed some ships' records in giving his name as 'William Pascoe', which Barrow abbreviated to the surname only in editing the Journals of Clapperton and Lander. . Other ships' records and John Evans used the less common form 'William Pasco' On his own Richard Lander was very variable. His manuscript Journal of the boat trip down the Niger with his brother and their joint final book varied between Pascoe and Paskoe. In his own book he always used Pasko. All the main characters in the book were real people, their names as well as place names being given, as far as possible, in modern form. , Only two personal names have been invented, both of women's names not given by Lander, Yetunde, Pascoe's first wife who deserted him at Katanga but later showed up again, and Miriamu, the slave wife he had from Kano.

As regards naval officers' ranks then, either Post Captains, the most senior below Rear Admirals, or Commanders below them, were commonly addressed as 'Captain', as Clapperton was after being promoted from Lieutenant. Sir Robert Mends commanding the *Owen Glendower* was a Post Captain in rank, with the position when heading a flotilla of Commodore, but this was not a rank.

It is unlikely that Pascoe, returning to areas he originated from, had initially any sense of being a member of an *exploring* expedition. While doubtfully a hero he deserves a better reputation than he has had. This book is inevitably partly fictional, as Pascoe's views and feelings are scantily recorded, and details of his personal circumstances when young have largely to be reconstructed from hints and general conditions. It is, however, probably the nearest approach yet to retelling a life of one regarded at the time as a mere African auxiliary to an exploring expedition.

Chapter 2 —
Abubakar Becomes Pascoe

As I think things over, I remember that the first question Mr. Evans asked me was 'What, er, um, is your name back home?' I said, 'I was Abubakar but now I am Pascoe.' He looked pleased and he could see I was also pleased, as I smiled. This made it easier for him to go on. He told me that people in his country knew little about Africa. He had learned as much as he could by reading about men who had come exploring, as he put it, but there was still much that people do not yet know. I agreed that he could ask me more about myself and where I came from another time. I smiled again and we left things there for the time being.

I like Mr. Evans and he seems to like me. He is not a ship's officer which makes it easier for him to speak to me, and he is a nice, quiet man. I do not see him giving loud orders to anyone. He is not like a seaman and I cannot see him climbing a mast to fix or reef a sail, or eating like us, or being punished as seamen sometimes are. His work is writing, writing, writing, and those who know him better say he is good at it. I can not really tell, as I cannot read or write, except that a friend taught me to sign my name.

I know that he wants to hear about my country, especially about a big river they call the Niger. I have told him about some big rivers I have seen but I do not know if one of them is really the Niger. He has been talking to me for many days, one day about this and another day about that. He always gives me time to think before I answer. Sometimes, if something is a little hard for him to say, he will hesitate and keep saying 'er, um'. It sounds funny but I do not laugh when I am with him, as I want us to stay friends.

One time he asked me about my home town and I said I came from *Birnin* Katsina He could not understand this at first .but in the end he saw that when I said that a place was called *Birnin* somewhere I meant the town with that name. So I came from the town of Katsina. Later I told him about other places like *Birnin* Bornu. He then asked me, ' How large, er, um, is this town Katsina?'. I replied, 'It is not easy for me to say, as I do not know how many people live there, but they are very many. It is one of the biggest places I know in Africa. When I thought for a moment I added, 'I can speak of Freetown which both of us have seen. I think Katsina is twenty times as big.'

One thing he wanted to know is whether, as people in England believed (for they had in fact heard of Katsina, as I was surprised to hear) was whether it stands on the banks of a large river which might be the Niger. 'No,' I replied, 'there is a small river from which the town gets water, but the nearest large river is three or four days' journey away.' Katsina stands in a large plain with no high mountains but many of the houses are built of stone, most of them just one floor high.

Going west from Katsina towards the setting sun is Zamfara at three days' distance, and two days beyond that is Alkalai, the capital of a country called Gobir, which is built on both sides of a big river. I knew that it had resisted Bello, the Fulani man who made himself king of the Hausa people, until he managed to conquer it, but that was years since. Some of these Fulani live in a town called Zulimi, one day westward of Katsina, white men with long hair and beards. They are very warlike. They live in huts made of mud and branches of trees, and they often move their houses. They go with their cattle which move in the wet and dry seasons.

In some other towns you find other white men with beards who we call *Turawan Gabas,* or white men from the east, Arabs or Moors. They wear cloths round their heads and have long beards They sell our people salt which they bring from a far country on camels, and we pay them with the cowries or shell money which are used in our country. I have seen dollars with these men but they are not in use as in Sierra Leone.

I do not know countries to the east or sun rising of Katsina, such as *Birnin* Bornu, fifteen days away, or Daura, half-way there, as I have never been there. *Birnin* Bornu is said to be much larger than Katsina, and they speak a different language there. My grandfather used to go here often He was a strong man and, as it is said in our country, 'One hell of a fellow!'

Mr. Evans asked me what our country produces on its farms, and I told him rice, guinea corn and yams. When it came to fruits I said, 'That is hard for me to answer, as some of our fruits are not the same as you will find in England, and I do not know what the white men call some of them. But I think I can say something like grapes, figs, apples, peaches, lemons and oranges' He asked if there were coconuts but I said I had never seen them until I came near the sea. He said that seemed right; some people had talked of coconuts at Timbuktu, but those who knew about things said they would only live near the sea. I said we do not have wine, but we make a strong spirit from guinea corn, our favourite drink. Our domestic animals are sheep, oxen, camels and horses, of which there are very many.

The king's palace at Katsina is very, very big, as large as all Freetown in Sierra Leone. The king when I left Katsina was called Agu Raji The king has a large army, both on horses and on foot. They use spears, bows and arrows, but not many guns. Elephants carry baggage when the army goes to fight.

We are Muslims. The imams in Katsina are many and there are fifty mosques there. All boys are circumcised, and they also have several lines cut on the face from the ear to the mouth, as you can see on me. As for our marriages, I can say, 'More wives a man have, more gentleman he be,' as the Hausa saying might be in English.

Our people make cloths, not wide cloths as you make in England just narrow cloths which we join together to make gowns. Gold is found in small lumps in the hills and is sold to the Arabs to buy salt. Many slaves are sent to the coast to be sold. A great item of trade brought north is cola nuts, very common amongst Africans. Some people travel for days with no food but its bitter juice. It comes from a country called Gonja which is south, towards the sea

By this time we had talked very much over many days, and I thought we had finished, but I found there was more he wanted to ask me about. When we met again he asked me how I had come down to the sea and along to Cape Coast and how I had enlisted in the Navy. I said that at the beginning I had travelled with about forty Hausa traders. I think I was about sixteen years of age at that time, but I can not be sure. Some traders had skins of goats or cows to sell, others slaves taken from local wars, roped together and closely guarded. Some of these would not be sold until we reached the coast, others to people we met on the way who would probably sell them again. All would want to buy and bring back cola nuts and things the white men brought. We were mainly going southwards but partly to the west as many trade routes go. Most of the caravan had horses or asses to ride. Usually we did not go over twenty five miles a day and we rested both at night and in the hottest part of the day. Such trading parties as ours were often seen in the towns and villages we passed through, and they provided us with accommodation and food free, as they welcomed our trade.

Four days after setting out we crossed a large river called the *Kwara Ruwan Dadi* or river of fresh water. We went over it in canoes, it being wider here than the river Gambia at its mouth. In spite of its name the water of this river is muddy and full of insects, not good to drink. It flows southwards and comes from the country of Gobir. Five days later we arrived at the banks of another river, deeper and broader, called the *Gulbin Gagari*. This could be what you call the Niger. It comes from Timbuktu, through Alkalai in Gobir, then through Zamfara, Nupe and Gwari, to a place called Zurum near Kaba, where the *Kwara Ruwan Dadi* joins it. The water of this river tastes salty and there are many hippopotami and crocodiles in it. We crossed the *Gulbi* at a place called Affo,, paying a canoe fare of three cowries each. Going on south for several days we saw some mountains one of which, called Wasony, is much higher than the rest, with a top white like marble. We saw many eagles there. We then crossed a small river called Eko and came down to a town of the same name by the sea, a town the white men call Lagos. Hundreds of people are sent each year from there to America as slaves.

We then turned along the coast towards the setting sun with the sea on our left hand. It took ten more days to reach Cape Coast. It had been a peaceful journey with no troubles on the way. 'So,' Mr. Evans said to me, 'er, um, this was the end of your journey and this was the place where you entered the Royal Navy, was it? Surely you had never been to sea and could not know what life at sea would be like?' 'Yes,' I replied, 'but…' At this point we were interrupted by a message calling him to the Captain on the bridge, and we could not continue further that day.

After Mr. Evans was called away I thought to myself, 'Just a minute, this was only one of a number of trading journeys I made, not the one when I joined the Navy. At the age of sixteen, with forty other men, most of them older, when I had never been to sea and did not know a word of English, I could hardly run off and join a ship just like that, could I?' That happened years later. When we came back from that first trip our family moved from Katsina to Gobir where my grandfather came from. There were some brothers there with places at the king's court. From Gobir after we had harvested our millet and guinea corn we went on trading trips most years, either to the coast or to Gonja to buy cola nuts. Many of our people do that after the harvest: we call it in our own language 'eating the dry season'. I could have told Mr. Evans much more if we had had more time. He may have thought I was speaking only of journeys from Katsina but later we went from Gobir. Some time I could tell you a lot about our life in both these places.

    We had various things to sell when we went south. Gowns made by our people were much liked by those to the south, and cloth caps for the head. Many of our people in Katsina made leather skins for holding water, also red or yellow cushions and horse bridles. Such things were made of either cow or goat skins. Such leather goods were also sold to the Arabs going north over the desert to sell in their countries and the white men sometimes buy them and know them as Morocco leather. Our gowns and dried meat were also made and sold to these Arabs. We also used to take south some of the goods brought to us from the desert to the north. You would be surprised how many things we could load on an ass, and we rarely had to take anything back because we could not sell it. Things we had to buy from the south to take back for trade were cola nuts and things the white men brought such as fine clothes and metal goods, plates and cups and other things. Often we did not need to buy much for ourselves on the journey, except food and perhaps soup cooked in the market for two or three cowries.

The same families might come each year under a known caravan leader who gave us a sign when he saw the stars and prayers as favourable. Each family gave him some goods as presents to give to various chiefs on the way. We dealt mainly with the Hausa people who had settled in the towns we would go through. When I began we used to go to the cola nut areas and then further on beyond them but later they would not let us go further on past Gonja. Some other times we went by other routes down to the coast. I used to play games with other young men in the caravan, games like what children in England call tag or hide and seek If we took care the elders did not see us, we could have fun with the girls in the villages too!

Some years my brothers and, I must admit, myself once or twice, had some slaves to sell. Then I came in the Navy and now we catch slave ships, sending the slaves to be freed in Sierra Leone. I have seen how bad it is for these slaves on those ships and now I hate this business. For me to say now to Mr. Evans that I could sell these poor people would be too, too shameful. Mr. Evans would see me as a bad man. So I have decided I cannot talk to him about such things. I will let him think that journey I spoke about was the only one and that then I just went to join a ship.

At the coast I sometimes met sailors, usually at taverns where we went for drinks and to meet women. Slowly I learned some English, and I could talk it a little. This helped me later when I did decide to join a ship. After I left Katsina I heard their king Agu Raji died and another took his place. A few years later these Fulani started fighting at Gobir and later at Katsina, saying we did not follow the Muslim laws properly. The fighting went on for years and at one time the defeated king came back but was driven out again. In the end the Fulani won. They changed how we lived, trying to make us good, not drinking or gambling. Trade then was very poor with all this fighting and many people left to go to Kano or some other places. Maybe ten years after I left Katsina, and some years since I had been home to Gobir, I found things too difficult for me. Then I heard at the coast that the English, who were very strong, were trying to stop this trade in slaves, so what were we to do? It might be a good thing to join a ship. Some men I met in taverns said men were wanted on the ships and we could live well there.

It was hard for me at first. The work was hard; the food was not what I was used to. I got into trouble when I did not understand an order. When there was a storm, *haba!* It was very bad for me. But I soon learnt that the first rule is always to do what the Captain says. And the seamen told me, using words they all know, 'When you have fun, look out for the Bosun coming round the corner, and keep your nose clean!' This way I never had really bad trouble. Some sailors helped me and I do not think it is a bad life now. I have been, oh, about fifteen years with your people, I know their ways and how they speak, and I can speak your language quite well, as you can tell.

We went to many places over the years, the river Gambia, the isle of Goree and others. Not long before the present ship came here we visited Copenhagen, Madeira and Tenerife. We have been in some fights with French ships in the war, and they were very frightening at first, but we did not suffer much damage, being very lucky. I think that if you take the years before I joined the Navy, my time in it and all, I must be well over forty years old now.

One more thing he asked me about was the name of the vessel in which I first enlisted. I had some difficulty remembering the name, but when he looked in the Navy List to see which ships had been to the coast of Africa and he read out the name of the 'Little Belt', I said that must be the one. He expressed great interest in this. He said it was the first voyage this new ship ever made. Also the year was, he said, 1808, when the law to end the slave trade was very new, and this was one of the first ships that came looking for anyone breaking the law. At that time they could only look for English ships, or those of France as the English were fighting them.

I could not tell you how I came by the name William Pascoe. I said, 'I did not know English names and I could only speak a few words. I had to accept the name they gave me. The First Lieutenant could not understand when I said my name was Abubakar. I think now that perhaps he heard Abu as Bill! A seaman said to me much later that perhaps he came from a place in England called Cornwall where the name Pascoe was common. In any case I accepted the name and so I became Pascoe.

There is one thing I do not feel happy about in what I have told Mr. Evans. He asked me if I was married. I said I had liked a girl I saw going to market or sometimes bringing water from the well. Of course in our way I did not spend time alone with her but when I found I liked her I gave her a few cowries as money. She liked this and accepted and gave the cowries to her father as a greeting from me. A few days later I took some more cowries to her father. If I had done this several times I thought he might agree to our marrying, but he said we were still young and we should wait. Then I started going on trading trips and by the time I returned things had gone wrong, so I never did marry her. I could have explained all this to Mr. Evans but I felt I should make it sound better. I had heard some seamen talk about their wives at home or the girls they hoped would marry them when their voyages ended and I thought 'If these men can have wives or girls waiting for them, why cannot I?' I know that if she has not since found a man she likes, her father will have found a man for her. So I did, perhaps, a little wrong in saying this, but I hope it was not too bad, and Mr. Evans seems to believe me.

Most of what I have told him is true, nearly always true. It would not be good to do anything else with him.

I may have added a little or taken a little away, but not too much. When I was young I used to listen to stories and I myself liked making up stories and telling them to my younger brothers and young friends. So that is what I have done here: nothing wrong in that is there? I have always been ready to tell stories and listen to those told by others. My shipmates wanted to know about my home country and I have told them a lot about this, sometimes true stories, some I made up. We had long evenings on the ships to pass, and telling stories was what helped us.

At the end I think Mr. Evans is pleased. He says he can now write about all these things we have talked about. He hopes some day the Captain will send his writing to London People over there will then know much more about my country – and me!

CHAPTER 3 — BELZONI

October –December 1825

I first knew something might happen to me when Mr. Evans sent for me to come quickly. He looked long at me, told me to be easy, then said, 'Ah, Pascoe, er, um, you told me some time ago how much you wanted to go home and marry your loved one, but there was no chance then. Now there could be a chance. You may have noticed a tall white man with a large beard, not a sailor, come aboard at Tenerife. He wants to travel to Timbuktu. Do you know where that is?' 'Yes,' I said, 'I have never been there but I have heard about it from traders, it is away to the north. It is a long distance. My country lies almost between it and Eko on the coast, which white men call Lagos.' 'Well,' replied Mr. Evans, 'er,um, this could be your chance. We do not want to lose you, but would you be ready to leave the Navy and go with him to Timbuktu? You would have to promise to stay with him all the way to Timbuktu and then until he comes to some place from which he can return to England. After that, you could go to your home. Would you, er, um, be ready to do this?'

My heart started to jump and to make such a noise I felt sure he must hear it. I did want to see my home and people again But I remembered how I had made up the story about the girl I had left behind, although he would never know it was not true. Also I had heard people say that things had changed much back at home, and it night not be good to go there. I had been away about fourteen years, and by now I was happy in the Navy. But, after thinking a little, I took a deep breath and I said, 'Yes, Mr. Evans.' He replied, 'That is good…. I will arrange for you to meet him. His name is Mr. Belzoni.' With a smile he added, 'He is what I have heard you call 'a big man' in England. If you succeed in this journey with him, I am sure he will pay you well and your name may become known too.'

The next day he called me to meet Mr. Belzoni. Talk of 'a big man', he really is so! I am a short man and he is so tall I had difficulty looking up at him. With his big beard he looked like an Arab to me. He also looked very strong. He asked me if I was ready to go to Timbuktu with him, to which I agreed. He said, 'I do not want any foolish behaviour. When we get to your country or near it you are *not* to leave me so that you can remain there. If you do anything like that

I shall pay you nothing, and I shall tell your king that you are a bad man and have broken your word. But if you do come with me to Timbuktu and then on to some place from which I can go home to England, then I will pay you a year's wages in the Navy, and give you to keep some things I will not need. Do you understand?' A year's wages, £18, would help me very much and I was pleased, so I said, 'Yes. Sir, I understand and I promise to do what you have said.' I had decided that I could accept this big man as my Captain for now, and I would do the things he wanted.

That was all we did then, and Mr. Evans went off with Mr. Belzoni to arrange things with the Captain. Two days later Mr. Evans told me to get ready to go. Then I said goodbye to those crewmen I liked and had sailed with for so long. After that I had to appear before the First Mate to be discharged from the Navy and then, very fast, the time came to be off. Mr. Belzoni and all his things were moved into the sloop *Swinger,* I joined him, and we were away.

Extract from the diary of John Evans. October 1823

Much has happened in a short time but I have been too occupied to record it in my diary until now. Sadly we were all affected by the sudden illness and death of our Captain, Sir Robert Mends on 4th September, due to some infection in the climate of this part of the world. He richly deserved the honours he had received from both England and Spain. He had fought bravely in many battles since the time forty years ago when, as a young Midshipman aged 13, he had lost his right arm in the defence of Yorktown in the American war. This naturally cast a gloom over the whole crew, especially his son who is a Midshipman aboard with us. For me it involved additional work, quite apart from the preparations for the funeral, as I had to communicate with the other vessels in our squadron As a result Captain John Filmore transferred from HM Sloop *Bann* to take command of this ship and the whole squadron, of which Captain Mends had been Commodore, and I had to help him become established.

    After we sailed from Chatham we put into port at Tenerife in the Canary Islands, from where we came on here via St. Iago in the Cape Verde Islands. It chanced that the famous Mr. Belzoni was there hoping to get assistance from the captain of some vessel to transport him to a place on the western coast of Africa. At first he had hoped to be able to go to the River Gambia and to follow the track of Mungo Park as the quickest way to reach the desert and Timbuktu there was then no boat going that way. Our Captain readily gave his permission to travel with us and to disembark at any place that he favoured. It was not my task to provide him with a cabin and other bodily needs but the Captain directed me, as a man interested in and knowledgeable about the exploration of Africa, to render him any other assistance he might need. This gave me amble opportunity to talk with him and to hear his own very interesting accounts of what he has achieved to date, and how he proposes to undertake this new task he has set for himself.

I know that before he moved in 1803 from Italy where he was born to London he had studied hydraulic engineering and he continued to pursue this calling in Britain. It was with a view to offering his own engines to improve the irrigation of fields bordering the Nile that he went to Egypt. As the well-known book he later wrote shows, there he came to know the explorer Burckhardt and this inspired him first to send back to London, with the assistance of our Consul-General, Mr. Salt, the massive sculpture of a head, called the Young Memnon , now a treasure of the British Museum, and other treasures. Then he searched for and was the first to find the tombs of several Pharaohs in the part of the desert that has come to be known as the Valley of the Kings, and a concealed entrance to the Great Pyramid of Cheops His greatest success, however, was to excavate the sand cumulated over many centuries which then allowed entrance to the wonderful temples at Abu Simbel,

I learned from him that he had been with hi wife to Fez in Morocco and had been given permission to cross the desert with a caravan to Timbuktu, the fabled city that nobody in Europe has yet been able to see and describe, but which for many years has been believed to be very wealthy and endowed with gold. It was his experience in the deserts of

Egypt which inspired him to this wish. To his great dismay, after some period of waiting and preparation, this permission was revoked. The reasons he could not discover, but he believes there had been some intrigue about allowing any foreigner to visit Timbuktu, which Morocco claims on historical grounds as its own, or to view the Moors' trade in this region. His pleas being spurned, he saw no alternative but to send his wife home and to cross by small boat to Tenerife in order to travel south and to attempt his exploration from there rather than from the north.

He stands very high, six feet seven inches, I believe, with an unusually strong body, and I could believe, when *I* saw him, the stories I had previously heard, of how he had represented Samson and Hercules on the stages of theatres in London and other cities, along with his wife, strong like an Amazon, they say. But he did not talk with me about this activity, which I believe was due to financial needs in his earlier days.

When I could do so I told Mr. Belzoni that we had an African man aboard who came from an inland country which might well lie on or near the course of his intended travels, who spoke fairly good English as well as the local African dialects. He was surprised and interested to learn this, and of course I arranged for him to meet Pascoe. After a short discussion Mr. Belzoni appeared satisfied and asked me if it would be possible for Pascoe to travel with him. I therefore composed for him a letter that he addressed to our new Captain Filmore, which read in part as follows:

'… having found a native of Hausa of the name of Abubakar on board the *Owen Glendower* now under your command who is desirous to return to his own country having been absent from it for 14 years,…..I take the liberty to request the favour that the said Abubakar may be permitted to follow me as Guide…'

This was written on 20th October. Being still new to our ship, and having no personal acquaintance with Pascoe, the Captain consulted me and I assured him that Pascoe has always been of good behaviour and shown himself to be reliable. Accordingly, the next day the Captain assented to this request, provided Pascoe was discharged from the Navy. He also instructed Lieutenant Scott, commanding Gun Brig *Swinger*, to sail southwards in search of slavers, and at the same time to afford Mr. Belzoni and this native of the country a passage to the English trading factory at the mouth of the River Benin, where he was to be afforded every assistance to land. After two days I had to say farewell to both Mr. Belzoni and Pascoe, wishing them success in their journeys, probably for me never to see either of them again. After one week, so I heard, they disembarked as intended.

Pascoe, London, July 1825

Soon after we sailed on the *Swinger* Mr. Belzoni sent for me to go to the cabin he had been given and asked if I knew the whole way to Timbuktu. I started to tell him that I knew the directions in which we should go and man y of the places we would pass through, but that I had never been to Timbuktu myself. Before I could say much of this he stopped me and asked another question, 'Timbuktu is in the desert, is it not?' 'Yes, Sir,' I replied and then started again to explain what I knew of the way, but he interrupted me again, saying, 'I am a man of the desert. I know the desert. I like the desert. How soon can we reach the desert?' I told him it would need at least six weeks, , if we walked very fast, or probably two months 'Can we not get horses or camels?' he asked, and I told him we would have to go a long way north before we could see such animals. The best we could manage in the south would be to find asses. Otherwise men would have to carry our loads until we got further north. He did not seem very happy with this and he kept on saying to himself, 'I am a man of the desert. When I was in Egypt I showed them how great the country was. When I reach Timbuktu I will show them how great that city is.' Then he dismissed me

After a week we saw land. This was near Benin, a country I had never been to but I had heard of it. As we came near the land we could at first see mangrove bushes growing above the water thickly. The air smelled heavy and dark as in places you do not want to go unless you have to. Beyond that we saw the coastline and a place where we could land, at a place called Gato, and there was a building of the factory up a little hill, where Mr. Belzoni could try to buy things he needed.

When we looked out from the deck what he saw was mostly wet and muddy land. There were some palm trees but coconut, not date palms. One firm path went up the hill between the swamps so that a man could walk on it. 'Where is the desert? I must get to the desert' was all he could say. The *Swinger* would soon leave us but Mr. Belzoni arranged to stay on a brig nearby called the *Castor* as he did not like what he saw on the land. Then he went to the factory to see what he could buy. I cooked a dinner for him but there was little else I could do then. I asked around and I found one or two traders who could speak Hausa or Yoruba, some of which I knew from my previous travels, but of the Benin language I knew nothing.

The day after we arrived an Englishman came in a canoe from the river which runs inland from there, where he traded. I later heard his name was Mr. Houtson. He was interested in what Mr. Belzoni wanted to do and he promised to take him to Benin City to see the chief or Oba, and when he was ready to set off he would come part of the way with him. Mr. Belzoni kept on saying to him 'I am a man of the desert. I must get to the desert quickly,' and all the rest of what he kept saying to me. They did go to Benin to see the Oba and when they came back he seemed more cheerful. It seems he had got permission to go through the country and a promise of some men as carriers and more as soldiers to guard us up to Hausa land. Mr. Belzoni went to the factory again to finish buying things and he made arrangements to leave Gato.

Mr. Houtson went to do some of his trading but told him he would soon be back Mr. Belzoni then started on his way with me to help him but he had only gone for a few hours when he started to feel very ill and he had to turn back. At first he thought that something he had eaten must be wrong for him and the trouble would soon pass. He tried some medicines he had but his illness got worse. Soon his flux got so bad that he had to spend most of his time in bed. Mr. Houtson came to see him several times but could not help him. Still it got worse. He had been a very strong man but I could see his strength going away. A man from the factory came to see him and I heard them talking. He was sure he was going to die and he told this man that what worried him most was how this would cause trouble for his wife Sarah. He had borrowed money for the trip but he could not earn anything as he could not write any book to sell. His wife would be left in debt. He gave some things to Mr. Houtson and his pistols to me. Then Mr. Houtson went off to do his trading saying he would soon come back, but Mr. Belzoni was worse. The day before he died he tried to write a letter but could not do so, and a man from the factory wrote one for him to a man he knew called Mr. Briggs in England, asking him to help his dear wife. His goods would be sent to England later on the *Castor* . Soon after that he got worse and died. Mr. Houtson was still away but the burial could not wait. I helped a man from the factory to bury him with a little ceremony.

There was I left alone, Mr. Houtson being away and the people from the factory paid me little attention after they had collected Mr. Belzoni's things to send to the boat. I had nothing to keep me except some small things of his I was allowed to keep. I did not know when I might be rescued or where I could go. It would be many miles to the north to reach Hausa country and it would be hard to reach there safely. I had been discharged from the Navy and in any case the ships were far away looking for slavers. As the days passed I got more and more sad and worried for myself. Three weeks passed with no hope for me. I thought little when the man from the factory passed by and said 'Who would think it was Christmas Day tomorrow?.' I made no reply as Christmas has never meant much to me unless we got extra rum or some special food then.

I was lying as sad as can be when Christmas morning came. Then, all of a sudden, a boy from a nearby village came and made signs for me to come quickly and he led me down to the waterside. Pointing out into the creek he showed me that there were four boats there being rowed by white sailors. I cried out, 'Ahoy, ahoy, ahoy!' They took no notice. Then I repeated, 'Ahoy, my name is William Pascoe, I came from the *Owen Glendower*. I need help to leave here.' Hearing me speak English they showed more interest and one boat rowed over near to me. I explained how I had come with Mr. Belzoni to go to Timbuktu but he had died of the flux and I needed to return to the Navy. This boat was then taken a little way out to sea to find their ship, the *Bann,* and to ask their officer what to do. Then it came back and picked me up to go with them to the ship while they finished their search for any hidden slaver.

I was soon signed on again in the Navy. I had thought I would be left there for ever and I was very glad to be out of my trouble. I rejoined the squadron again under Captain Courtney on the *Bann,* but I had to be an Ordinary Seaman again, like a new recruit. I was with them for eighteen months but near the end I was transferred to the Sloop *Ranger.* After we reached Chatham I was discharged on 8th July 1825, as it shows on my papers here, and ordered to go to London and report at the Admiralty.

I found two naval officers together there. One told me he was Commander Hugh Clapperton who was going to lead an expedition or group of men to go to Africa, where he had been before, and the other was Commander Robert Pearce,. who was to be his second in command. They knew somehow that I came from Hausa land and could interpret for them there, but my actual position would be as cook to Captain Pearce, as they had also heard that I had experience in cooking in the Navy. They said I would receive pay as a seaman, food and grog money, so that I would lose nothing compared to what I would receive in the Navy. I decided I liked the idea of serving these two officers going to my country so I accepted. Captain Clapperton said he already had engaged a servant for himself.

When in England I saw Mrs. Belzoni and told her where and how her husband had died. She gave me some corals and other small things of her husband's. Other than these and the pistols I got from Mr. Belzoni, all I got out of my travels with him was serving on a smaller ship, a lower rank and less pay, 24 instead of 30 shillings a month!

Chapter 4 — The Niger Expedition Begins

<u>John Barrow, 2nd. Secretary to the Admiralty – London, June 1825</u>

Well, Commander Clapperton, first I congratulate you on your recent well-deserved promotion. Next, I appreciate your coming to see me within a few days of your return to England following your hazardous travel over the desert with Major Denham an d the late Dr. Oudney, without any delay to enable you to recover from your exertions. What I have heard of your travels and your visits to Bornu and Sokoto is most interesting. Countries that we could previously only talk about seeing some day have now been made real to us. I only regret that you have not yet been able to con firm what I am convinced is the truth , that the River Niger flows eastwards across Africa to join the Nile. That still remains to be proved, as we hope we can soon do. Your coming to see me so early after your return proves how anxious you are to augment our knowledge of that part of the world.

This time you say you wish to enter Western Africa from the south, from Whydah or Benin on the coast. It was good that you obtained the agreement of Sultan Bello at Sokoto to send a messenger to meet you at Whydah during this July, although you will now probably be unable to reach there so early. I trust that when you do arrive, even if you do not find a messenger awaiting you, you can at least retrieve a message left for you. It was also good that the Sultan agreed to take steps to end his subjects' participation in the foreign slave trade, which is a major objective of this Government. From Whydah I believe you will have a considerable distance to travel northwards in order to pass over the line of the Kong Mountains which geographers assure us cross the continent from west to east, preventing any great river coming south to enter the Atlantic Ocean. Indeed, south of these mountains only short rivers or creeks run down to the ocean. Having passed these mountains you would have to continue northwards before encountering the River Niger running eastwards towards the Nile. However, I agree that it is a possible, perhaps desirable, line to follow and, since you wish to make this approach, I laud your ambition to succeed in this way.

You are aware of Major Laing having started from Tripoli towards Timbuktu, as you have answered my request before you arrived home to send advice for him. We believe he is still far from this objective. The chances of your meeting him for some time are not great, but we will allow for this possibility.

I shall, of course, have to seek the agreement of Lord Bathurst at the Colonial Office, and the concurrence of the Treasury to providing funds. Kindly draw up a statement of your objectives and requirements as soon as you can, to enable me to act. Meanwhile we shall have to give thought as to how many persons should accompany you, and who they might be.

You may have heard how in 1823 the celebrated Mr. Belzoni of Egyptian fame attempted an approach to the Niger and Timbuktu by nearly the same route as that you desire to follow, but unfortunately he died soon after landing near Benin. He had with him as interpreter and guide a Hausa man who originated from an area not far from where you visited when you went to Sokoto. He had served in our Navy for over ten years and is still a seaman on a vessel which I believe has now arrived at a port in this country. We have a report on him which we received from the Captain of a vessel he was on earlier, and if you can spare a little time now, I will have a clerk bring this for your perusal It may be as assistance to you to engage him for your mission.

Contact this office when you can let me have your document listing your requirements and intentions, and I promise you that I shall make every endeavour to obtain the necessary agreements as soon as I possibly can.

<u>A month later</u>

Captain Clapperton, I am delighted to be able to inform you that Lord Bathurst has welcomed the information you have delivered concerning your recent journeys to Bornu and Sokoto. He has, with commendable expedition, approved that you should make a fresh entry into this area, with the support of His Majesty's Government and bearing its authority, in order to take this favourable opportunity of establishing intercourse with the interior of Africa. This will probably put an effectual check, through the powerful chiefs you have met, to a large portion of the infamous slave traffic carried on in the Bight of Benin, as well as extending the legitimate commerce of Great Britain with this part of Africa, and at the same time add to our knowledge of the country. His Lordship; does not hesitate in adopting the arrangements you have made with Sultan Bello for certain articles of English manufacture to be sent to him by the sea coast; that an English physician and a Consul should be appointed to reside at a certain seaport; that Sultan Bello would despatch messengers to bring up the articles of commerce and send a proper person to transact all matters of business between the two governments, through the intervention of the English Consul ; and he welcomes the Sultan's readiness to adopt measures for putting an entire stop to that part of the slave-trade carried on by his subjects with foreigners. You will also be supplied with gifts to take to the Sheikh of Bornu, with whom you have already had amicable intercourse, and who you should visit afresh in order to negotiate satisfactory arrangements in conjunction with the British Consul already established there since your earlier visit.

It has been agreed with this office that you will be accompanied by Captain Robert Pearce, your senior by a year in the Navy but evidently content to act as your second in command. As well as his naval experience he is an excellent draughtsman. Dr. Morrison, a surgeon, is knowledgeable in natural history while Dr. Dickson, also a surgeon, will look after the health of the mission. Columbus, who you recommended after his crossing the great desert with you ,and the servants of Captain Pearce and yourself, will complete the party. Now that these matters have been determined, along with the financial arrangements we have earlier discussed and agreed, it remains for me to wish you all success in this praiseworthy enterprise, together with my hope for information on the course of the elusive River Niger across Africa to join the Nile.

At Badagry on the African coast, 6th December 1825.

We are all having to work hard here at Badagry but I am happy to be serving this expedition as cook to Captain Pearce, a nice man. We have to get all our loads off the ship on to the shore, and that is much work, I can tell you. There is nothing like a harbour here, or any way to moor a ship near the coast, and the boat must stay at sea although that is often rough in the wind and the current. The local men, who work as fishermen, must lower the loads into canoes, and they know how to do this difficult work without dropping them into the sea. Then the canoes are paddled through very strong surf, finding just the right moment to land. Even they make mistakes sometimes: the canoe carrying Mr. Houtson capsized and he was pulled from the water only just in time so that he did not drown. Yes, this is the same Mr. Houtson as I had met when I travelled with Mr. Belzoni. As I shall tell, we met him near Benin again, and he directed us to come here, where he has a house.

We had been three months coming from England on HMS *Brazen* so I am glad now to have this work to do, even if not interpreting, which will come later. We had stopped at Whydah, along the coast from here, but I heard that Captain Clapperton did not find any messenger as he had hoped or any message either. So we sailed on past Lagos for several days to the east until we came to Gato, that place near Benin where I had landed with Mr. Belzoni before. Mr. Houtson was still there doing his trading, but he said the Oba did not like the English as they tried to stop the slave trade which cut what he earned. So we went back again to Badagry, but first we passed it by and went to Whydah, as Dr. Dickson wanted to land there and to make his own way to Sokoto. The gentlemen parted from him sadly but they talked of meeting again, perhaps at a place called Ijana that we would be going through. It was at Badagry that finally we stopped and landed and Mr. Houtson said he could lead us from there to Katanga in the country of Oyo.

When the loads had been taken off the ship and safely landed, that was not the end of our troubles. Where we landed was not the mainland but just a long stretch of land coming many miles from Lagos to our east. This land was only one cable-length across and the loads had to be taken up and carried to its other side. Then they had to be taken in boats again across a long creek which I heard also came from Lagos, many miles away. It was only then that we finally reached the mainland near Badagry. Men we hired did all this carrying but we had to watch things all the way to see that nothing was stolen or got lost, and then we had to arrange the loads in the proper order. All this took us several days but we got it all done with nothing being lost.

Since we came here a man I talked with told me, 'The slavers hide slaves in small boats in this long creek or in small side creeks. Their ship at sea watches until it sees the coast is clear and then the slaves are brought out quickly and off they go! They must have seen your naval vessel in good time so there was nothing to see here, was there? You did not know any of this, did you?' He gave a little laugh as he thought this very clever.

On the *Brazen* the gentlemen shared cabins and messed with the ship's officers. I had a hammock and food as I have done many years now. I prepared food for the officers but otherwise I was like a passenger on the naval ship, a new thing for me. The gentlemen did not agree to my being a crew member as they might want me at any time. I find Captain Pearce a good Master and I do whatever he needs me to do.

Apart from the gentlemen we have two servants, Richard Lander who works for Captain Clapperton, and me. I do not know Richard Lander well yet, but he has told me he served first in the West Indies as a boy and later in South Africa. He seems to have no worries about this journey, telling me he sees his master, Captain Clapperton as 'the soul of adventure' Many of his friends in London and at his home tried to tell him there was too much danger in coming, but he pushed all this talk away. As we both work for our masters, who seem to be good friends with each other, I hope Richard and I can also be friends. I think of him as 'Richard', as his master calls him, but I always speak to him as 'Mr. Lander.' He calls me just 'Pascoe' and he seems quite easy with me.

The other man with us is called Columbus, a black man like me. He comes from the West Indies but I think he ran away from his slave master on a ship. He has done much travelling since then, including going over the desert with Captain Clapperton and another man, and they say he speaks Arabic and other languages. I do not like him at all and I keep away from him as far as I can. I know that Richard likes him even less, having once said some small thing that you or I would not bother about. But Columbus then said to him in his loud voice,' I shall one day have the pleasure of seeing you parching with thirst on the back of a camel and, rather than give you a drop of water, by God you shall perish there: that will be my revenge.' He thinks he is superior to Richard and me, as he is paid by the Colonial Office, while we work for our Masters, who pay us. In fact he has been sick most of the way here, and both Richard and I are glad that he has left the ship at Whydah with Dr. Dickson.

Whilst we were on the *Brazen* we saw two Spanish ships caught. One had thirty five slaves on board, the other was waiting to take on two hundred from the shore. They were sent back to Sierra Leone in their captured ships to be freed there. We watched this happen but I was not part of the boarding party, as I am not in the crew. We thought it a good thing but I knew that in peacetime we could not touch a French ship that we saw even though she had two hundred slaves on board.

When we were leaving our ship to come ashore all the officers and some of the men lined up to say goodbye to us. We black men who come from this country can go about without any trouble but these sailors looked so sad as if we *could* not come back alive. I have heard it said that white men landing in our country are going straight to their graves, and 'how few come out though many go in.' Trying to make things more cheerful Richard got down into a canoe and played a tune on a thing he carries, which he tells me is called a 'bugle-horn.' The tune, he says, is called *'Over the hills and far away'* which he chose as we are going far away, though he did not know if there are hills we shall have to climb over! Perhaps we shall have more tunes from him as we go on.

Everyone has been well up to now, whatever anyone may say. We expect to leave tomorrow and start on our journey. I shall be glad to see the back of this place as one of the King's wives treated me badly. After three months at sea I was ready to see a woman but it was she who came after me, offering me a bottle of rum. The King heard of it and threatened my life if I came near her. So I stayed away and did nothing. She waited until she saw me outside and then threw a heavy stone hard at my chest, and it hurt! I have seen before how these women in this Yoruba country are big and strong. I called her names and I want nothing more to do with her. Richard joked that it was my fault, but it was not. I will find another woman at another place to keep me company. So now I am ready to go!

7th December 1825

Yes,. we are off, as I said yesterday. Not very far at first. Carriers had been arranged but it took a long time to sort out the heavy loads, about forty in number, that they are to carry. Richard and I had to do this. Next morning Captain Pearce and Dr. Morrison came back to see the loads were all brought forward. The day after that there was a long argument with the local headman and in the end he said it was not for him to arrange carriers for us. Men we already had from Badagry as guards took their places as their headman was afraid he might have to go back and report failure.

Captain Clapperton, as our overall commander, told us all, 'I want to get on as fast as we can manage. As we go inland things will get better for us and our health. Captain Pearce and Dr. Morrison please go ahead with the beds and our own loads and take Richard with you Pascoe, you follow with the carriers and the heavy loads as far as you can get. I will bring up the rear with Mr. Houtson. The day had nearly finished when we all got away. Because of what the Captain had said those in front went on walking into the night. Coming at the rear new boots troubled the Captain but he changed to slippers only to have these fall off and get lost in the dark. Then he found that the local horses, being small in this country, were difficult for him with no saddle and he tried to walk. As he could not see he trod on several lines of ants which hurt him very much. He could easily have lost his way altogether but a village helped him with torches and guides. Even then, it was midnight when he finally caught up with me where I had stopped. We slept on the ground in the open that night, and it was noon the next day before we found Captain Pearce, Dr. Morrison and Richard with the beds. Only then could Richard bathe his sore feet. After that the Captain saw to it that the loads and people did not get too far apart, but he still made us press on as fast as we could go.

We soon met other problems for only five days after starting the white men began to fall sick, first Dr. Morrison, then my Master Captain Pearce, next Richard and then even Captain Clapperton himself. Still he ordered us on and on. He kept saying it would get better further on and in my own country where he had been before there was much less sickness. Hammocks would be the best thing to move our people on but this was difficult, for all the people around said that in this Oyo country they do not carry anyone in them. They all said, 'Men are not horses.'

The way this was settled shows the difference from how I had seen things in the past. When I came with parties of traders the villagers always helped us with food and places to stay but all was quiet. But seeing the white men coming to visit them was wonderful to all the people around. At every place many, many people men, women, and even children came to welcome these strangers. Most say they are here to bring them peace, although I hear a few voices saying they mean harm to the King. Everyone from far around wants to see this happy visit and all the noise is friendly. Sometimes the singing and dancing go on all night. It is this joy of seeing their white visitors that has made them ready to help even by giving them hammocks.

At the beginning, while we were sorting out the loads and how we would travel I was separated from Captain Pearce, but afterwards, especially when he started to be ill, I stayed with him. I did all I could to look after him. He could eat little solid food but I made him good soups and some light meat from chicken when he could eat this. I hope he will soon get better. At one place, while Captain Pearce stayed behind to rest, Captain Clapperton took Mr. Houtson with him to visit the local chief. His main followers lay down flat on the ground to salute the chief, as is their custom, covering their heads and clothes with dust. Our people gave some rum for the chief and his followers. There were many people, men and women, filling the veranda of his house and all the open land in front of it. They clapped every time the chief spoke in a friendly way to his visitors. The Captain told them that in his country a man could have only one wife, and they laughed and laughed at this strange idea, as their big men have many wives. I feel the same way as them, and if I could have many wives I would do so.

Next day we came to a place called Ijana, which was where we had hoped to see Dr. Dickson and Columbus, but there was no sign of them. We had heard that they had come some of the way from Whydah, but no more. Here the countryside was open, up a hillside, unlike the earlier part where the country was covered with thick trees, with only narrow paths to travel along. I could not say how many people live here, certainly a large number. Thousands have come to see us, and there are farms everywhere. The chief sent us much food and has given us a good place to stay. Other people too gave us a goat and yams. I was surprised when the chief sent us twenty five gallons – yes, twenty five gallons of rum, so that we could give all his people a dram, to make them think well of us.

I have had my own big success here. I think the good spirits must be with me to repay me for all I have suffered in the past. Some men may do better and have many wives, but I now have one at least!. Her name is Yetunde and she is a beautiful girl, round and with a good body. I love her and I am sure we shall be happy. We have married here according to their customs. I know she does not like the idea of leaving the Yoruba people she knows and coming into the Hausa and Bornu lands. For me, I think we should go on with the Captain. Life is good for me now.

Some of our people have good days and bad days. On one good day for him Captain Clapperton went with Mr. Houtson to visit the chief in his house, the others staying behind to rest. I could stand near and see what went on. Again there were very many people, and what made them most happy was when they saw their chief join hands with the Captain and Mr. Houtson to do an African dance together. The chief made a bright red dress he was wearing look even brighter when he changed it twice. They went round, hand in hand, several times, as he kept looking at one or the other with his old face. They turned about and went slowly back and forwards and then back and forwards again. Captain Pearce was brought in his hammock to see but he could not stay long for all the noise.

We have stayed some days at Ijana and the gentlemen's health has got worse. I did my best to help Captain Pearce but both he and Dr. Morrison have got weaker. Richard too is very ill. Once Dr. Morrison tried to bleed him on the forehead but he could not hold his instrument well and it dug right into Richard's head. The noise he made was like an animal being slaughtered. Richard still got worse in the next few days and the doctor tried to put a blister over his head, but this made Richard like a fighting man, not knowing what he was doing. I thought he might die but after some time he became quiet though still ill.

Before we left Ijana I heard Captain Clapperton say to the sick gentlemen, 'I am sorry to see you both so unwell, and I believe you need rest and fresh air to help you continue the journey. I hope you will agree either to stay here until you have recovered while the rest of us go on, or to go down to Badagry with Mr. Houtson to rest there or on the *Brazen*. I think this would be best for you and for all of us.' But Captain Pearce did not like this and said, 'Weak as I am, I want to continue. Even if I should die and be buried here, that would be better than leaving you to continue alone.' Dr. Morrison agreed with him saying, 'No, no, no, I want only to go forwards, not back.' Nothing that Captain Clapperton said would change this so we went on, using the hammocks. But next day Dr. Morrison had changed his mind, seeing that he was delaying the whole party. . He agreed to go back with Mr. Houtson who therefore took him back.

We had with us a man called George Dawson, a seaman who had volunteered at Badagry and been taken on as a servant to Dr. Morison and he like the others was by now very ill. Beyond Ijana we had a cold morning after some unusual heavy rain in the night, although it was a dry time. He was unable to keep himself upright on his horse but was so weak he kept falling off onto the wet road and having to be helped to get back on. Once his horse slipped and threw him down, right into the water. He struggled back on but could only just make it to the next village and in the afternoon he died there. He had to be buried the next morning with all of us there and Captain Clapperton saying prayers at his grave. The Captain himself had a bad cold at that time.

Until then Captain Pearce had remained cheerful although ill, and both Richard and I did our best to keep him like that, but George Dawson's death made his spirits fall right down. From then on he got weaker and worse until he too died. This made Captain Clapperton very sad as they had been good friends for years. It was sad for me too, to lose my Master, who was a good man, less than a month after we had reached Badagry and landed. Once again Captain Clapperton had to see to a burial and say the prayers for the dead man. Our going on was slow as the Captain himself was not well and he decided we should rest a little. That evening Mr. Houtson came back alone, saying they had only just got to Ijana when Dr. Morrison died and he had seen to his burial. This was in fact the same day as when Captain Pearce died, so it was bad news for all of us. Dr. Morrison was the doctor who was going to treat any illness and keep us well.

I know that after my Master Captain Pearce died Captain Clapperton wrote a letter to the Captain of the *Brazen* sending some of the dead man's property and some drawings I had seen him make, to go to his brother in England. He then said to me, 'Pascoe, I have seen how you served Captain Pearce faithfully. Now that he has unfortunately died, I should like to take his place as your Master if you will agree to work for me as cook and interpreter. I will give you the same terms as he did.' I at once agreed and from then he became my Master and Captain. He kindly gave me Captain Pearce's bed and some other small things he had had.

I started cooking regularly for the Captain, and soon I was able to show him what I could do as a cook, from my experience in the Navy. At one village he was given a turkey, which I had not seen in this area before. The next day I cooked it, and I was happy when the Captain said it was as well cooked as any turkey he had eaten in London. All that was missing was some good wine to go with it!

But most days we were feeling sad. There are three white men dead within one month after our arrival, when we still have far to go. Perhaps those men we had parted from on the *Brazen* were right in their thoughts about the dangers to white men coming into this country. Both our Captain and Richard are sick and I have to ask myself is it to be like the time I went with Mr. Belzoni and he soon died. How will it be for me if this continues? Will I be left alone, separated from our ships, discharged from the Navy and with little idea what I can do? I was fortunate after Mr. Belzoni died but even when I did get back into the Navy I was left poorer than before. Apart from the few things Mrs. Belzoni gave me in England I have very little of my own and who would pay me now? If I was alone, not with a party of traders, would the people take me as a slave and sell me at the coast? That could easily happen. This all fills me with fear and worry but my good spirits have so far stayed with me. The Captain and Richard stay alive and we go on. Sometimes they are able to walk or ride their horses, other times they have to be carried in hammocks, but at least they have not died yet and left me alone. To my surprise the Captain keeps going even when ill, and Richard seems determined to continue serving him. At times when he has seemed better I feel unhappy at how he seems to be watching me, but as long as he remains alive and busy serving the Captain I do not worry too much. So on we go towards Katanga!

Chapter 5 — At Katanga

<u>January – March 1826</u>

'Poor Pascoe,' I heard a voice say, 'so ill.' This was almost the first time the Captain had said anything to me that was not an order. I was very sleepy, the fever having come very suddenly, making me first sweat and then go cold. I was so surprised that I could only just make my eyes open, as I said, 'Aye, aye, Sir.' Later I was pleased that the Captain had spoken to me like this. I know he is a good Captain and I had seen him keep on moving even when he was ill. It had been bad to see the three white men die from fever in a few days, and I had been worried that I could find myself alone again and poor, like when I went with Mr. Belzoni. Now here was the Captain looking well but I was getting fever myself. I fell back to sleep.

The next day I was much better. This was how it used to be when I was younger and before I went to sea. I had fever then many times and I thought my body was used to it. We had been in Katanga about a week when I fell ill. We were living close together but I had a small room to myself with Yetunde. Before coming here we had come through the mountains at Shaki, a place I had seen more than once before in my journeys from Katsina to the coast. After that we came towards the rising sun, and people said we were very near to the kingdom of Borgu to the north. We were afraid men might come from there to attack us. We also passed villages that had been burned by Fulani raiders from across the river, but those Fulani we saw still living nearby with their cows in the bush were very friendly and sometimes gave us milk.

I say we were in 'Katanga' as that is what we people from the north call it. In our language this means a big wall, and that is a good name for the town. It has the biggest earth wall I have ever seen, bigger than Katsina. It was the first thing in the town we could see from a hill top where we climbed and then looked down. After we came in through a gate we had to walk on for a long time, perhaps an hour, before we came to the house of the King or Alafin as he is called, after passing some rocky hills standing in the middle of the town. There are many houses and the big ones have carved wooden doors with posts holding up the roof. Many of them are carved with animals, snakes and lines of soldiers with drummers, very fine. The Yorubas or local people call the town 'Oyo' but to me it is Katanga.

After the fever left me I went to a market and started talking to some Fulani men. I said we soon hope to travel north but we were delayed by a civil war in Nupe. 'No,' said one of them, 'there is no civil war in Nupe. You could go that way quite safely.' When I went back to our place I told the Captain who was pleased to hear this. He wanted to go on through Nupe and he thought the Alafin was being difficult and not helping us to travel on. After that I heard some people say there was a war and others saying there was no war, so I do not know what to think. Richard seems to think there is fighting there, but the Captain continues to think there is none.

The Alafin is very kind to us, sending us much food. When he comes to see us he dresses like any other man and he brings things himself too. But many times we are hungry. How can I explain this? There is a simple reason – the man who brings the food eats it all himself!. When I say 'the man', he is not really a proper man but a very, very big body with a tummy so big you could not believe its size. He is the sort the King could have to guard his wives. In our language we call such a person *marmata* . Richard keeps trying to tell me what it is in English, but I do not understand it. He keeps saying 'You' something but I do not know what it is. His name is Ebo but I shall just call him 'the Fat Man' He eats and eats and eats to fill this great big belly of his. Nobody else could eat as much. He goes for the best things, honey, good meat and tasty fruits. What we get is the driest and least tasty bits. The result is that we go hungry, the Captain, Richard, Mr. Houtson, Yetunde and me. After some days I found a chance to speak with Richard about this. I rubbed and patted my tummy, making a sad noise. He smiled at me and said, 'I know. I am hungry too. I know the Captain feels it too. He has said things to the Fat Man but those only made him get angry and give us bad milk as a result. The Captain does not want to worry the Alafin about things. He is trying to persuade the Alafin to arrange for us to go early but he is told the road through Nupe is not safe. So I do not want to worry him about the food.' I did not feel I could speak to the Captain myself so I left things, but I wish we could have a good meal.

There was something else I did not feel happy about. When I was sick my wife Yetunde met some young girls in an evening market and they helped her to know some other women, and soon she got to know some of the Alafin's wives. When I was well again I heard how she was meeting these wives. What I did not like was that she must have been drinking with them as she sometimes came back to our house singing and laughing and making a great noise. I tried to make her be quiet but she did not take good notice of what I said. The Captain said bad words about this and he said she must keep quiet or she would have to go. This upset me greatly: I love her and I am sure she loves me, although once or twice I have been worried she might have some young scoundrel near her. I told her I would beat her if she did not behave.

The Alafin and his people seem happy to have the white men come to visit them. They say they would like us to stay a long time. I would be pleased with this as I know Yetunde is not anxious to go to the Hausa country or Bornu. People here think we can help them get peace in their country. They did have peace until the Fulani over the river at Ilorin made the people there rebel against the Alafin who has always been their ruler. They had been his slaves, the people say, but now they are his enemies and could bring their war to Katanga where there is no fighting now. The Captain did try to entertain them by firing rockets one night and they enjoyed this but the Alafin said perhaps such things should be kept for warfare.

When we had been here for about two weeks they had a big festival and headmen from many of the towns under the Alafin came to greet him. Then we could see how they do things following their customs. I know from my own country that when a man meets somebody who is more of a big man than he is he has to bow down and be like a poor servant, but I think the Yoruba pass all in this way. These headmen are big men in their own towns but when they meet the Alafin they have to take off all their clothes from the shoulder down to the waist. Then they lie down flat on the ground in all the dust and dirt and kiss the ground so that the dust covers their heads. I said to Richard, 'Here come the sand-eaters,' and the Captain heard my remark and thought it very funny, although he had to stop himself laughing until we had left the Alafin and gone back to our own place. Then he told me he thought I was quite right about this.

These customs that they have here remind me of how it used to be at my home town when I was young. Our kings and chiefs are Muslims, of course, though the Fulani say we are not good ones and that we do things wrong. Our great festivals are the ones that come at the end of Ramadan and the later one when we kill a lamb and eat it together. .The king always leads what we do at these festivals and goes with his chiefs to the prayer ground and then takes part in the celebrations that come afterwards. These chiefs and their men come in their best clothes, with white gowns and blue or other coloured turbans, riding their horses. The king goes ahead and takes his seat outside his palace unless there is rain when he may go inside. Then each chief rides up with his people slowly until they get near the king and at last ride up fast, charging until they rein in their horses suddenly, coming to a stop in front of the king and making the horses raise up their feet while they raise their own fists in salute. When each chief with his men has done this, they go off to the side and the next chief comes with his men to do the same thing. Dust is thrown up and there is much noise as the horses charge up. It is all very exciting to watch. The chiefs and their men salute the king, but they do not get down in the dust like the Yorubas do

If the king goes inside because of the rain and has taken his seat, it may be a big yard where he sits under a cover, but when the chiefs and their people come in the space becomes very full. Everybody wants to be there. The big men come in first and sit near the king. Then those who are not so big come in too. Each person knows where his proper place may be. Sometimes a man will come in a little late and in order to reach his place he may have to climb over the legs and feet of those already inside sitting with their legs in front of them. A man may have to allow somebody who is bigger than he is to take his place while the smaller one has to move back to find his proper place. At last all will be in their places and you would think there was no more space for anybody at all, it is so full, but some late person may still come and have to be allowed to get to his place, climbing past those already there. Then the king begins to greet everybody and say whatever he may want to say. He uses a man with a loud voice to speak out his words, a he does not want to shout himself. After all that, singing may begin, or acrobats or snake charmers, all wanting to show their skill to the people, while the king may go further back into his palace to rest. The people continue their feasting and rejoicing for as long as they want. Away from the palace and especially in the villages the people offer chickens and goats to the spirits of the rivers, woods and other places. It is said the Fulani now try to stop all this, which they say is bad for Muslims to do. I think the customs in Katanga are rather like those we have in the Hausa country.

As part of these customs here they put on plays which we could enjoy. These begin with loud music from drums, horns and whistles. Their drums are different from our Hausa drums. The drum has leather straps down its sides. The drummer holds it under his arm and squeezes it to make it make its sound higher or lower. I cannot follow everything in Yoruba land, but they say this is like the drum talking in their language. The drum is sending a message from here to there. In fact, at any place when we come there the people seem to know we are coming and this is how they are told. At the play there is also much singing, mostly from the women, and all seem to be happy during these plays. In my country I have seen plays like this in our festivals and in the villages where not all the people are Muslim, but I hear that Sultan Bello wants them to go more to the mosque, not to take part in plays.

The early part of the plays was good . The actors came on covered in cloths that looked as if they could not see to move about, but they did move and leap about and dance as if they could see well. Then two of them lay down and one went inside the other's cloth so that they became like a long snake. The snake then put out its head with a long tongue, trying to attack the man who was giving it orders as to what it should do. In the end he took a stick and used it like a sword until it seemed nearly dead. These actors were good, but I have seen acting like this long ago in my home town.

The best part of the plays came when a man came in covered in cloth and then removed it, showing himself underneath as a white man. He was covered in thick white stuff which made it hard for him to move about, but he played his part well. The actor made himself look like our Captain, standing very straight and proud. When they saw this everyone laughed and laughed and they cried and rolled on the ground. The Captain, Richard and Mr. Houtson tried to look pleased too, and they applauded the act, but I think they were not really happy about it. It is something I have never seen before because, of course, there has not been a white man that anyone could copy in our villages.

It was when everybody was happy after these plays that Yetunde forgot what I had told her and went to visit the Alafin's wives,. coming back drunk and making a noise. The Captain sent for me and said, 'What did I tell you? If that woman would not keep quiet, she would have to go. Well now, she has had her chance and she *will* have to go.' This made me more than sad. I felt a big loss and I went down on my knees and said, 'Please, Captain, I beg you to give her one more chance. I love her so much I could not bear it if she had to leave me. Please, please again, be kind to us. I will make sure she does not do this again.' The pain of it made tears come to my eyes, but when Richard said to me later, 'Why are you weeping and crying like this?' he was telling a lie. I told him I did not weep, even if I was very upset. Anyway, the Captain agreed to give her one last chance. Then I spoke strongly to Yetunde and I gave her some beating so as to be good.

We had been in Katanga about a month when the Alafin came to us with the Fat Man. I know the Captain had begun to feel angry about the delay in telling us we could go, but this time the Alafin said everything was almost ready. The road was clear for us to go, not though Nupe but by Borgu. He could not be sure of our safety if we went by Nupe and he did not want to be blamed if we came to any trouble or harm. The Captain thanked him but then decided to tell him how the Fat Man had been stealing the food he had been sending us. The Fat Man protested loudly that this was not true, saying he had added some of his own goats with the food. The Captain denied this angrily, saying that he himself had bought these goats in the market, and he would not argue any more with this bad man. The Alafin said nothing about this but he gave the Captain a duck and some rice which was not easy to get at this time.

PASCOE, PRINCE OF GOBIR

A few days later the Alafin said we could go when the customs were over and his headmen had gone from town. The Captain was pleased, and he noted down things that the Alafin would like to be sent from England, a brass crown, some fine yellow and blue cloth, a large coral, some bright carpet, a drum of the English kind and half a ton of cowries that he could use as money. He said he was writing to England to have these things sent. The Alafin again gave us a duck, some rice and come cola nuts. We had to wait another ten days before he said a messenger from Yaro, the chief of Kaiama, was ready for us. He would himself give us a messenger and a horse to take us tomorrow when we would leave, the headmen having just gone back to their own towns.

We went to bed after packing all our things and we slept well, ready for setting off in the morning. When it dawned I woke up but found the bed beside me empty. Where was Yetunde? I sprang up and looked around the room and outside. No Yetunde. Then I noticed that the coral beads and other things given me by Mrs. Belzoni in England were not there. Then I remembered how she had been unhappy about going on into Hausa country and Bornu. I thought too how I had sometimes had the feeling some young fellow might be going after her. Soon I became very angry and I started to curse her in both English and Hausa, '*Shegiya,* bastard, thief, *barauniya,* harlot, *karuwa.*' Even if the Captain knew some Hausa from his previous time in our country I was so angry that I did not care if he heard me. When Richard asked me what was the matter I told him with more strong words. When I had calmed down a little I added, 'She must be mad to leave such a man as me this way.' How much sympathy do you think I got? Richard gave a little laugh. The Captain just shrugged his shoulders and said he was not at all sorry to see her gone.

Chapter 6 — Bitter Honey

<u>March 1826</u>

Out in front were six lovely girls, each one carrying a light spear. That was good to see though I wish I had been closer. They had reached the age at which they could be married but were still maidens, with firm breasts and good round bodies. Now this was something I had never seen at home or in the Yoruba country: for small children, yes, but not for grown girls – all they wore was a string of beads round their bodies and a thin white cloth tied round their heads and sticking out some way behind. Maybe they had heard what the white man likes and what does not please him, for before they came in where we were they laid down their spears and tied a red cloth round their stomachs, hiding part of their beauty. When they came out they took all this off. Alas, this was the only chance I had then to see these lovely bare girls. I would have wished to see more of them!

The Chief of Kaiama came without delay to see us after we arrived. Behind these girls he came, looking like a real chief on a fine horse with his mounted warriors. Their horses are much bigger than those the Yorubas have. We found Kaiama in Borgu kingdom to be a large town with many people. This was after six days on the road from Katanga. The Captain was on a little Yoruba horse given to him there. Richard and I walked until near here, where the Chief sent an escort with horses for the three of us. There was a saddle for the Captain but we had a hard ride without one. The escort were rough men who took goats and chickens from the villages we went through. I know the Captain was angry about this but could do nothing.

We parted from Mr. Houtson at Katanga, where he started back to Badagry with his boys. One of them had been Yoruba interpreter for us after an earlier one ran away with some of his other boys, when something had frightened them. Now I have started to work as interpreter into Hausa at last. With Sultan Bello in Sokoto the Captain could speak Arabic, as he told me. He learned some Hausa too in his eight months in our country, but he still needs my help much of the time. The people of Borgu have their own language which we know as *Bussanci* or the language of Bussa, their main city, but nearly everyone knows some Hausa. Traders with

Gonja where you buy cola nuts cross the Niger from the east and pass through Borgu, many through Kaiama. Some settle here just as they do in other places where they trade. In fact, everywhere we have been from Badagry onwards we can find somebody who speaks Hausa

Soon we met a large caravan of Hausa traders coming back to Kaiama from the west with their nuts. They wanted us to go with them to Kano in the north. The Captain has not made any agreement with them yet, however, as he is not sure if they may take a long time, or want to go to other places.

I hear that the name of the Chief of Kaiama is Yaro, a surprise as this means a boy in Hausa. I think he may have another name in *Bussanci* but I do not know what it is. In my country you may speak of a man who helps or goes as a page with a king or other 'big man' as his boy or ' *yaro*.' My brothers in Gobir used to be called *'yaran sarki'* or 'king's boys.' That was before the Fulani caused us trouble and my brothers had to run away. But why the Chief here should be called a boy I do not understand. He is under the King of Bussa but he does not act as a 'boy' to him.

The Captain gave gifts and talked for some time with the Chief with my help He said that King George IV of Britain had sent him and ordered him to go to Sokoto and Bornu. He wanted the Chief to help him with 36 carriers for our loads, which he agreed to do. We started with 40 loads but some contained gifts given to chiefs on the way and some things were used up, so the number slowly gets less. He told the Chief how anxious he was to leave soon so as to get to the dryer and healthier area of Bornu before the rains came, so he did not want to stay long.

The Chief understood that the Captain is a big man serving his king and he offered him his daughter as his wife while he was here. The Captain gave him many thanks and accepted. He goes to where she lives each night while we are here, so he has this comfort. Of course nobody made any such offer to me! I still have no wife since that bad woman ran away, stealing my things. That still hurts me very much, as I thought she had looked at me as a good husband for her.

While speaking to the Chief the Captain pointed to Richard and said to me, ' Tell Yaro this is my son who has come with me from England to help me.' I was surprised as I knew he came from a different town from the Captain. So I put it as I thought he must mean it and said in Hausa to Yaro, 'This is the Captain's boy', using the word *'yaro'*. The Captain stopped me, hearing this word and said, 'I did not mean them to think he is my boy but my son. They would think it strange if I said anything else, and I want them to think he is my son.' So I told the Chief what the Captain now said, that Richard is his son. I said no more, as I could see the Captain was looking angry with me. But afterwards I did not know what to think.

On the Friday nobody worked in Kaiama, while the Hausa and other Muslims went to the mosque. In the afternoon Yaro came galloping on his horse with his followers led by these lovely girls who ran alongside giving him spears to throw at any animals around. A man came behind to give the girls more spears. Later there was horse racing and Yaro won the races as he had the best horses. The following day we left Kaiama.

It only needed three days to the next place Wawa. On the way I thought about what the Captain had said and I still could not see why he called Richard his son. If he had just called him his boy people would have seen that as good. Richard is still working as his servant. although I have seen that since Captain Pearce and the others died the Captain is talking with him much more and even discussing how things are and what we should do. In the evenings they chat together and smoke cigars. Sometimes I hear Richard play his bugle-horn and they sing songs, while I go to my hut and look for a companion. However, as long as this does not change how he works perhaps I should not bother too much. We shall see more as we go on.

The name Wawa is a strange one like the Chief's name Yaro. In our language *wawa* means a fool. It may mean something else in their language. When we arrived we had to wait some time to see the Chief, and the Captain was getting impatient and sent a message that he thought we should go back to Kaiama. The Chief sent to say that he was dressing so we stayed until he came out. The greeting was friendly although the Chief wrapped his sleeve round his hand so that he would not touch the unbeliever, as he regarded the Captain. I do not know if he is a serious Muslim but he calls himself Mohammed. He is not a Hausa man and he may have a different name locally. We were shown a good place to stay in the house of an old widow. She was following their custom that they keep after the husband has died, for at least a year or until they marry again, that I have not seen anywhere else, with a rope tied round her head, another one round her neck and a third one round her body.

Another widow who soon came to visit us was quite different, with no ropes round her and no sign of mourning. Her skin is fair as her husband had been an Arab, and she said quickly that as a white woman she was very happy to welcome these white visitors. The Captain said nothing to this but Richard looked very surprised. I know our people would agree in calling her 'white'. She came with some female slaves, of which they say she has a thousand, but they stayed outside. Her clothes and the gold rings on her arms show how rich she is. She is also very, very fat, as much as the Fat Man at Katanga who used to steal our food sent to us by the Alafin. She could have been lovely when young and even now if I wanted a wife she would have been all right for me. Alas, she did not want the likes of me! She made it clear soon that she wanted a white husband as she started to try and attract Richard to marry her. She might have been about the Captain's age but Richard is young so she thought he was the one for her. We are told this is 'the Widow Zuma', a Hausa word meaning Honey, and she saw herself as being very sweet as well as white.

I was not able to stay all the time in the hut. I may be needed if the Captain has to settle matters with a Chief, or to understand and talk with somebody if there is any difficulty, but for much of the time he can manage without me. Of course Richard does not speak any Hausa yet as it is only a few days since we left Yoruba land. What I did see in the hut – and I could also hear some talk from outside – was that the Captain was very amused as the Widow was talking with Richard. The Captain sat on a mat with his back against the wall of the hut, going puff, puff, puff on his pipe and laughing quietly to himself. She sat on a mat eating cola nuts or chewing tobacco while trying to get Richard to agree to marry her. He sat on another mat throwing his arms and shoulders about and trying to say no, no, no to her without being too rude. I do not think he knows much about women and he has never had a wife. He looked very unhappy and clearly did not know what to do. I though he made poor work of this. After some time the Widow Zuma decided to leave them, but I expect she will come back again soon.

When she did come back she did not repeat her efforts with Richard but turned to the Captain instead. He called me in to explain to her he was not free to do this, as he was under the orders of King George IV to go to Sokoto and Bornu, deliver his messages to them and then return to England to report to the King. She said no matter, she would come with him to Sokoto, indeed she would go with him to anywhere in the world. I think the Captain does not understand how anxious she is to marry a white man. He thinks this is all a game and he is not serious at all. He believed that he had shown her he could not marry her but she thinks she can still get him to do this. I think there could be trouble here, as the Captain is wrong about it. But he has not asked me, so what can I do?

Between visits the Captain worked on his plans. He was told by a leading man in Wawa that two white men with some black men came twenty years ago in a large boat to nearby Bussa, but the boat sank and the men drowned. At first this man said there had been no fighting but later he said there had been some shooting, started by the white men. Some books and other things had been taken from the boat after their death, but the Captain would have to ask about them from the King at Bussa. The Captain said this agreed with the story he had already heard about a white man called Mr. Mungo Park and his death at Bussa. He must go to Bussa and ask about this and see if he could get any books or other things.

The most direct way to Sokoto would be to go first to Bussa, then to Yauri, but people said there was fighting between Yauri and men coming from Sokoto. Some messengers who had recently been at Yauri advised against going that way. He could go to Bussa safely bur instead of going on to Yauri he would do better to go a little south from Wawa to a place called Komi where he could cross the river Kwara, which he believed to be the River Niger that he wanted to see. He got the agreement of Chief Mohammed in Wawa to help us with men to take all the loads to Komi while he went to Bussa and then came back. After crossing the Kwara he could go northwards to the city of Kano, the great city he had seen before when on his earlier journey. However, he still could not reach agreement with the caravan leader we had met at Kaiama to carry our loads there, as he asked for money first but the Captain insisted he could only get money to pay him when they reached Kano. He knew that once there, a trader could give him money in return for a paper which the trader could use to get money sent from Tripoli.

I was nothing to the Widow Zuma, of course. What she wanted was a white husband, not a *yaro* like me! But she had seen me interpret for the Captain and she thought I could help her to convince him to accept her as his wife. She had many slaves, as I have said, so she gave me one to be my own wife. I was happy to have one again, so I thanked her and said I would do what I could, which I thought was little.

In fact she thought things were going well for her. The Captain agreed to come and see her house. It is made of separate huts, like other houses, but much, much bigger because she is rich. The Captain thought he had convinced her to forget about marrying her, and that he would be safe in going to her house. He went alone. I do not know what happened there, but in a short time he came back with a face black like thunder and saying to himself 'That is a bad woman, and I will have nothing more to do with her.' Off he rode to Bussa, less than a full day's journey away. He told us that after seeing the King of Bussa about Mr. Mungo Park and his books he would soon come back to Wawa. Richard and I should prepare all the loads and, with the Chief's promised help, take them to Komi. After he had said farewell to Chief Mohammed he would join us at Komi.

Only a short time after he left, who should suddenly start off also for Bussa but the Widow Zuma?. Her going was a noisy one, with many of her slaves, both men and women, some on horseback. Her own horse, which she rode, must have been strong to carry her weight! It had a red saddle cloth and was covered with bells, brasses and belts. She wore a bright red cloak of silk with gold on it, red trousers and red leather boots. She had on a large white turban, and round her body were many charms, wrapped in red, green and yellow leather.

In front of her were musicians playing drums, fiddles, guitars and flutes, blaring out a loud noise until they were all out of sight. She first called at our place and told Richard she was going to follow the Captain to Kano or wherever he might go, perhaps she had no idea how far that might be. Richard seemed surprised and worried but he waved her goodbye and wished her a safe journey.

Then Richard said to me, 'Come, Pascoe, let us get all the loads ready and then we can ask Chief Mohammed for men to carry them to Komi as the Captain said.' We were busy with the loads and he kept saying to himself, 'Monday, *Litinin,* Tuesday, *Talata* ….' You see, he was trying to learn a few Hausa words every day, either ones he had heard from me or ones he had picked up elsewhere. Today he was trying to learn the names of the days of the week. We had not finished with the loads and so were not ready to go to the Chief for help, so we were surprised when a man came from the Chief's house and told us to go immediately to see him. He meant this for Richard but of course I had to go with him to interpret.

When we reached the Chief's house he said at once, 'You are not to leave Wawa. Both you and the loads must stay here until the Captain comes back.' We said, 'We believed we were to take all the loads to Komi and wait there for the Captain's return, and that you had agreed to help us with carriers'. ' No, no'he replied 'you must stay here. I am worried about what the Captain and the Widow Zuma may do. You must wait until they come back. I am sending men to see you do not go away. Do not argue and go to your place.' We could not understand this, but we saw that we must obey. The next morning we went to see him again and beg for his permission to go, but he was angry and gave us no further reason. One thing more he did say was that the Widow Zuma should have had his permission before giving me the slave woman to be my wife, and the Captain did not ask him either. I would have to send her back to the Widow when she was back here.

Back in our place Richard began to worry much. 'I must go and see the Captain and tell him to come back and arrange things with the Chief. But how am I to get away and go to Bussa? I cannot take you with me as you will have to stay and guard all our loads.' We talked about this for some time until I said, 'Mr. Lander, I do not know if this will succeed, but I think we could get help from the young boy who has been helping with the preparation of food and other things. If he could manage to get you out in spite of the men supposed to watch us, he could guide you all the way to Bussa. Of course, he does not speak English and you still have only a little Hausa.' 'That would not matter,' Richard said, 'The only person I need to speak to is the Captain, and if I have to speak with someone else, I will manage somehow.' The boy was willing to help, and some food was prepared and given to our watchers which kept them busy long enough for Richard and the boy to get away.

So first the Captain went off alone, then the Widow Zuma had gone after him with all her people, and now Richard had gone off with the boy. I was left alone – and I had been told I would lose my wife I could only wait for the others to come back. The Chief allowed me to walk in the town, as long as I did not go outside it or try to take the loads away. I talked with some of the local men, and I learnt that the Widow Zuma was the daughter of Chief Yaro of Kaiama, which made her a 'big woman' in people's eyes. Her husband had been a rich Arab trader from whom .her wealth came when he died. The Chief was afraid she meant him harm

After that I went to the market. With come of the cowries the Captain gave me from time to time to meet my own needs I bought some food, and that left me with just two cowries. It was nearly night time and I knew that traders want then to finish trading and go home, so things might be cheap. With my two cowries I went to a man with a small heap of cola nuts to sell, five of them. Usually my two cowries might buy me two cola nuts but I wanted to get more if I could get them. I asked the man if he would sell the five nuts to me. He pointed to them and said *Do*. I know this means One in their Bussa language. So I said, 'You can do more for me than that.' After a little time he said *'Pla'* and shook his head to show that this was all he could do. I knew from my previous visits that this means Two. I then pretended to get angry, saying that this was not the way to treat a stranger and a visitor with such important people. I was alone and I needed the nuts to keep me going. We argued and argued until it was nearly dark, when he wanted to go away, and at last I won. Looking angrily at me he said, 'Very well, then, if you must, give me the money and take *Pingi* - all the nuts. So I gave him my two cowries, picked up the five cola nuts, thanked him for his kindness and went away happy!

Late in the day after he had gone to Bussa Richard returned back in Wawa but said he had not seen the Captain He believed he must have turned off the road leading back to Wawa to follow the river bank down to Komi, where he would expect to see us already waiting for him. Richard had been received kindly by the King and his wife at Bussa, a much smaller and quieter woman than the Widow Zuma. He had been unwell and very tired so that he could not prevent himself falling asleep in front of them, but they left him alone to sleep. The boy had explained to them why he had come, looking for the Captain. He had also seen near to Bussa the place in the river where they said Mr. Mungo Park had died.

At almost the same time as Richard the Captain arrived back but coming back from the opposite direction, from Komi, after four days away. Like Richard he had found the King and his Queen at Bussa very kind. He too had seen where Mr. Mungo Park died, but found people did not want to talk about it, regarding what had happened as something they were not pleased about. They said they had no books from the boat, but the King *of* Yauri happened to send a messenger at that time and he claimed he had books which he would return if the Captain went there, which he said he would not be able to do. The Captain said it was correct that he had gone straight along the side of the river to Komi, and he was surprised not to find us there with the baggage. Soon Mohammed's son had appeared there, coming from Wawa, telling him he must return to Wawa with the Widow Zuma. Only then would he be allowed to go with his people and loads. He became angry and said that he had no business with the Widow, and that he could not be expected to tell her what she should do. That was up to the Chief. He did not know where she was, although he thought she was not far away, as she had sent him some food. Leaving Mohammed's son to find the Widow, he rode his horse the few miles back to Wawa.

When he arrived back Richard told him what I had learnt in the town. There seemed to be some trouble between the Widow and the Chief, and Mohammed wanted to see them both before he let us go. He was afraid she had some arrangement with the Captain. Then the Captain laughed and said, 'Why did I not see why she wanted to marry me? She wanted to use me for her own ends.' Soon his anger died down and he went to see Chief Mohammed, taking me to interpret. Smiling and thanking Mohammed for all the things he had done to help us, he talked of his visit to Bussa and how good the King and his Queen had been to him there. Then he said he had been surprised not to find us and the loads waiting for him at Komi, as the Chief had promised to help us move them there. The Chief did not show any anger but quietly explained the reasons for his actions. Some time back the Widow had used her slaves in a rebellion, trying to remove him as chief. He had defeated the slaves and captured the lady, but when she said she was very sorry he let her go. Several times more something like this happened. but each time he forgave her. Then we came to Wawa and she seemed to make a special friend of the Captain, who visited her at her house. Next the Captain allows her to give me a slave woman although neither of them had got his permission. When he goes to Bussa, at once she follows him with a great number of people, telling us she was going to follow him to Sokoto or Kano. He had learnt that at her own house she said she would come back with him to take power in Wawa and everyone in the town knew this. All this looked to him as if they were plotting together against him – how could he think otherwise? Until the Widow Zuma came back and confessed and gave up her plans he could not agree to us going. Also he repeated that I must send the slave woman back to her.

The Captain replied that he was very sorry if it seemed to the Chief that there was any plan between him and the Widow Zuma. He did not know her before we came to Wawa, he had made no plans with her and he had no wish to harm or disturb the great Chief of Wawa. He himself had simply to serve King George IV and to do what he had ordered him to do. When she first came to see him there had been one of Mohammed's chief people with her, but he had given no warning of what she might try to do. He was not to blame. Also it was up to me, Pascoe, to decide about the slave woman. Naturally I quickly decided I must obey, and I sent her back at once. I was not too sorry, as I did not much like her.

We had to wait to the next morning for the Widow Zuma to appear. She rode into Wawa at the head of all her people, in all her fine clothes. A drummer with an ostrich feather in his hat led the way and the musicians played loud and long. Then she heard news of what the Chief was saying, the music stopped, and as soon as she reached her house the drummer, musicians and her slaves were sent away to hide themselves. Off came the bright clothes she had been wearing and she put on the most simple and plain clothes she had. She came to the Chief's house and went down on the ground on her hands and knees and said she did not mean to cause him any trouble. He told her she was behaving very badly after all the times he had forgiven her and she must forget any plans she had against him. She told him a lie about having gone after a runaway slave. He said he could not believe her but after some more talking to her he sent her away. Then he told the Captain that as she had come back and had repented, we could continue on our way tomorrow. Next day we were on our way, in Komi with all our loads, ready to cross the River Niger

I had to leave Wawa without being able to settle one mater. Besides the slave woman that the Widow Zuma had given me, I had arranged with her to buy one of her many slaves to become my wife but we had not completed this. I got part of my money back before we left and I hope can get the rest back later, but now she owes me this money.

Before we came into Borgu people had said they were rogues and thieves here. Men often claim to be good themselves and they say bad things about their neighbours. In fact, we had had help from the people in Borgu, and nothing was stolen from us. I thought of how kind Chief Mohammed had been to us. He understood it was all the fault of the Widow Zuma who had tried to make use of the Captain against him. Many a chief would have made bad trouble for us, but he had shown he is a good man. It would have been better for us if the Captain had not thought it was all a joke. Enough of the Widow Zuma, who is not sweet honey for us!

Chapter 7 — Over The Niger and on to Kano

April – July 1826

'Well, here we are crossing the Niger for the first time' said the Captain in a loud voice as we were being paddled by canoe ferry 'the river that men have been seeking for a long time. If you go north from here, to our left, you would come to Bussa, where the bold Mungo Park died after he had led the way to the river. If you go south, on our right hand, I believe it must lead to the sea in the Bight of Benin, whatever else anybody may say. It remains for us to find that way to the sea, after we have first been to Sokoto and Bornu.' I thought, 'How brave these men have been, when others have died, to come so far through difficulties and being ill, both the Captain and Richard.' I felt brave myself too. I usually left it to others to speak, but I felt I must say something. I called out what I had heard so often on board ship when we had had a victory, 'Hip, hip…' and I was glad to hear the others join in with 'Hooray'! Then Richard felt in his bag and brought out his bugle-horn and gave us the tune I had sung many times with my shipmates, *Rule Britannia,* and other tunes. Afterwards the Captain said more quietly to me, 'I expect, Pascoe, that after all your years in the Royal Navy, chasing slave ships and releasing their unfortunate captives, you do feel one of us in singing this song?' 'Yes, Sir, of course I do' I replied, although I knew that if I had not been with these men, I could not be sure that never, never will I be a slave.

This was after three days we had stayed at Komi, as the Captain had been sick. We had sent over our baggage, then the horses, before crossing ourselves. We then came into Nupe country with rich farmland. Many were Kamberi people, busy farmers who worry nobody. We learnt that there was really a civil war amongst the Nupe, which the Captain had doubted earlier, as to which of two brothers should be their ruler. Most were pagan but those who were Muslim had called on the help of the Fulani from Sokoto, and they seemed to be winning the war. Ten days later we thought we were near where Mohammed el Magia, the Muslim one trying to be ruler, was living, but we heard that he was two days' journey away. We did see the Queen Mother of the Nupe, with one eye, who advised the Captain to go and see him.

The Captain did go off, taking as interpreter into Arabic a man from Murzuk who has lived here for years and speaks Nupe. I stayed behind with Richard. He was away four days and when he came back he told Richard he thought badly of Mohammed el Magia. He last saw him going off to attack a village already badly damaged in the fighting. However, one good thing was that he came back with a small horse to add to the two he already had, that I could ride.

Since we left Wawa it has got hotter and hotter, weather to make you sweat: it is that time of year. I remember how it was before I went to sea, and I was then used to this season before the rains come. Now I have been away from it for a long time. The Captain and Richard kept having days when they do not feel well and I know this weather is bad for them. The fast of Ramadan also started at the time we were leaving Wawa. As so many of the people here are not Muslim this does not stop our getting food at any time, but some Muslims look at me and ask me why I am not fasting. Often I do not want to eat in the hot time of the day anyway but I do drink water when I feel I need it. Sometimes I smile and say that as I am travelling I need not fast now. I will make up for it later. Other times I take no notice of these questions and walk on. I do see that many people who keep the fast and pray five times a day still drink beer or palm wine after they have broken their fast at night Just like the pagans they are sometimes drunk. I like a drink, as you know but I try not to get too drunk and annoy the Captain as my wife did at Katanga.

An odd thing happened at one place. The carriers suddenly put down our loads and ran off. This must have been when they saw other men running towards them, and they must have been frightened there would be a fight. Then these other men picked up our loads, saying nothing to us, and they ran ahead as fast as they could go. Once they put down the loads to get their breath then, as if on a signal, they picked them all up again and went on running with them. It was some time before we on our horses caught up with them, at a town we wanted to reach. At last they put down our loads. We could see they did not mean any harm to us, but all this was very strange. The only trouble was that when we came to pay them they showed they had expected us to pay much more! But they went off quietly.

The Captain and Richard had much fever, often at the same time, and our progress was slow. It was three weeks after crossing the Niger that we reached a large town called Kulfo, on the bank of a small river Maiyaro. We would usually expect to do this in a few days. On the way we had passed through smaller towns, crossing rivers by bridges made from crooked parts of trees and too narrow for more than one man or horse. Thatched houses crowd round two big market squares, open daily, but with bigger markets two days in the week. I have seen many traders from our Hausa lands and Bornu to the north, from Yoruba to the south and from Borgu and even Gonja to. the west. They used to come from Benin to the south as well, but that is more difficult because of the civil war. So many roads used by the traders meet here. You can buy different kinds of clothes, many types of food and peppers, goods the Arabs bring from Egypt and Mecca, things from Europe that have come from Tripoli over the desert, almost every kind of thing is here in the market. You can also see tailors, people spinning and weaving and other craftsmen here, many of them also trading. I have been round the market with the Captain when he has been well, helping him to know what all these things are, where they come from and what is their price. I know he goes home and writes about these things. Slaves too are bought and sold here, but most of the time they are kept hidden away in houses.

After we had been here a few days the new moon was seen and there was rejoicing as the fast of Ramadan came to an end. The next morning everybody was out in their best clothes and both Muslims and pagans were happy. After the Muslims had said their prayers for the Id there was dancing in the streets, singing and playing music. All drank as much as they wanted until some were fully drunk and rolling about. The noise was very great and there was little sleep all day except for those too drunk to stay awake. Of course I enjoyed my share and I am glad to say the Captain and Richard were well enough that day to have a little too.

But I have mentioned how the weather was getting too hot, meaning the rains were near. On the very night when all were celebrating a great storm arrived and spoiled all the rejoicing. I know from the past how you can be sweating in the heat, with no wind at all, and then the first sign can be a wind starting and getting stronger, throwing up horrible dust. Then you get thunder and lightning but if this is the first storm you may be unlucky and have no rain, only wind, dust, then silence and worse heat. But this time a strong storm did come, with too much noise, wind and really hard rain so you could not see across the street. Thunder and lightning went on and on and seemed to be hitting the ground all around us. People rushed to take into their houses everything they had outside. Roofs were blown off houses and even some houses were blown down. There were screams of fear from women and children and what seemed to be like war-cries from the men. A small town called Bali near Kulfo was hit by lightning and the thatched roofs caught fire, jumping from one house to the next. When the rain came it put out the few bits of fire in Bali that had not burnt the housesdown. At our house the roof of one hut blew off but other parts were all right. Next day I saw people from Kulfo go over to Bali to help and give them things they needed until they could build their houses again. In the past I have been used to the storms at the start of the rains and the fires they cause, but I do not remember such a strong one as this.

I know the Captain has sent out people to Yauri to the north and to a Nupe town called Raba on the Niger. He did hear that somebody there might have books from the boat of this Mr. Mungo Park. They came back with no success. We did hear one story here, however, saying that the king of Bussa did send people to attack their boat. This was at the time when Sultan Bello's father had begun his uprising of the Fulani, and the king of Bussa thought the white men he heard were coming down the river in a strange boat must be some of the Fulani. The whole event had made his people afraid, especially as they found some meat in the boat, ate it and many died. From the present king of Bussa we had a friendly message and a present of a little mare, and some foodstuffs sent by his wife. She advised us not to eat any meat cooked by Nupe outside Kulfo, as it might be poisoned. This has made us very careful.

We had to wait a long time before the Captain and Richard became well enough to go on. Most of the time they stayed in our lodging quietly. We were in the house of a widow called Ladi, who was a big trader in beer and palm wine, which she brewed. Of course she had many customers and this did not make for quiet. There were two men who did the washing and other things for us, but when the Captain and Richard were ill I had to watch them, or they could be idle or drunk. The Captain thanked me for doing this as well as working as cook and interpreter, but one day he said he wanted to change things when everybody was well again. He said that then, while of course he was the Captain, he wanted Richard to be his First Lieutenant, and I could help him when I was not busy as cook and interpreter. I did not like this very much, as I thought Richard and I were equals as his servants, and I did not want to feel I was under him. However, it could not apply while they were both suffering from fever.

In fact, this went on for seven weeks and all that time we had to stay in Kulfo, and I had no problem then. The Captain is worried about the delay, as it has been raining nearly every day since that storm. I know how much he wants to get to dryer places to the north. Another thing that worried him was that we needed so many carriers. He decided to sell horses, other than the Bussa mare that he would ride. With the money he bought bullocks, as they could carry many of our loads Even when we did finally manage to go onwards Richard soon got the flux. He had to lie down on the road from time to time and roll about to beat the pain he had. Sometimes the Captain had to wait and call Richard to come on after him, making smoke signals to show him the way.

Even then, with the Captain pushing us to move on, we soon left the Nupe country. When we had passed a place called Kurege we had to cross a stream that was full of water because of the rains. The loads were taken off the bullocks and we carried them across, with the servants we had following us. Of course both the bullocks and we ourselves got very wet.

Half way, my foot slipped and .I lost hold of the Captain's shot belt. Down it fell, deep in the stream, and we could not find it. The Captain can be very angry sometimes and I was afraid he would shout at me, but he saw how it happened and luckily he did not blame me too much this time. .

Then we came to the country of the Gwari. In under two weeks from Kulfo we reached their capital Birnin Gwari. I remember my father telling me how he had come here when it was joined to Katsina kingdom. That was before the Fulani attacked and drove our people back. We found a road full of rocks going north from the town which they say goes on to Katsina; There were caravans of traders on the road to or from Kulfo, but not many stayed in Birnin Gwari. It is a small town, even though it has a very big wall round it. The town is east of the road and on the other side there is a long hillside, with the wall going up, up and over it. The Chief was nice to us and we stayed there two nights before going on to Zaria. On the road I was picking up a stick to make a fire but I felt the stick moving in my hand. I did not stop to look at it to see what it was but at once I threw it away as far and as fast as I could. It could have been the end of me, for it was of course a snake, grey marks on it that made it look like a dead piece of wood. The full truth of this I only knew when I woke up, for the shock of feeling it move in my hand made me fall down in a faint. For this I thanked my good spirits – yes, I do have some good spirits, not only bad ones, - and I bought a chicken to sacrifice to them The Captain told me to be more careful in future. I think Richard was too sick to say anything then, but later he laughed at me about it.

Zaria is a very big city with a high mud wall like Katsina, with rocky hills round it and even inside. Much of the land has been cleared for farms but all along one side of it are many tall trees called *rimi* trees. It is not the time now, but when the weather is all dry they have seeds like cotton when it has just been picked, which can blow all round the place. When this stuff is collected it can be used to fill cushions or pillows to make things to sit or lie on. You can see that people cut the side branches to use for firewood or other things, making them stand very tall, straight and narrow, like poplar trees in England, the Captain says.

We hear that the Governor is out of town. He is not called a king as he is appointed by the Sultan at Sokoto, but he governs the large area round the city for many miles. While he is away a man called Abdulkarim is in charge. He has given us a good place to stay in his own house, and sent us food.

We have spoken with some people. The Captain said how good these *rimi* trees look. An old man said they had stood there for many years. Those coming from other towns say they are special to Zaria, where they are taken as signs of how old the city is and how it will last for many years. He then said, 'We in Zaria have a saying, even though we have good women, we can depend on the *rimis* even beyond the virtue of a maiden.' The Captain laughed and said, 'That is a strong saying. If I could come back in a hundred years do you think I would find them still standing?' The old man also laughed and said, 'I believe they would still be here, even beyond a hundred years.'

There are many other trees you can see, including the date and oil palms, pawpaws and melons. They are growing all kinds of guinea corn, millet, rice, yams, sweet potatoes and other crops, a wealth of stuffs. Houses and farms are all round the place in the city, with cattle, sheep and horses. Most houses are thatched but some have large rooms with flat clay ceilings, which the richer men have. On the top of some roofs are ostrich eggs, but I have not seen any ostrich here. Near the Governor's house, which is like a village in its wall, there is a big mosque with a tall tower or minaret. The only way I can tell you how tall it is is to say it goes up as high as the mainmast in a ship of the line.

The Captain talked much with Abdulkarim and I interpreted between them. First the Captain said who he is and why he has come here. He wants help to go to Kano, and Abdulkarim said he would give help and send a messenger to show him the way. Then Abdulkarim told him it was a new city built by the Fulani when they took the city twenty years ago after a two-day battle. He showed where the walls of the older city still stand. The old king who lost the battle to the Fulani went away with some of his people to a hilly place far to the south. He still resists attacks from Zaria and claims he will come back. There are many Fulani people in Zaria, but in the district around it they rule many Hausa people and in some places pagan farmers. He said there was much game in the whole country, antelopes, guinea fowl and other birds, and further south there are elephant and buffalo.

Our stay in Zaria was pleasant, but when leaving, with Abdulkarim for the first day, the Captain could not agree with him. Abdulkarim thought Britain was just a small island in a big sea, and was unable to fight any strong battle. The Captain tried hard to put him right, but they nearly had trouble between them. We then had not only bullocks but also a camel, which the Captain had bought, as it would be even better for carrying loads. Before we came here you could never see a camel.

The route towards Kano was a little east of north from Zaria. With all the rain the country was green, one farm after another. The guinea corn and millet stand half as high as a man. Trees that have fruit have been kept but other trees have been cleared away. After passing Likoro with its walls, the next day we came to a place called Romo, a word which means a soup with meat, but it is in such a bad state that you can hardly get anything there! A day later we could get cows' meat at Auchan, where they had killed a bullock because of the great feast of Id el Kabir, just like we used to observe this feast in my young days. The Captain had his pocket watch stolen after he had put it up in the rafters of the hut. There were few people who could have been the thief, and soon we found it was in fact one of our own bullock drivers. So the Captain got his watch back, and he spoke strongly to the man.

I have seen houses like this before but none can b e found near the coast. Farmers are now busy hoeing and weeding, and there are many women together threshing corn from last year's harvest on a stone floor.

The Captain took me up a granite hill outside the town where we could see all around. The ground is flat but you could see hills back to Auchan some days' journey back, and north to Kano. We reached this very big city the next day, the seventh day from Zaria. As we got near we had to cross a wide river, but not very deep, running eastwards. 'This,' said the Captain, 'must be the river the Arabs have said goes to meet the Nile, and some people like Consul Ritchie have supported this, but you can see it is too small to go all that way.' He also talked about it being nearly eight months now since we landed at Badagry. After he goes to Sokoto, where he wants to go soon, then come back and has gone to Bornu, the second place he must go to, he hopes we can be back on the coast before another eight months have passed.

Chapter 8 — Bad Spirits

<u>August – December 1826</u>

'Mr. Lander,' I said, 'why should I not go outside the town?'

'You know that when the Captain went to Sokoto to see Sultan Bello he wanted us to be ready for his return, when we will all go to Bornu.'

'I know that, but Sokoto is a long way. With all this rain it may take him a long time.'

'That may be true but, as the Good Book says, "Watch therefore, as you do not know when the master of the house comes." He could come at any time, and we should be ready.'

I said no more.

The Captain had indeed started to go to Sokoto as soon as he could be ready. He had been with us in Kano only three days, and on the fourth day he started his journey. I do not know what orders he gave to Richard. To me he said only that I should wait for him and be good. From what he had said before I think he may have meant Richard to be like his Firs Lieutenant, but he did not say so to me.

One thing we heard very soon after we came to Kano. That is, that war had started between Sokoto and Bornu. When he went to the house of Alhaji Hat Saleh, an Arab who had done things for him when he came to Kano before, he was told that all trade had stopped between them. This had even prevented the Arabs' trade over the desert to Tripoli, as Bornu could shut that route. Another route further west through Katsina was uncertain because our people driven out of there by Sultan Bello were now fighting from a place further north. People hoped that the Captain could help to make peace and remove the difficulty. The Captain hoped that Bello would see that as he was somebody from outside he could still be allowed to go to Bornu I thought this was un certain as he had been there before and had been friends with the ruler , and Bello might think he might want to join with them against him.

I soon found a wife for myself in Kano. She was a widow and needed a man to look after her. First she wanted to go to the village where she used to live before to see her family, and bring her things to Kano. I did not want her to go alone, in case anything bad might happen to her. This is one reason why I wanted to go outside Kano for a few days. I thought Richard was being too hard in saying I could not go. I would also like to take a pair of our pistols with me and shoot some guinea fowl or pigeons that I could bring back with me. If the Captain had ordered me to do any thing or not to do it, of course I would have obeyed him, but Richard was a servant like me and I did not see why he should try to give me orders.

Twice again I argued with Richard that I had good reason to go out from Kano but he would not listen to me. My wife said many times that I should either go with her or forget about her altogether. . After two weeks of worry I decided I must act, even if Richard did not agree. I would go with the wife, but because Richard was being difficult I would forget about shooting birds this time. Not saying anything to him I went off with my wife to her village. We reached there the same day as we had started, and we were there two more days. In one more day we would have set off back to Kano. She talked with her mother as she got ready to collect her things and come back with me to Kano. Of course she also wanted to see neighbours before saying goodbye to them. But then, all of a sudden I heard a horse come fast into the village and a voice that I recognised. He was speaking some Hausa badly . It must be Richard as nobody else in the whole country, except the Captain who was far away, could speak like that. He had learned some Hausa by then but it did not sound like a Hausa man speaking. I could only think that somebody had told him where my wife had lived before and he had followed me here. I had intended to go back to him in Kano the next day and I did not like him coming to me in this way. There was little time to think what I should do now. My wife pointed out into the yard but it had little cover for me. The best I could do was to go behind a pile of yams and crouch down. It was not a good place to hide and almost at once Richard saw my clothing sticking out from behind the pile of yams.

Running towards me he made an angry sign for me to come out and he called loudly in English 'Come out, you bad man. I told you not to go away from Kano and here you are, hiding yourself.'

'Yes, Mr. Lander, here I am. I told you I needed to come here with my wife, and I do not know what is wrong with that. Tomorrow I was going to come back to be with you in Kano.'

'I have to look after things while the Captain is away, and you have to do what I tell you.'

I said no more, but I made a sign of drinking to my wife's mother, who went inside and brought out a bowl of milk which she offered to Richard after bowing down to him. Taking and drinking it started to calm him down. My wife also bowed down and gave him some *kosai* or bean cakes which they had in the house. All the people there could see that he was angry but they did not know the reason.

My wife began to weep and to tell Richard I was only helping her in coming home to see her mother and to gather her things. We did not mean any harm to him and if this was wrong in some way then please, please would he forgive me. She went on saying this and adding to it, but she was speaking very quickly and Richard probably did not follow even a half of her words. But it was obvious that she was pleading with him to forgive me and in the end he became quiet. Of course we set off with Richard as soon as he was ready to go, with my wife still pleading with him. When we got back to our house in Kano he felt it necessary to scold me once more and to make me promise never to do anything like this again. Then he said that, since I did promise, he would not say anything more about it also I did promise. Then we all went to lie down and rest.

Not many days after that something happened that surprised me greatly and that made me think that perhaps Richard had some truth on his side. Suddenly the Captain reappeared, and we did not know in advance he was coming. It was rather like what Richard had said about his Good Book. The Captain had steered a little north of west, as you would say at sea, and had been through many wet areas and across streams, but in the end the rain and the rivers made him turn back to Kano. This was after meeting Sultan Bello's

Gidado, one of his chief men. He had come this way to see things were good in the eastern areas under the Sultan but now wanted to go back to Sokoto. He advised the Captain to wait with him at Kano until the rains became less. I was glad that I had not been away from Kano when the Captain arrived. To be fair to Richard, I do not think he told the Captain anything about my having been away, as he had promised to say no more, and perhaps he had realised I had some good reason.

After two or three weeks in Kano the Captain went off again, this time with the Gidado and his men. Having them with him would make it easier when they came to bad places. They went by a more southerly route, going first to Bebeji that we had come through on the way from Zaria, and then to the west.

Richard and I had little work to do. Most of the loads were locked safely in a room, but we checked them often and saw that our guns were clean and ready. Of course we had to find food for ourselves and this took us many days to the Kano market. It is the biggest market I have ever seen, much more than the Katsina, Katanga or Kulfo market. There is a food area, where you can buy guinea corn, millet, yams, cassava, tomatoes, onions, fruit, vegetables, and almost anything you could name. Then there is an area for cloth, either simple lengths of cloth or gowns and other things made up by a tailor, also fine clothing from Egypt and other countries. The butchers have their area, and near there you can buy cooked items to eat. In other parts you can find paper, scissors, knives, pieces of tin and other metals, glass, brass or coral beads, even good drinking water can be bought as the ordinary water in the town is not good. At the edge of the market there is a place for selling animals, sheep, goats, cows and others, and there is another area for selling slaves, men in one line and women in another. Every day you see a big crowd in the market. The traders have to rent bamboo stalls from the chief of the market, who also fixes prices of common things. What he says is law. I even heard of a man who had bought something expensive but found it to be bad, and the chief of the market could tell which trader had sold it and he made him pay the man back. They have a custom that when a price has been agreed and paid the seller either returns a small part of the price or adds a little more of the grain or other thing sold. This they call the *gyara* or benefit. This market is well arranged but we saw one problem: when the rains are heavy water floods in from some ground nearby and sometimes the market cannot be held., but when it is dry this market is a great thing for Kano.

After the Captain left us the second time, with the Gidado, I decided I would try to keep my promise to Richard, even though he often made me feel bad by giving me orders as if I was his servant. I did not want to fail the Captain. Things continued like this for six or eight weeks. As we did not see the Captain again I thought he must be well on his way to Sokoto. As I say, I tried to be patient and not to argue with Richard or go against what he said, but in time I became angrier and angrier in myself. I did not want to fight with him, but when I tried to get him to agree that we should go out together with pistols to get birds, or if he did not want to come, then I could go alone, he would not agree. He kept saying, 'No. We must wait here until we have news of the Captain. You may not go.' I felt I was bursting with anger, and in the end I could bear it no more. I know this was wrong, and I ought not to have done it, but one night I went off without telling him, taking my wife with me. I had a pistol for shooting birds, and I took six scissors so that I could trade them for food. I did not know how long I would stay away. I just felt I needed some time away from Richard. As it was a direction I had seen before on our way to Kano I headed south towards Zaria. After two days I came to the place called Romo that we had stayed in for a night before we came to Kano.

Richard somehow succeeded in finding out the direction I had taken and he followed me. I knew he was still not well, but he was able to come on. He had with him a man who did some work for us. He also hired a number of men in Romo to catch me like a criminal. I was no criminal and I had no thought of committing any crime, but Richard's following me made him imagine all kinds of crime I might commit.

When he and these men found me I made no resistance – why should I? – I explained to Richard that I had only done what I often talked about with him, shooting birds for all of us to eat. I said I could not see why he should think it necessary to come to me like this, and I would very soon have come back to him in Kano. I was sorry and I would try not to give him any more trouble. In the meantime, with her being upset by finding me in trouble again, I lost my wife who left me and went back, to her mother. After saying to Richard what *I* thought he only said, 'Oh, very well,' and we went to rest.

I have said I know I had done wrong in coming away from Kano without telling Richard, but it was after we lay down that the bad spirits really entered me. I could not rest but I felt very hot, burning with anger and a strong feeling that I must go away. I had no real idea where I could go and whether I should stay away from Richard altogether. What I could do and where I should live I could not think of then. My mind was put all wrong by these feelings, and I was driven to wanting just to get away. Once before, long ago at the time when Sultan Bello's people had first come to attack our people, I had had the bad spirits in me then. I had not had them again later until now when they had come, many spirits in force, to trouble me.

When I could be sure that Richard was asleep I got up quietly and prepared to leave him. Not knowing how long I should be alone and where I should be, the spirits led me to take our pistols, all the money Richard had with him, clothes and other things. I k new he had more money back in Kano and I had to take what he had here from his sock m which he had tied it. I knew there was a dead sheep outside, which had been slaughtered but not yet cut up by the butcher. I dragged it in and put it on my bed, covering it with a cloth, and I put a cap on its head. Then I went outside and ran off in the darkness. I knew nobody would be about then, so I got away easily. Where to go, I did not know. When I had gone some way I found an unused stall in a small village market and I lay down to rest. The spirits started to be quiet and I went to sleep. When I woke up it was morning, and by then the spirits began to give me some peace. I began to think better and to ask myself what I should do now. How could I be led back first to Richard and then to the Captain after what I had done? How long I was like this I do not know. It may have been some days later when I was seized by men who said they were sent by the Governor of Kano. The 'Little Christian', had complained I had stolen things from him. I knew they must mean Richard by 'the Little Christian', but how they found me I do not know. We were some miles from Kano and I was taken back there and put in a room, all chained up, as if in a prison. Later I was given some food.

It was some days later that Richard came to see me, and he was still angry with me. He said the Governor was out of town but would see me when he came back. He also said he had received a letter from the Captain, who had reached Sokoto. He hoped soon to see the Sultan, who had been away fighting the Gobir people. He had had the fever but hoped to get better soon. After another week or so he came again and said he had had another letter from the Captain, saying he had been well received by the Sultan but he found him most unwilling that he should go to Bornu and he did not know what to do. He thought some Arabs were saying bad things about him to the Sultan. However, he thought he would still come back to Kano before going anywhere else. Richard said that the Governor of Kano was not yet back, and I should have to wait until he did come back.

I must have been in this prison for about two weeks before I was eventually called before the Governor. I decided not to argue as I thought the Governor would not understand my problem with Richard. He only heard Richard's story and then he spoke to me strongly and made me swear not to leave Richard again. Then, at last, I had my chains removed and I was set free, going back with Richard to our house. Next day Richard was called to the Governor's house and told that he had received a letter from the Captain saying that both of us should go immediately *from* Kano *to* Sokoto, taking all the baggage with us. Richard could not see why there should be this sudden change of plan unless something bad had happened to the Captain. Then, two days later, the Governor sent for him again and told him to get ready to leave quickly, the next day. I know this was said, as Richard had taken me so that I could interpret and make sure there was no mistake. .

So off we went, the next day, and both Richard and I were troubled, but for different reasons. Richard was troubled about the sudden change in plans and he was afraid something bad might have happened to the Captain. I was troubled, as I did not know how things would be with me if I got to Sokoto. They had fought with Gobir and had taken most of their country but were still fighting with them, as the Captain's first letter had shown. There was also still unfinished fighting with Katsina. Things I had heard from time to time in Zaria and Kano showed how things had changed very much in these countries since Sultan Bello's father had started all of this trouble. I was very unhappy about going to Sokoto at all.

We had all the loads with us and a camel. The Governor of Kano gave us five bullocks to carry the loads, and there were four men to look after them, as well as a messenger. It was now dry weather, not like when the Captain had left us. The harvest was now over. The wet ground had dried and the rivers got much smaller. We could therefore travel quite fast but this brought me nearer to Sokoto. People were talking about the fighting with the people of Gobir and I did not like this. Everywhere we were welcomed and given food and places to stay. They seemed happy to see the 'Little Christian'

After we had been about a week on the road Richard suddenly fell badly ill. Soon he was calling for my help – yes, me who had been in chains for him so recently. 'Help, Pascoe,' he said, 'I feel I am dying and will leave you soon. If I die, have me buried and then go as fast as you can to Sokoto and give everything to the Captain.' Of course, I said I would, and I *was* sorry for him. I knew he was trying to do what he thought the Captain wanted. The next day he felt much better and he made some men prepare a bed to carry him on the back of the camel. Going through the woods was difficult as the branches caught at the bedding. The Kano messenger helped by using his sword to cut the branches off. At the next village the Chief came to us, happy to see the Little Christian. He said he was a very good man as much as anyone else, although some people tried to tell him this must be wrong. The next day Richard was able to ride a horse and we went on for some days.

Now that Richard was better and less needing my help, as we got nearer to Sokoto, I became more worried. If I was to keep away from that place and the danger that, as a man from Gobir, I would have my head cut off, I decided that I must leave very soon. We went through a large area of bush with many wild animals in it, and signs that elephants had been there. Then we came to a place called Sansani, not a town but a large open area where the Sultan's armies could gather together from different places before going to fight. For fear of robbers coming to steal our things Richard had the baggage put in the middle with all the men sleeping around it.

Those bad spirits came into me again and gave me no peace. This, I thought, must be my chance. As I meant to go right away this time I would need to have enough things with me. After everyone had gone to sleep I managed to open some of the boxes and I took a gun, two pistols, a cutlass, some money and a number of knives and needles of various sizes which I could trade with. Where I had been lying I put a pillow in a sack with a cloth over it, and then ran off.

I did not succeed. Richard did not sleep well and was worried that his camel had gone outside, and soon he found that I was missing. At once he cried out and he got the Chief nearby to send out twelve armed men on horses. I was going back the way we had come, through the bush with animals around. Some hyenas came near and frightened me. I left the things I had on the ground and went up a tree. I stayed there all night. Then, wanting to go down and move away I fired the gun to scare off the animals. This was my mistake.

The men who were looking for me heard the shot and came quickly. They saw the things on the ground and soon saw me too up above. They told me to come down at once and if not they would shoot me. Of course I climbed down and let them take me, saying nothing. I was put on the back of a horse and then they galloped back to where Richard was, calling out their success in catching 'the bad man.' Richard asked me why I did this bad thing after promising him to be good. I told him how frightened I was of having my head cut off in Sokoto and how the bad spirits had seized me. The Chief of the village wanted to cut my head off right there, but Richard said no, I should be tied up with ropes and chains and put in their prison.

They tied me up so badly that my arms swelled up much bigger than usual and it was very painful. I showed my bad arms to Richard the next day and he had the ropes undone but left me in irons in their prison. I was there a whole week. By this time the bad spirits had left me and I could show Richard how sorry I was to have displeased him. Then he let me out. An escort of fifty soldiers had come from Sokoto to take us and the baggage, using the Captain's camel, so we got ready to go.

The Kano messenger secretly gave Richard a letter from the Captain, which showed that he thought we were still in Kano and had not asked to have us brought to Sokoto. Richard was very angry and said this must mean that Sultan Bello had told lies to make the Kano Governor send us up to him with all the baggage. Probably he was planning to kill us when he had got us in Sokoto. The Gidado's brother in command of the escort promised us there would be no harm done to us in Sokoto. The Sultan just wished to see the two Christians, he said. The next day and a half were a tiring walk across the Gobir bush, a difficult part with no water sources. Then we rested two days and the next day went on into Sokoto. With various things delaying us on the way it had taken nearly a month from Kano and it was three months since we had seen the Captain.

After our arrival I saw him just once. That was when Richard told him the things I had done, how I had run away from him three times and stolen guns, money and other things. 'Yes,' he said, 'that agrees with what I have heard from the Kano Governor through his messenger, and it is very bad. I easily get angry when people do wrong. I cannot forgive you, and I must dismiss you here and now. I will not pay you any wages or anything else.' I did not want to argue with him or to try to blame Richard. All I wanted was mercy. I sank to my knees with tears running from my eyes. I rubbed my hands together and then held them out in a pleading way in front of me. I said nothing but silently mouthed the words, 'Mercy, please.' I was so sad to have to leave the Captain I had tried to serve for so long.

As I say, I did not want to argue with him or to say it was Richard's fault, although it was the Captain's having left me under my fellow-servant to obey his orders that had started it all. I did not think he would listen to me if I said this. I only wanted to get wages for my service and I went to find a lawyer who could advise me. He asked me my name and I said 'Abubakar'. Then he asked me for 200 cowries if I wanted to consult him. I said I just lost my means of getting money but I put down 100 cowries. Then he said:

'Were you the man who was with the Great Christian, as men here call him?'

'Yes,' I said, 'I was with him.'

'What do you want now?'

'I want the money I have earned.'

'Everybody in Sokoto knows what has happened, and everybody can see you deserved punishment.'

'I only want the money due to me.'

'Abubakar, you have much to be thankful for. You have come here alive. You have reached this city of peace and justice, where you can repent of your sins. You have a place to stay and you are given food. Above all, you should thank God that you still have a head attached to your body. Anyone else in Sokoto would have expected your master to have cut off your head. Thank God he has not done so. That is all!'

My bad spirits had brought me to this low point. All I could do then was to go away and weep.

Chapter 9 — In the Depths

December 1826 – March 1827

I cried aloud and I wept. How could I survive? I had lost my post, I was without my pay The Captain had at first agreed to pay me as a seaman, but in the Navy there was always a long time between pay days, and in any case, here in Africa. there was no time for issuing pay. Now he had said there would not be any pay at all I was not very far from my old home town but Sultan Bello had defeated Gobir and sacked the capital, although men from Gobir were still fighting him. Katsina was almost as bad. So trying to go home did not seem good for me. I did not know any craft except being a sailor and cooking, and the sea was now far away. Most of all .I was no longer with the Captain who I had tried to serve well. I had quarrelled with Richard, that servant who had tried to order me about, but I had never meant to do anything wrong to the Captain. Now he had driven me away and cut off my pay. That was the worst thing, which made me feel I was being made to walk the plank and fall into the deep sea, from which I could not escape by swimming.

To sleep that night was impossible, and the next one, but soon I started to see a little light shining into my dark depths. I was a free man and, as the lawyer said, I still had my head on my body. I had a place to sleep, as the Gidado was always a kind man – he had asked the Captain to forgive me – and he let me stay in his compound. I still had a little money that I had not spent, not much, but some, and I could try to find a way to earn some more. It would be hard but I could try to keep myself.

I went to the market to buy some food from a woman who had many customers, for it was said that she cooked very good food. She had a large pot in front of her, selling *tuwo* and I had to wait while other customers were served. *Tuwo*, guinea corn or millet pounded fine and then boiled until it becomes thick, is like the white man's porridge that I have eaten many times on board ship. It can easily make you feel full and strong. If you have money you can get it made from rice, with a vegetable soup or even with meat, but I was saving my money so I had it plain, as it was. It was very good and I thought the woman must be a better cook even than I am.

I said to her, *'Tsohuwa'* which means an elderly lady, perhaps not very old, a word used when you can say this politely, 'this is a very good *tuwo* that you make. May I come again some times to eat here from you, and can you let me have a little credit for the next few days? I have little money and no work now, until I can find a way to earn some more.' In spite of my troubles I did manage to smile, and this seemed to please her. She agreed to what I asked her, but then also asked me if it was true that I had come to Sokoto with those Christian white men, as she had heard. I said this was so and I let her know that the Captain would not let me work with him any longer.

She thought a little, and then said to me, 'I think I know how you may be able to earn some money if you are prepared to work. There is a place outside Sokoto where they grow tobacco and it is sold here in the town. Some Muslims do not agree to smoking but some others allow it. What many people like but find hard to buy is snuff. If you can buy some dry tobacco leaves and grind them into small pieces you will get snuff to sell.' 'That seems a good idea,' I said, 'let me try it.' She told me where to go and how to buy it. She called a young boy and sent us off together. At the tobacco farm they had put some rope between trees and hung the tobacco on it to dry in the sun.

When I came back with dried tobacco leaves I had difficulty to find how I could grind them small to make snuff without the wind blowing it away but I solved that. Then I had to decide how to make the snuff into bags for me to sell. The tobacco leaves themselves were too dry to make bags with them. I found I had to cut other leaves from trees which were less dry so that I could use them to make small bags in which I could put the snuff. Most people who use snuff have little horns in which they keep it, so I could sell it in my bags from which they could put the snuff into their horns. It took me a day or two to work things out but then I made up some bags and took a place in the market after paying the headman to give me a place. Soon I had my first customer, then another one and, in the first day, about six. But what I had not thought of was that they would ask for credit, as they said they needed to make sure it was good stuff that I was selling them. I had had to pay for the tobacco, of course, and the market place, but they were not paying me at once. My *tsohuwa* let me eat on credit for some days, but my customers kept on finding reasons why they needed a longer time to pay. I think they found my snuff good but they would not pay up. After a week like this I found I did not have the money to go and buy further tobacco leaves and I could not continue in this way. I would have to find some other work to bring me money.

Where I stayed in the Gidado's compound there was much talk about how the Captain's affairs were going. I heard he was not happy and had said bad words about the Sultan and the Gidado. They welcomed him when he came to Sokoto, but he had been angry to see Richard arriving with me and all our baggage which he had not asked for. He had thought we were still back in Kano waiting for him to come back when we could then go off together to Bornu. Richard told him it was the Governor of Kano who had made us come up to Sokoto, pretending that the Captain had sent a message calling us to go there. He saw that this lie must have started from the Sultan who wanted to get us into his power. What did he want to do with us? Even Alhaji Hat Saleh, the Arab trader who had helped the Captain in the past and had welcomed us to Kano this time, had been made by the Sultan to follow us to Sokoto to show the Sultan he was not keeping any of our goods back in Kano. He was angry about this and he blamed us.

I heard that the Sultan and Gidado had told the Captain strongly that they meant him no harm. Only they did not want us to go to Bornu now that they were fighting a war with that country. They were worried that things we might have to take to Bornu might be used in this war against the Sultan. I heard that the Captain had been so angry that he had used hot words against the Sultan which people thought might cause him trouble. I did try to see the Sultan myself one day, not to say or do anything against the Captain or to complain about what had happened to me, but to ask if the Sultan could do anything to help me, but he said he could not. I did not like it when the Sultan showed some signs of wanting to keep me for ever to mend weapons for him, thinking that my time in the Navy would have taught me how to do this. I did not want this at all.

I went back to my *tsohuwa to* talk about what else I could do. She continued feeding me with her *tuwo*. I then learnt that her name was Giwa, meaning the Elephant. I do not know how she got this name: for a man it would be a very good name. Even a chief may be called a lion or elephant, meaning someone who is very strong and powerful. She is a strong woman and perhaps that is how the name first came to be used. So I shall call her *Tsohuwa Giwa,* the Elderly Woman Elephant. I also heard that she was not born in this area but is a Yoruba woman. She came to Sokoto some many years ago and people like her because of her good cooking.

She saw how my selling snuff was not doing well, as people were too slow to pay me. The only other thing she could suggest was that I should go towards where I used to buy tobacco leaves, but not so far, and cut and bring in firewood to sell. This would be hard work, especially as we were now in the Ramadan fast which I had to keep now that I was in Sokoto. It was also the very hot time again, just like when we left Wawa a year ago. As it was all I could find to do I decided I must get on with it. She had become a good friend to me and I wanted this to go on while I worked away bringing in firewood to sell. I made bundles of wood and tied them up with ropes like the tobacco farmers use to tie the tobacco up to dry. When I reached town with my bundles I could sell the wood in small amounts or even singly.

I did not have any meeting with the Captain or Richard although I saw Richard in the street once or twice. I know they heard things said about me, just as I heard about them. In any place, one person gives news to another person and then it is passed on until it comes back to the person who is named in the first place. This always happens. From what I heard Richard started saying things that I did not like. He kept saying that the woman I was with was very, very old, bent over and ugly. And that I was only staying with her because of her *tuwo*. I know my *Tsohuwa Giwa* is not now young and does not have a beautiful face but he made things sound much worse than they are. I think this is because he feels bad about me and therefore everything about me is bad too.

Another thing I heard about was how bad the war was for the Sultan. In towns where fighting had taken place many people had been killed and the men from Bornu had advanced a long way into land under Sokoto and captured many of the towns. They were said to be even at the gates of Kano, with the people shut inside in fear, and they were afraid that Bornu might capture that city too. People in Sokoto were very worried, especially those top men like the Gidado and also those who were usually trading with Kano. I could see why they did not want us to go to Bornu or give them any help. But as the Captain still thought he must go there, things became more difficult between him and the Sultan. Some said that Bornu had tried to warn him to be careful in case the British became too strong, but he did not show any sign of doing us harm, he simply wanted us to go away in peace. Sometimes the Sultan or the Gidado sent the Captain gifts of food with nice messages and nothing was done to stop him when he went out, as he often did, riding horses with Richard and even shooting birds and animals to eat.

I became very good friends with my *Tsohuwa Giwa* and we wanted to marry. The Gidado agreed to this and he helped us arrange things. I made the declaration of faith before an Imam and he married us To hold a ceremony afterwards I needed to borrow some money and I was lent 3,500 cowries by Ben Gumso, an Arab who was friendly. We got in some good food and invited people to come. I am not sure how this happened but some how we found we also had some drink, which was not easy to get in Sokoto and must have been brought from outside the town. I must admit my new Islamic rules did not seem strong enough when I found the drink something I liked, but the drink was strong. By the end of the evening I was less able to stand up than I expected. My wife was also affected but less so and she was angry with me about this. Who did bring us this drink? And from where? I forget, or perhaps I did not know at the time, I was too busy enjoying it!.

You may think this makes life sound good for me, but most of the time I was working hard bringing in the firewood and selling it in the market. If I had not done this, we would not have had anything to eat. But then a new thing happened that really took me back into the depths. I heard that the Captain had fallen ill and was not getting any better. Something was not right in his body, clearly, but in addition I think he fell ill because he was worried. Not being able to go to Bornu meant to him that he was not completing the duties given to him by King George, which troubled him very much. The news of his illness made my spirits go down again. By then it was over two months since Richard and I had arrived in Sokoto, while the Captain had been even longer, and I wondered how much time there might be before we could move out of Sokoto again.

Mallam Mudi, the Gidado's brother, had been friendly, and I think it was from him that I first heard of the Captain's illness and that Richard had sent word to call me to go to him quickly. At the time I was bringing in firewood to sell. My wife heard Richard's message and of course she told me as soon as I came back with the wood. At once I dropped it down and went over to where the Captain and Richard were staying. When I arrived there I could see at once that things were bad. Richard came out of the hut but he was very thin and was so tired he could hardly keep awake. He told me the Captain had the flux very badly and there was nobody else to help them. Some men they had hired would not work during Ramadan, and a girl he had got Mallam Mudi to send him to help with fanning the heat off the Captain started well but soon got tired and ran away. He was fanning the heat off for hours as it was then so hot. He had to move the Captain himself and wash his clothes several times a day. He said he had been doing all this alone for over a week . The Captain had now agreed to my coming back and Richard would be very glad of this help. He could not manage by himself. If I would promise to work with him to help the Captain then he would take me in to speak with him. Seeing how bad things were, I was nearly crying and I said I would be very happy to help and to do all I could. I believed I could do well, and it would not be more difficult than my present work of bringing in firewood.

When he had spoken to the Captain in the hut he took me in to him. I was sad to see him lying there unable to move or to do anything to help himself. In this hot weather he was sweating much and was obviously uncomfortable. Even as we spoke Richard was fanning him but this did not seem to help him much. He greeted me and I fell on my knees before him saying, 'Captain, oh Captain, how sad I am to see you ill like this. I pray God every day to help you get better, amen. I know I have pained you and I am so, so sorry. Forgive me, please forgive me, and I will try always to be good to you. I will try to be your helper. Please forgive me, I beg you. I weep for you. If I have been bad I will try not to do it again. Just get better, with God's help. I beg you again, forgive me.' He then said, 'Pascoe, it is good that you are now sorry for the bad things you have done, and that you have given me this promise to do good things and avoid the bad things. If you will keep this promise then I can forgive you what you have done in the past.' 'Yes. I promise, Sir, and I will keep this promise.' 'Good,' the Captain said, 'I forgive you entirely, and what has happened in the past will be forgotten entirely. Work with Mr. Lander and do what he needs you to do, and we will be together again.' 'Thank you, I thank you from my heart, I thank you a thousand times. To help you now is what I most want. Thank you again.' This was what I really wanted most.

I could see he was tired and so I left him, sad to see how he was but happy to be forgiven and to be back with him again. All my time in the Navy I had known that to obey your Captain was the first thing, and as I was with my Captain again I felt that this was very good. I went to Richard and promised him too that I would help. To show this I first took the Captain's clothes to wash, then I made him some soup from a guinea fowl. Richard went back in the hut to fan the hot air off the Captain and he spent a long time every day doing this. Each day we carried him outside to get some cooler air. He said the Captain had not eaten anything for a long time except some soup, and I continued to make some for him any time he felt able to eat.

Richard spent much time listening to the Captain while fanning him. The Captain seemed to be talking mostly about people he had known in the past and places he had visited. Richard also read to him many times from what he called his Good Book and he and the Captain said prayers together. Nobody came to visit him except for an Arab who had worked for him, who brought some bark from a tree and said it could help to cure this illness. He boiled up the bark, although Richard said it would be safer not to use it, but the Captain said he would try it. Then he drank the water in which the bark had been boiled. The next day the Captain felt worse and said he was sorry he had drunk it, but after that he continued much the same for some days.

Then one day he said he felt much better. Richard shaved off his big beard, and he started to talk of getting well. I cut up some guinea fowl meat very small and he was able to eat it. Next day we were all just getting up and dressing for the day but suddenly I heard a loud cry from Richard. He had gone in to see the Captain but he was surprised to find him sitting up in bed with his eyes looking all around him, when he had not been able for days to move himself at all. This happened when I was still outside, but a further loud cry from Richard made me go in, to find him laying the body of our dear Captain back on his bed after he had died in his arms.

It was hard to believe that the Captain was no more with us but Richard's grief was obvious. I too was extremely sad, but we had to accept God's will. Richard told me to bring some water, and together we washed his body. Mallam Mudi, who had come to visit, also came in and the three of us moved his body outside. The Captain had been a big man and it needed the three of us to do this.

    Richard sat there for some time in sorrow, then he moved himself to send word to the Sultan that the Captain had died. He asked for permission to bury his body and to say where this should be done. After some time the answer came back from the Sultan who sent four slaves to help take the body and make a grave. We had to put the body on a camel's back and we covered it with the Union Jack. Then we made quite a long journey through the streets of Sokoto, out of a gate in the walls, and on to a village called Jangavi, There the slaves dug the grave but then went some distance away, arguing and making a noise. Richard read some prayers from a book, crying as he did so. Then we lowered the body into the grave and the slaves covered it with earth. Richard and I stayed some time there, each with his own prayers and his own sorrows. Feeling very sad and alone, and in the deepest depths, we then went back, saying nothing but carrying our separate feelings, to where we were staying.

Chapter 10 — Recovering Some Hope

<u>March – July 1827</u>

What could happen to Richard and me now that our Captain is dead? But I soon had to ask myself, would Richard live at all? When the Captain was ill Richard worked hard and was worried. After his death Richard went back all the way to the grave to see if the nearby villagers had built a shed over it as they promised. Finding they had done nothing he went again with some slaves to do this. Then he lost all his strength and collapsed with fever. He lay still on his bed. I had to feed him and do everything. I was not sure he could even see me sometimes. If I had not helped him I think he might have joined the Captain in a grave. This lasted ten days, and then suddenly he felt better but could still do little.

Before the Captain fell ill and I was called back I lived in the Gidado's compound and there was much talk among the men living there about the Captain. Some said they expected the Sultan to punish him for what he had said about him. Others said the Sultan and Gidado did not show any anger and sometimes sent the Captain a messenger with food and good words. Those who knew the big men best said that it was the Arab Ben Gumso, my friend who lent me money when I was getting married, who persuaded the Sultan to do nothing about the bad words used against him. Ben Gumso has been a favourite of the Sultan since the time a poisoned arrow injured the Sultan in a battle. Ben Gumso cured him by sending him a powerful charm written on wood that he could wash off and drink, something our learned men are good at. They say he advised the Sultan that as the Captain came as a messenger from the King of England it was best not to do him any harm, as the English might then come and cause him trouble. He should leave him in peace until he wants to go away, as long as he does not go to his enemies in Bornu. Now the Captain has died, for which the Sultan cannot be blamed, and it is said he hopes Richard will go away quietly.

A few days after Richard lost his fever the Gidado and Malam Mudi came to see him. They had always been kind but they said the Sultan insists they see all his loads. They were surprised to see how little money we have but they made a list of everything for the Sultan. Later they came again and said they must take guns and some other things, but the Sultan will pay for them through Alhjaji Hat Saleh when Richard reaches Kano. Richard was pleased to hear that the Sultan now speaks about his going to Kano, but to make sure the Sultan will be good to him he gave some presents to Ban Gumso, as he knows he is a friend of the Sultan.

Not long after this he was called to make a final visit to the Sultan, who did not call me to go with him. Richard had therefore to struggle with his poor Hausa. From what he told me afterwards part of his meeting with the Sultan must have gone like this:.

Richard – Sultan I thank you for your kindness in letting us stay so long in your country and giving us your friendship; with food and help. I am only sorry my leader and father, the Captain, cannot be here to join me in this. Now I seek your permission to leave Sokoto and to go first to Kano and then back to Britain.

Sultan Bello - Well, son of the Captain, we also grieve that he is dead, may he rest in peace, amen. I hope you will continue to think well of us. Now I agree that you may leave us and go first to Kano. There you can arrange with Arab traders to lead you over the great desert to Tripoli, from where you can sail to England. May God give you a good journey. Abubakar (that is me) will stay here with me and I will find him good work to do

Richard – Thank you. But I do need Abubakar to come with me. As you can hear, I still do not speak Hausa well and I need him to interpret for me.

Sultan Bello - Surely if he comes with you to England then after what he has done the king will have his head cut off?

Richard - I do not think it will be like that. Our king does not know what Abubakar has done. For any crime less than murder or mutiny in a distant land he will not be executed. Besides, he may earn the king's favour by helping me as the good interpreter he is.

Sultan Bello - Is not what he has done mutiny enough? Your father served your king by fighting on the sea, he made you his lieutenant, and Abubakar rebelled against you, as the Governor of Kano has told me. What is this if not mutiny?

Richard - I can see your concern, but my father forgave him before he died.

Sultan Bello - Farewell, then. May God be with you, amen.

Richard tells me he had to continue arguing for some time, but in the end the Sultan agreed to let me, Pascoe, come with him, as long as I am sent back as soon as we reach Kano. This Richard promised to do. To me he added, 'We will see.'

Before he went to see the Sultan he asked me whether I wished to stay with my wife Tsohuwa Giwa in my home country, or to come with him. I thought things would be bad for me if I stayed. Up to now I have been seen as being with the Captain even when he dismissed me. Now, with the Captain dead, if Richard left I would be alone and unprotected. I was a stranger, I had been with the Christians for a long time and I might really be one of them, even if I had made a poor effort to live like a Muslim. The final thing was when I heard a man say, 'What kind of a Muslim is he if he drank wine just after seeing the Imam?' Then I knew I might be made a slave, or punished or worse. Before Richard asked me I knew my answer would be to come with him. Tsohuwa Giwa said she was happy to have me with her, but if I wanted to go ,*shi ke nan,* so be it. She had lived for years alone and she could manage. I think I have been wise to agree to go back with Richard, I cannot say 'back home' as I do not have any home now since I joined the Navy and my home became one ship after another.

    The Sultan promised Richard a camel to help with the loads and some food to start us on our way, but we did not see either. We prepared our remaining loads, much fewer by now than at the beginning. Richard said we must take the Captain's books, papers and prayer book, his naval uniform and instruments, and some rocks and arrow poison he wanted to take home. Fortunately we have our camel and some horses to carry things.

When we left Sokoto we went to a large open space we had seen on our way from Kano. We found lots of people, who came in groups to stay there overnight. There were hundreds and hundreds of them. Some were Arabs who wanted to go north over the desert, some to go east like us to Kano or other places, but some would go on to the pilgrimage to Mecca. Some would go south or even southwest to trade in Gonja or down to the coast. First all of us had to go one way, to cross a wild area called the Gobir bush because my old home Gobir lies beyond it. It is now the hot, dry weather and in the Gobir bush there is no water, no villages, only small trees, but what it has is plenty of wild animals and dangerous rebels who are ready to attack and kill people who are alone or in small numbers. After a bad night when we were bitten by many mosquitoes we were all ready to be off when some horns sounded a signal for us to go. Everyone wanted to stay close to the others until we were over the bush when they can begin to divide up and go their different ways. We found ourselves with the Governor of Bauchi, who was quite friendly, with his people.

Before we got out of this bush some people met trouble. The Bauchi Governor, whose country is east of Kano and Zaria, had come to pay homage to the Sultan, and to give him a regular gift, including fifty slaves. The Sultan knew that Bauchi lost many men in resisting the Bornu forces, and he told the Governor to go home with his slaves to make up his numbers. Having walked all the way from Bauchi and started back, carrying heavy loads, these poor people could not keep up and many were falling down and dying of thirst while the Governor goes on. Richard too is suffering. I do not know if he brought too little water in his leather bottle, or if he lost some of it somehow, but he too has difficulty and he lay on the ground unable to go on, with his thirsty, exhausted horse beside him. He sent me ahead to look for water. Many people came past him and refused to undo the cords round their water bottles to give him any help. This went on until one young man came along and saw how he was and let him take a drink from his bottle. Those around him said this was a foolish, or even wicked thing to do for an unbeliever. He held up a double-barrelled gun he is carrying and asked, 'If a white man let me have this, how could I refuse help to another white man? We are all the same.' He stayed to come on with Richard until they reached me. By then I had found some water and was sitting down to enjoy it. Richard was angry with me that I had not come back to find him. I was tired, as I told him. I admit I had a small return of my bad spirits then, but I am glad to see he is all right. I shall be more careful in future as we depend on each other.

    One place that we passed was strange to see. We went up a small slope of rocky ground well away from any village, a place where nobody can farm. At the top the land slopes down. What I saw was a line of ten or more *kuka* trees close to each other. You see such trees near villages, where people use their flavourings. I have seen such trees many times and now I am back in a land where they are common, but *kukas* usually stand alone, not in groups. They stand quite tall and have very wide trunks, but sometimes they are hollow in the middle. I have even seen them break apart, one piece falling this way and others falling that way. They stretch out their arms, all twisted up, as if they want to grab something. Here they seem to be trying to grab each other. It is a curious sight and although we soon passed them, I think this something to remember.

The young man told us that before he reached Richard lying down on the ground he had seen 30 or 35 of the Bauchi slaves also lying down, some dead from thirst and others were dying; He did not know what happened to the remaining 15. This made me think back to the time when I sailed on the *Iphigenia* and we came to Lagos, five or perhaps six years ago. I told Richard and the young man about this. A big ship can not go into the lagoon but Captain Mends sent boats in to see if there were any slavers around, as we had been told to expect. I was in one of the boats, leading the way, and we soon found a ship flying the Portuguese flag. It looked like a slaving ship although the Portuguese had by then promised not to look for slaves in these waters. Our lieutenant called out a warning that we would attack if they had slaves on board. He ordered us to go aboard with muskets primed and bayonets fixed, but they quickly hoisted a white flag. It cannot have been over 100 tons with a small crew. As we went in they did not try to resist but stood with their eyes down, ready to be arrested. As we came to the hatches we could hear many voices below decks, and an awful smell hit us. Our lieutenant called out that they should not be frightened, we were going to free them. I do not think they could understand his words but I think they did realise what we might do, so they went quiet. When we went below we found as many as 175 men and women shut up in a space so small that they could hardly lie down. They had been on the ship only two or three days but in the heat, being without water, they were clearly suffering and the smell was terrible. Some, I found out, were Hausa people captured in a war and I could speak with them before they had to be moved away.

We could not just send them back on shore. Those who brought them and sold them would capture them again, although some might be able to run away, and wait for another ship to take them off as slaves. By the Navy's rules we put enough of our crew aboard to sail the ship with the slaves to Freetown to be set free. The Portuguese were held on our ship with the Marines guarding them. We then sailed along with the slave ship to Freetown. We left the slavers there to be judged by the court and we sailed home. I do not want to see anything like this again.

Once we passed the Gobir bush the road was easy in the dry weather. The Bauchi Governor talked in a friendly way with Richard. He seems to accept that his slaves are lost and does not seem surprised or worried. Our young man with us said he doubted if any of the slaves ran away. Usually a slave accepts his position and stays with his master as a part of his family. If he behaves well it is unusual for him to be sold and sent away. The time passed quickly and with the road dry it has taken no more than three weeks from Sokoto to Kano. Of course Richard went straight away to see Alhaji Hat Saleh and show him the Sultan's letter. The Alhaji complained and grumbled that the Captain and Richard had been the reason why the Sultan had made him go to Sokoto. against his will. When there he had been in danger of his life until he could convince the Sultan he had not kept any of our loads back in Kano. He agreed now to pay the Sultan's bill but he said he was not ready to lend Richard anything more, trade being bad After he paid him, he was ready to do some business with us and he sold Richard a slave woman to be his servant. By this time Richard has become fed up with paid servants and he is ready to take this slave woman as he can rely on her better. When we get to the coast he says he will free her.

Then Alhaji Hat Saleh, reading the Sultan's letter, reminded Richard that he had agreed to send me back to Sokoto. Richard argued with him, saying that his being with me from Sokoto showed how much he still needed an interpreter. This went on for some time but in the end Richard gave the Alhaji a large present. The Alhaji then said he would stretch what was in the Sultan's letter and allow me to go with Richard as far as Kulfo. .Then I must come back to Kano without fail, and he will send me on to Sokoto. I was there when this was agreed, and to make it definite the Alhaji put an oath on me saying, 'You come back, Abubakar, or the Devil himself will come and seize you to bring you back.' I nearly broke down on hearing this. I fear God, I fear strong men, but most of all I fear the Devil.

What a problem I have! I want to go with Richard to Kulfo or anywhere else, but to be caught by the Devil there and dragged back would seem like the ending of my life. I said to Richard that in that case I could not go with him and he tried to make me change my mind but I could not. I stood there terrified, and he went quiet for some time. Then, saying no more about Kulfo or going there, he spoke as if a new thought had come to him,

'It is a pity,' he said, 'I thought that you could take this slave woman as your wife, since you have nobody now, as your old wife stayed in Sokoto.' I was too much concerned about the Devil to say anything at first, but little by little the idea of a new wife came into my mind, fighting to give me new power against the fear of the Devil. In the end I said, 'Yes, then perhaps I will come with you.' So Miriamu, as she is called, came to live with me and to drive out this fear of the Devil.

Next day we set off from Kano but at the river we saw on our way from Zaria Richard remembered we had not brought the tent poles. He sent back for them an Arab he had taken on again as a guide. I know he had cheated our late Captain of Captain Pearce's sword and much money. In my opinion he should have been dismissed since, since! In a heavy rain storm that night it was difficult but we managed to tie the tent up to a tree. The rain was so heavy that it brought the whole tent down on top of us and we got very wet. In the morning when there was no sign of the man Richard sent me to follow him back to Kano. I brought the tent poles from the place where we stayed, and went back, feeling very cross about not seeing the man.

Back on the river bank we found the water much lower than it was yesterday and we took off our clothes to cross the river with the tent poles, meaning to come back for our clothes. As we were going up the south bank four horsemen charged up to us. Pointing spears at me they shouted, 'Hey, Abubakar, what about the money you borrowed from Ben Gumso at the time you married? Pay up, pay up, or we shall arrest you and take you back.' 'I agree I borrowed this money,' I said, 'but I left clothes and other things in Sokoto which are worth a lot more. Ben Gumso can take these things to make sure he does not lose.' They were still ready to take me off but then Richard stepped in and said, 'Very well, then, here is the money. Leave him with me.' Even then they seemed to think we were cheating them, but they took his money, which was not a large amount to make them come all the way from Sokoto. I did not care about the things left there. What did make me angry was that after being paid they went and took all my clothing that I had dropped on the other side of the river! Richard had to hold me back from going after them, naked as I was. He pulled out from the loads a mat which I could put around me until further on he could buy some new clothes for me.

After another wet night we crossed another river and passed the town of Bebeji. that we went to on our way to Kano. Not far beyond there we reached a fork in the road. To the right one road would take us to Zaria and on to Kulfo, back on the way we had come. The road to the left, Richard said, would take us to Funda, a new name for me. He says the Captain warned us against going to Kulfo. Chiefs there and in places beyond might be against us because we had been friends with the Fulani with whom many of them were at war. Richard reckons that going to Funda will be our shortest way back to the coast, and that from Funda we can go down the river by boat. .So he thinks we should try that road. Starting this way we went past a town called Damoy, leaving Zaria to the west of us, and we were steering towards Bauchi over to our east. Soon after that we met two men who asked us where we were going and we said to Funda. Then they rode off on their horses in the direction of Zaria, riding fast, as if they might be messengers in a hurry to see somebody

When the Captain was alive Richard lived near him and they spent long hours in the evenings talking to each other, smoking cigars and sometimes singing songs, for which Richard brought out his bugle-horn. Now Richard showed more desire to talk with me, and I too am ready to spend time talking with him since my Tsohuwa Giwa is not with me, although I have started to know Miriamu better. We talked mainly as we walked along. I told him much about my younger days and my trading journeys, as we were traders as well as farmers. I enjoyed listening and telling stories to my brothers and other people. They would tell me about things they had done or places they had seen. It had been like that too in the Navy where telling stories was a way of filling in evenings when we were not on watch.

Thinking about this for a while I said to Richard, 'Mr. Lander, what we suffered in the Gobir bush has brought back to my mind a little story I remember hearing when I was young about a merchant who set off at dawn with many goods for trading piled up on the backs of two animals, a donkey and a mule. The day became hot and they were going far. The donkey was suffering and it said to the mule, 'Can you make things easier for me by taking some of the loads off my back? They are too heavy for me to carry.' The mule answered him,

'You are a strong donkey. I am sure you can manage your load.' Some time later, as it got even hotter, the donkey spoke again, 'Everyone knows the mule is stronger than the donkey. I do not think I can go much further.' The mule snorted and said, 'You are talking like an old woman. Don't trouble me further.' Soon after the donkey felt sweat in its eyes that made it unable to see well. Just then they came to a bad place in the road, with big holes and rocks sticking out, and the donkey collapsed into a big hole. The merchant beat it with a stick and pulled its tail but the donkey could not rise. At last the merchant decided, 'All I can do is to find some labourers at the next town to bury the dead donkey in a big hole, Then he undid the loads on the donkey's body, moved them and put them on top of the loads already on the mule. Then they went on, not making any stop to rest or giving the mule any food or water. Many of our tales have a moral attached to them, as I believe many of the stories in your Good Book have, and this one is that the mule found that by not giving any help to the donkey, it had made things worse for itself.'

Richard said, 'A very amusing story it is. But do you not think that by failing to give me any water while you were drinking yourself in the Gobir bush, you were not being like the mule in your tale?' He gave a little laugh, which made me feel better, as it was a sign that he would not blame me too much. I thought it best for me to say nothing.

The next day, he asked me about my life in the Navy. 'Did you have often to climb up the rigging to fix or adjust sails, or move heavy guns about?' 'Mr. Lander, I did things like that when I joined my first ship, as a landsman, and I think I could do these things now if I had to. But after I became an able bodied seaman, I found myself in the galley most of the time. Like all seamen I had taken my turn as mess cook along with the other seven men who messed with me, but this did not mean doing much cooking, as the meat which I had then to collect from the store and take to the ship's cook went into the ship's oven for cooking. However, I found I pleased my messmates with the plum duff and pease pudding I made. Before long I went as assistant to the ship's cook and once when the cook was ill I took his place. He was registered as a chip's cook at Greenwich, being an old seaman with a peg leg, as many of them have, and so I could not be a ship's cook. I did quite well though, enough to start making food for the officers. Then I became the cook to the Captain on HMS *Leven* some years ago, Captain Bartholomew his name was, and I served with him for almost three years Poor Captain Bartholomew! All that time we sailed around Madeira and other islands off Africa surveying but he died and was buried at the Cape Verde Islands. Only the Marines in their smart uniforms were taken ashore to see him buried before the Governor there. We crew attended a service on board. As at other times when the command 'Roman Catholics and Jews fall out' was given I went to the service on board. Allah or God, it is all the same isn't it? I know some of the hymns but I never got any further.

After that I went to the *Iphigenia* where the Captain Sir Robert Mends had his own cook, so I did not cook for him. However, I was by then regarded as a ship's waister, as we call it, doing work that does not usually mean our going up the rigging or moving heavy guns about. The second time I sailed with this Captain in the *Owen Glendower* he too died and we had to bury him. So that was how it was until I went with Mr. Belzoni and then again I started with you and our late Captain.'

By this time we found ourselves walking alongside high mountains on our left. These cut off the sun from our view in the morning as they rise up higher than mountains I have seen at Freetown or in the Yoruba country. Beyond them is said to be Bauchi country. There are villages high up in the valleys and Richard said that the people are called Yam-Yams and people say they eat men. Sometimes it is people caught in battle that they eat, but I have heard tales of passing traders being taken and eaten, but I do not know if this is true. We do not see the Yam-Yams themselves very much here, as they keep away from the Fulani and Hausa who sometimes take them as slaves. They go about naked, with no clothes at all Some call them Bauchi men, as they are like those who live in Bauchi over the hills. I hear they do sometimes trade with other people, but they are very poor and have little to trade with. In the villages you can see fetishes hanging down outside the houses, as these people are not Muslims.

We saw a number of slaves at one place being taken off tied together with ropes made of bullock hides round their necks. You would think they would be miserable but these people were singing as they went along, although many of them showed signs of having smallpox and I do not know how long they can live. Richard asked me if it was usual to see slaves being taken off for long distances, like these ones and those we saw in the Gobir bush. I said that in the past days I had seen slaves being taken just short distances, but now that Sultan Bello had such a large country under him it seems that they are taken longer distances to be given as presents to him or other big men.

The road we were going along went up and down and it was tiring to walk on, but after some days it finally came down and became more level. We crossed a big river called the Kaduna River and then came to a town called Zangon Katab. Many of the people in the town are Fulani or Hausa, and many of them come from Zaria to trade, but some are more like the Yam-Yams in their faces but wearing some clothes. The market was busy, trading on one side for cattle and the other side with slaves for sale. Beyond there we were back in the hills, often with water from the rains falling now almost every day and running down into the valleys. This made it difficult for both horses and men to walk along. On some parts of the path there was little room, for one side had a steep slope going down while on the other side the hill went up. Our horses have had trouble on these paths and one of them with a wide load on it actually hit the hillside with its load and fell off right down the slope. We quickly scrambled down to it and were amazed to find that it was alive and even able to walk when we pulled it up from the path. It was stopped in falling by the rope round its load catching on some small branches. This was a lucky escape as I do not know what we should have done if it had been dead. I thanked the good spirits looking after us.

Just after that we turned a corner and we found the hills were ending and before us there was a long level stretch, which makes it much easier for us. Richard says we have now been seventeen days since leaving Kano and that only another two weeks should bring us to Funda after which we can go on the river. To get there, he believes, we need to turn more to the west. By this time we had reached a place called Danrora. We slept happily, but early next morning we saw four armed horsemen go to the chief's house and point towards us. After talking with the chief they came to us and said, 'You will have to stop here. We have been sent to take you to Zaria and you must follow us.' The chief confirmed this order, saying it would be to his death if we did not do what these men said. My first thought was that we should go on our way as we wanted, but Richard seemed crushed by this happening and wearily said that he was sorry but he feared we must do what they said. So we turned back and followed them to Zangon Katab. The horsemen pointed to a route different from that we had followed, going northwest, but before we could even start Richard was attacked by the flux and was not able to go anywhere. This lasted four days and by that time the horsemen were tired of waiting and rode off, leaving two local men to look after us and telling us to come on when we could.

The first day was awful. Our road went through thick bush with lots of terrible big flies. There were many of them and they came at us from both front and back, and the sides too. Their bite felt like having knives stuck into your body, and blood came out wherever they bit you. Not only us, but the animals suffered too. I was riding an ass and it was so troubled by these flies that it threw me off its back and then it rolled about on the ground. Richard had trouble on his horse while Miriamu, of course walking along with us, .complained all the time. Everyone among us was glad when we came out of this bush and the flies left us. Then we came to a village of the Yam-Yams or Bauchi people where we could at least rest, but they could offer us little food as they were so poor. But as a special feast with the white man coming, the village chief roasted a dog and made a sauce in which he boiled up parts of a snake that they caught. Richard ate some at first but when he heard that it was not a fish as he had thought, he would not eat any more, only corn in water. I gained from this as I much enjoyed the snake with its wonderful flavour! I could eat the roast dog to with pleasure.

Next day we went to the River Kaduna but it was much stronger and deeper than we saw it at Zangon Katab before. Our guides tried to make us go across but Richard refused after trying to put one of our loads on a raft that nearly sank as soon as it touched the water. They cursed us but we told them to go if they wanted and report to their chief in Zaria, and we went back to the Bauchi village. Richard was ill again and we stayed there two weeks. He just ate corn but I was happy when they brought roast dog again. Then the guides came back, with no curses this time but a request for us to go on. So we followed them to the river again and this time we made a stronger raft on which both we and our loads were able to cross. When we went we lay flat on the raft and the guides swam behind and pushed us across. The animals had a worse time, being carried down stream and being exhausted when they came out at the end. The one paid servant still with us, Mohammed, would not continue and he stayed behind, but Miriamu and I put the loads on our animals so that we could go on.

We were to the west of the road on which we came south to Zangon Katab, with hills to our right which were high but not up to those over in the Bauchi direction. We must have gone first on one side of these hills and now we were going back on the other side. This road took us to the town of Kauru, where the chief is a Hausa man like many of the people in the town although there are Yam-Yam villages all around. They gave us good food and accommodation and we rested there for three days. Then we crossed a river north of the town and went over more level country until we reached the large town of Igabi. This is very clean and rich, unlike the poor and dirty Yam-Yam villages we had seen. From there, we had to spend one night in the bush, then we arrived in Zaria. The Governor was away but he had commanded that we should be well fed and given good accommodation, and he came back in the evening.

Next day we saw him and he has been very pleasant to us. He said that we would have had trouble at Funda because they were at war with Sultan Bello, and it was for our good that he had us brought back. Richard said he thought the Governor just wanted to see us, as he had been away when we came before with the Captain on our way to Kano. The servant Mohammed who ran away from us came back and wanted to continue with his work but Richard refused and sent him off. Not wanting another hired servant, he bought a slave called Jaudi, an Idoma man . Later we visited the Governor's son, who seems also very kind. He even allowed us to see his wives in the compound, although they ran away frightened when they realised a Christian man was there with them. Richard also obtained help from the Governor's son in a way he did not expect: he gave him a female slave. Richard was pleased with this and thanked him very much, but he felt unhappy and did not know what to do, when the Governor's son said this was given as his wife! He had never shown any sign of wanting a wife. He did not think he was old enough or in any position to keep a wife. Our return from Sokoto has thus added three members to our party – Jaudi as the servant, I have a wife Miriamu from Kano and now Richard has one too. Abuda is her name. I think we are now alike and can both be happy about this: Jaudi and the wives will help us more than paid servants in our travelling, and the wives will keep us feeling better in our beds. What Richard will do, I do not know, except he says he will give both Jaudi and Abuda their freedom when we reach the coast. We have now come a long way out of the depths where we were before.

Chapter 11 — At Peace Together

<u>July – November 1827</u>

'A fine cock-and-bull story that is, Pascoe, if ever I heard one!' said Richard. 'I hope you know what that means don't you?' I replied. 'Yes, Mr. Lander, I know well enough what it means I have heard seamen say that when a man has told a story to his mates. It means you do not believe any of what I have said.' I shrugged my shoulders and smiled as there was no point in arguing with him.

I had been telling him of the time when the Fulani began to make trouble for us in Gobir Up to then we had been living quietly as farmers and traders. Only sometimes there was some trouble with the people from Katsina. Mostly we farmed our millet and guinea corn and when we had harvested them many went trading in the months before we could farm again, Some of my brothers were *yaran sarki* in the king's court, so they stayed at home, but other brothers and neighbours went off to 'eat the dry season' in order to trade in Gonja and other places in the south.; We had heard that the Fulani, who lived in our country, were saying that our king was not a good Muslim and was doing bad things by allowing old customs to go on. They said he was oppressing the people but not many of us felt like this and we did not expect it to come to a war. Then they came and attacked us at Lake Kwotto and after this there was much fighting with them.

    I told Richard that my brother was a brother of the King of Gobir – you know we use 'brother' to mean anyone related to another man. He was leading an army against the Fulani and I was with him. We were fighting strongly but needed some extra support. Suddenly my brother was changed as if by a miracle into a white elephant and he charged into the enemy, trampling many of them and scattering their army. But then they came back and attacked him with bows and arrows until they were sticking out on all sides of his body. He was weakened by the attack and he lost much blood, until he went off the field of battle, carrying me in his trunk He went into the bush and dropped me gently down and stood there. I was shouting out loudly for somebody to come and help. God's power had given him strength ;as an elephant, but now He made him stand still, unable to move or do anything. We were there for three hours, and I watched as I saw trees and bushes grow up around him until he was all hidden and nobody could see him or do him any harm. Only then was I able to move away and save myself.

This was the story I told Richard and now he had said he could not believe any of it. This is a trouble I had with him: sometimes I told him something that was quite true and he might or might not believe it. Other times I told him what was just a story, like this one, and again he might or might not believe it. This time he did not. I never knew what to expect. Did he not play at story-telling when he was young? But I know my rank in Gobir better than he does.

This was when we were on our way from Zaria to Birnin Gwari, which took us only five days. The Chief was friendly again and said he had expected us to come earlier as he had heard we left Kano since. Richard explained the delay as being because we tried to go to Funda but were taken back by force to Zaria. The Chief said he was a friend of the king of Funda and could get us there safely, but Richard said we would not try again as we had no suitable present left to give the king. So after four days at Birnin Gwari we went on towards Kulfo and arrived there after another eleven days on the road. We found ourselves welcomed by the same landlady as we had before and she has made us stay in her house, turning out some lodgers there. She made much lament over the Captain's death, weeping with her friends. By this time a horse we had ever since we were at Katanga and a bullock obtained recently at Zaria were both worn out and with difficulty, as they were in a bad state, Richard sold them and bought some asses instead. What saddened him more was a horse he called Bussa Jack that he had from Bussa crawled from its stable in the night to come just in front of where we were staying, and then died there. When we came with the Captain bad health kept us there for weeks, but this time we stayed only five days. As the landlady makes and sells beer I was able to take two leather bottles to drink on our way.

It was because of that beer that I made a small mistake when I was telling Richard more about our troubles with the Fulani. Much of it was the simple truth, not like the earlier story about my brother and the elephant. As my talking ran on I made a mistake by saying 'that happened when I was captured.' At once Richard, who did not seem to be listening, woke up to ask, 'Eh, Pascoe, what is this about you being captured? How and when did this happen, and what happened afterwards?' I saw that I had begun something that I did not want to talk about but I just had to say something more. So I said, 'Well. Mr. Lander, this was a year or two later than what I told you about before. I was out one warm night when the moon was shining, dancing with some people of our town to the sound of drums. Suddenly several men with sticks and bows and arrows surrounded us and took us captive. Where they came from we did not know, and they came at us without any sound. We saw from their dress that they were Fulanis. Their leader said that as men and women were together dancing, we were doing bad things not allowed by our religion – but you know that we are Muslims just as they are – and they took us away and kept us as prisoners. 'What happened then?' said Richard and I tried to change the subject by saying something about the road we were on.

Of course he wanted to know more, although he did stop asking questions just then. Later when we were walking on he came back to this. Little by little I told him about what had happened to me. I had not told this to anyone for years. It is not something you want to tell to anyone else. I told him now as he and I had grown almost like friends together and I had started to like him. I wanted to change what I was saying and to add in parts that I made up, but I do not think I was successful. Perhaps you can tell whether it sounds like the truth., as I tell it now.

'The Fulani who captured us said that we were now their slaves. I was taken away from the others and sold to a trader from Gonja, where we used to go to buy cola nuts He forced me to go to his home and he made me work for him. He did not feed me well, and several times he beat me when I had not done anything really bad. So I ran away, taking as many of his things as I could carry'. Richard said, 'This was where you learned to steal from people, like you did with me, was it?' I replied, 'Well, you did not ill-treat me like this man. You only tried to stop me doing things I wanted to do.'

'Anyway,' I continued, 'I have never been very successful in running away, as you have seen. This time I did not go far, and he found me the very next night, dancing and drinking with about twelve women. So there I was back again as a captive. Because of what I had done he sold me again, this time to a man from Ashanti. My new master sent me and other slaves he had bought to his own country. He treated me much better than the first man, and I lived on his farm. But then one of his wives came to like me and she misled me into doing things I should not have done. My master found out and I was then tied up with other slaves – this man was a dealer in slaves – and I was marched down to the coast, to the port of Whydah. The Portuguese have a fort there and I was sold to one of their people and put on a ship; sailing to Bahia in Brazil.'

'With chains or ropes round our arms and legs we were forced to lie down next to each other, almost touching in very little room. We had to lie between decks that were one above the other, only a short distance apart. There was no chance we could do what a man has to do in a clean way, and the air was soon foul. We were threatened with whips and these were sometimes used when they thought we might try to fight them. It was my good fortune, however, that we had not gone far when an English ship came up and made us stop. Sailors came aboard and the Portuguese looked frightened. I only knew a few words of English then but I saw these must be the British Navy. They took the Portuguese away to their ship, but it was too small to take all of us slaves also. They told us, or showed us by signs, that we must keep quiet while they took us to what they said was Sierra Leone. There we were told that the town was called Freetown and that we were free and no longer slaves. For now we must, however, be good and do what the British Government told us. After some time we saw the Governor again. He said we could have land to farm on, or we could join either the Navy or the West India Regiment of soldiers. I was one of the few who said I would serve the Navy which had rescued us. I went to Cape Coast and found a ship. When they saw I was fit they took me on as a Landsman, not having any experience as a sailor'.

'When I was in Freetown I heard that the ship was called the *Daring,* a small Gunboat. Much later I heard that it had been in a battle with two French vessels. It was damaged and the officer in charge had it burnt to avoid capture. The crew joined other ships in the flotilla but in another fight with the French some were killed. These included the officer in charge of the *Daring,* Lieutenant William Pascoe. By that time I was already in the Royal Navy but after we reached England and were discharged I decided to take the name of my rescuer, and used it when signing on for another ship. That is how I came by my present name.'

'I hardly ever was involved in fighting myself. On our ship the guns were run out and fired often to keep the crew practised, but we rarely had to fight with them. By the time I joined up, the Navy had beaten the French so much that they did not usually come out to tackle us, and not very long afterwards the war ended and the peace came'

'Well.' said Richard at the end. 'You told me before that you had volunteered at Cape Coast, but this now tells me much that I did not know before. I can not say you had no offence in becoming a slave, but I realise it all began when you were seized in a wicked capture.' All this was said a little at a time over several days as we walked west from Kulfo to the river Kwara or Niger. There we crossed over at the same place as when we were coming. We had trouble to make our slave Jaudi come with us in the canoe, as he had never seen such a large bit of water in his life and he was frightened. At last, when we got him into the boat, he sat there with his eyes shut, shaking with fear, and when we reached the other side he could hardly stand up. From the river we went up to Wawa but it was not easy, as the rains were falling very heavily by then and the journey was slow. When we were not talking together I went in front, with Abuda and Miriamu and Jaudi following, then Richard at the rear.

Reaching Wawa, we were greeted like old friends by Chief Mohammed, and he wept when he heard the Captain had died. He said that as we went to Sokoto he was astonished that these enemies, who had attacked Borgu, had allowed us to get safely away. Before long he caused the people of Wawa to join us in a ceremony to show sorrow for the Captain's death. For this he cut up some goat's meat into small pieces and joined them with a large bowl of *tuwo,* which was all soon eaten up while prayers were said. He allowed us to try to go to Bussa, as Richard wanted to see the king and his queen who had been kind to him before, and he went with me, but the road was so bad in the rains that we only reached half-way there. Before then, my ass had such difficulty getting its legs out of the mud that in the effort I was thrown clean off its back, to land in the mud, getting it all over my clothes. That made Richard decide to give up the attempt.

We hoped after getting back that we could go on our way very soon, but the Chief made us do some things for him first. He had seven muskets and two pistols that he wanted us to clean for him. They bore the Tower mark, and he was probably correct when he said that they came from Mr. Mungo Park's boat that had been lost twenty years before. When we had done that it was still not enough. He made Richard write out several charms on pieces of wood to ward off bad luck and evil deeds, even when Richard said he did not know how to do this. I don't know what he wrote but Mohammed was very pleased when he was given the charms. Just before we left Wawa we were worried when the Chief sent for us again, in case he had more work to be done, but we found that he only wanted Richard to promise to come back again before long, and he gave him a list of things he wanted to be brought for him from England.

One thing we could not do at Wawa was to see the Widow Zuma. Richard asked about her but the Chief said that after what she had done before she would not be allowed to come out while we are here. He probably did not know that she has been able to send out her favourite slave woman at night to bring us messages and sometimes gifts of food from the Widow. Sometimes she has other slaves with her who sing to tell us how much the Widow loves Richard and how sad it is that the Captain has died. As I remember things when we came before, Richard tried so hard to say 'no' to her and turn away, but this time when he could not see her you would think he really did return her love. Perhaps it is different because he has his own wife now. When the time came to leave Wawa she was able to send her slave to see us outside the town with a loving message. She said we should see some man comes to her from England, to marry her and to become chief in place of Mohammed. She never changes! To me it was better that she also sent two calabashes of honey for us to eat on the way!

It took twice as long as before, six days, to go from Wawa to Kaiama, because of the rains and the bad state of the road. One river that we crossed had so much water in it that Richard's horse slipped and he fell right into the water. To make things worse, his foot was stuck in a stirrup and he nearly drowned before we could get him and his horse out. One of our asses became too tired to continue so we decided to leave it at a village. The ass did not like being left and it set up a very loud and sad noise, and the other ass joined in. Poor Jaudi was in charge of them and he was made to cry by this. The whole journey was difficult but Abuda, like a good wife, bathed Richard's forehead and feet to help him rest.

It is hard to know how to please the king of Kaiama, Yaro, though he had been pleasant to us before. This time the first thing he said on out arrival was 'How dare you, Little Christian (a name which everyone now gives Richard, a short man like me) arrive without first sending me a messenger, so that I can prepare?' 'But I sent you your own messenger three days ago' said Richard. 'Not good enough,' said Yaro, 'go back five miles and send me your messenger.' So Richard was turning to go back but then Yaro changed and shouted at him, 'I will forgive you this time, Little Christian, but watch it another time.' Then he became friendly and lamented over the death of the 'Big Christian', our Captain.

Before long his manner changed again and he said sharply, looking angry and ready to become our foe, 'What business did you have with the Fulani and why did you go to Sokoto? I do not think they were very kind to you and your leader died when with them.' Seeing how angry he appeared to be I stepped in and said, 'The big Christian was under orders from his King George to go and see the Sultan and try to make peace between them and their neighbours and with England.' As he still looked angry I added, 'The little Christian and I were waiting at Kano for the Big Christian to come back from Sokoto and then we would all have gone to Bornu, but the Sultan made us go to Sokoto by telling us a lie.' After this he seemed to lose his anger and to be friendly to us again. Otherwise I think he might have punished us for being friends to his enemies.

After this beginning we spent five days at Kaiama, and the king's women gave us all the food we needed. I spoke before of how girls without any clothes used to march in front of the king. This time we found that he made it a rule that all women near him should never wear any clothes. We saw that when they were away from him they had as much liking for wearing clothes and ornaments as any other women. Men, however, as the superior people, should wear clothes before him! For the rest of our stay he was kind and friendly to us. At the end he gave Richard a strong small horse .He also told him that if the British king wanted a man to go to Bornu he would be happy to guard him and to take him there, as the ruler of Bornu was above him.

Going south for three days in land soaking with rain water brought us to Moshi, a village on the banks of a river of the same name. This is the boundary with the Katanga or Yoruba land. The Kaiama messenger with us said that the Moshi was a feminine river and did not like anybody to speak about any masculine river like the Niger, and was probably offended because Richard had already asked about it, which all sounds rather silly. Nobody gave us any food there, while everywhere else people had always given us some. The river was running so fast that nobody would send a boat across with lots of charms put on it to protect it, but then it sank on its way back. The food and anything else it was carrying fell into the water, and the main result was that we were blamed for offending lady Moshi! However, I had seen that although the chief denied having any food, he had in fact a large store of yams down by his farm. He did agree that we could cut some grass for out animals, so I went to cut this and reached out my hand to grab two good yams and put them into the bundle of grass I was to take back for the animals. We were there for several more days, still not given any food, but going to his farm each day for the grass, each time I managed to get some yams for us, even when he came to the farm with me! I think this made Richard look at me with much more pleasure than before. In fact, as I accepted that he was the leader between us, I think we were by now at peace together.

It was when we reached this far that I thought how fortunate it is that all the talking together that Richard and I have done made him forget all about the promise he made at Kano to send me back from Kulfo I might then have been sent back to Sokoto and become Sultan Bello's slave. Of course, I did not say anything to remind Richard of this!

When we did finally get across the river, another three days brought us to Katanga or Oyo. Next morning the Alafin sent word for us to await his coming to us. He stopped outside our house with five hundred of his wives, dressed from the waist down. We heard later that there were four times as many of them altogether, as every house has to give one to him. They stood in front of us with one knee bent, holding a light staff, singing very sweetly. Part of this, we were told, was to greet us, and part to show sorrow for the Captain's death. They all think this is due to the Fulani having killed him, and of course the Fulani are their bitter enemies. At the end of their singing the women went quietly away and then the Alafin came to greet Richard.

There was an awkward time when he complained to us how the Fulanis are troubling him. He showed anger when he asked why we had gone to Sokoto and given them presents. I had to step in again and explain this, as I had done at Kaiama. After that it has been good between the Alafin and Richard again.

While we were at Katanga all our needs were met but this had nothing to do with our old friend, Fat Ebo. We did indeed see him: he has been promoted to one of the king's top councillors and he was prepared to make a joke about how he dealt with us before. He still has his great big belly and I do not think we can trust him any more than before. Once he asked Richard to give him his best ass but he refused and later we found the ass standing with poisoned arrows on both sides. Nothing we could do would stop the ass getting more and more sick until it was hardly living. At that point Richard made Jaudi and me take the ass outside and cut its throat to put it out of its misery. This was the only bad thing we suffered from the Fat Man and he was pleasant in manner, but I do not trust him. He could not do much else as everyone could see that Richard was well liked by the Alafin and in his favour. So much is this so that the Alafin pressed him to stay and become their Prime Minister or war chief. He promised him houses, horses and everything else. He even brought some of his young daughters to Richard, all naked, and said he should make his choice among them. Richard said he must first go home and see people there and then come back to take up this kind offer. Alas, nobody made me any offer like this! It was a restful month we spent there, and at the end the Alafin sent us off with messengers to make sure everything was good for us on the way to Badagry and the coast.

Chapter 12 — Parting

<u>November 1827 – April 1828</u>

'Well, Pascoe, we are now nearing the end of this journey in your land, which has lasted almost two years since we came to Badagry. My thoughts are very strongly on my going home, finding some work, marrying and setting up a family. What about you, Pascoe? I noticed that after we reached your own country you decided not to stay there. Then why did you decide in the first place to come with the Captain? You could have stayed where you were, serving on a ship. Was it to go to your country? Or to get money? And what do you intend to do now, return to the Navy or what?'

'Mr. Lander, I have thought about these things. No, I did not come for money or to get rich. What I was promised was a seaman's pay, food and grog money, the same as I would get on a ship. I did think of returning to my country, but what I saw there did not make me want to stay. I could indeed return to the Navy, although since the end of the war with France there has been less chance for a seaman. That started to happen ten years ago now, at the end of the war, but I have continued to be signed on in some ship or other since then, and this could go on. I like living in the Navy but one day I may become too old. When I met our Captain with Captain Pearce, my first master, I liked them, and I thought it would be good for me to go with them. Now perhaps the time has come for me to find a place to live on dry land in Sierra Leone, Cape Coast or some other place. There I can farm and live with my wife Miriamu. I shall be happy if she will stay with me. I do not know what more I can say. You and I, Mr. Lander, have had some troubles but also some pleasure. I wish you will be happy in whatever you find to do.'

We were on our way by then from Katanga to Badagry. At Ngwa we saw the grave of my first master, Captain Pearce, may God give him rest! Part of it has been washed away by the rain and the fence around it has fallen down. Richard gave the chief a little to repair it. Later we saw also the grave of Dr. Morrison at Ijana, in good condition.

I think it was before we got there that Richard pointed out to me a local man with a white skin, lighter than his own, but with hair like mine except that it is white. I have seen people like him in Hausa land too, but it was a surprise to Richard. It was also on this road that we had a fight with some thieves who stole from merchants on the road ahead of us. The merchants were running back towards us in sheer fear, crying out that we should also go back if we wanted to keep our lives. Richard told them they should join with us in fighting for their goods, but they were too frightened and would not join us. Richard did not want to be held up by having the road in front blocked by these men, so he said that we – the two of us, with Jaudi and the very few helpers with us – should attack the robbers. He said that if we could get the goods, we had a right to keep them in the law of the land. We had only an old musket we got from the Alafin and a damaged pistol. Crying out loud we charged and I fired the musket. At once all the robbers jumped up and ran off as fast as they could go. They looked at us from the bushes beside the road but they did nothing. What a wonderful lot of goods we grabbed, ignoring the merchants who had done nothing!. Richard made us carry them back to the town, where the chief bought them all. I thought Richard should have the money but he refused, so we divided it between ourselves. That has made us richer and we are happy. Our wives want to buy better clothes. We thanked Richard for this.

At one place Richard gave a woman his shirt and some other clothes to wash, for which he would pay her with a few needles. When she brought them back he cried out with surprise, 'We have been looking for things that belonged to Mr. Mungo Park, the white man who died at Bussa, but it must be his son who has also been looking for him. Look, at the bottom of this shirt is written 'Thomas Park.' This woman says just a few days ago he died at a place not far from here. She was given this shirt and it has got mixed up with mine!' 'Will you take it back to England?' I asked, and he said he would.

When we reached Badagry what a great welcome we received! King Adoli was happy to see Richard and made him live in his own bamboo house while he went into a small hut outside. But when they heard the Captain had died they wept and made lament, like other chiefs we had met, so loudly that you would think it was their own father who had died. All the people of Badagry seemed pleased to see us and they gave us food.

Only one thing made me worry: there are several Portuguese living in the town. There can be only one reason for this; they are trading for slaves, buying them every day and hiding them away. Along the coast from Badagry I know there is Whydah with its Portuguese fort. From my time afloat I know that the Navy cannot touch them there but slaving is their business. Now there are perhaps eight or ten of them here, so their wicked business must be doing well. I have no reason to like this at all. You may remember that when we first came I explained that Badagry's creek is so good for hiding captured slaves and then rushing them out to their slave ship when they are ready. There is no vessel for them here now, but they are probably at sea, doing ordinary trade along the coast. They show themselves to any British naval ship that is near, when they are not carrying any slaves or shackles for them, so that they look clean to our seamen. Then they wait for the Navy to go away before they get the people here to put out all their canoes and do everything to get the slaves out to sea as quickly as they can. Of course this is the business not only for the slavers themselves but also for Badagry. They have no other trade here to live on.

Nor is there any trade to bring any British ship here, as the British do not trade for slaves now, and some other countries are doing the same. We have no way to send word to any British post to come and help us. I know that Richard is trying to get some man who will take a message along the coast in a canoe to Accra, Cape Coast or anywhere else, but he has not found anyone to do this. I think they are afraid of the Portuguese, who they know are not friends of the British. So far the ill will of the Portuguese towards Richard is not obvious, and they speak quietly to him. I know he has even done some business with their Captain Morrison, who seems to be the best of them. But they are spreading bad talk among the people. They do not want Richard to be able to go to anywhere else, as they think he will call the Navy to come and trouble them. They even tell the king and his people that the Navy may come and attack their town. Maybe they even plot to do harm to Richard himself. If they can do that, what will happen to the rest of us? Abuda, Miriamu and Jaudi are still slaves, and the Portuguese would claim and seize them. Of course I am a free man, but if they can learn about my dealings with their slavers in the past, I could be in trouble too.

After some days we found King Adoli and all the people being less ready to welcome us and act in a kindly way to us. It seems that the talk of the slavers is working on them. Richard has told me he is finding the Portuguese more like an enemy every day. We hear the chiefs are arguing among themselves about what to do. Then one day they sent a man to call Richard and tell him that at noon he must go to their Council place, a large hut standing away from other ones. There he is to answer complaints against him of causing danger to the town. We soon see that all the town is full of people expecting to see a big event. Word goes round that their priests will make him take a test by ordeal. Quickly this becomes general talk. It is the first time a white man has had to face such an ordeal, but it will have the same result whether he is white or black. They say their gods are always fair: if the accused person dies he must be guilty; if he lives this must be because they see he is innocent but nobody can remember when this last happened.

I get together Jaudi and out wives, Abuda and Miriamu, and tell them we must pray for the best and remain calm. I send Jaudi to the sea coast to bring a large calabash of salty sea water. I make the women build the fire and heat up the water. Then we come together again and we pray hard, those of us who are Muslim to Allah, and Jaudi to whatever god he follows. Then we can only wait but I go near to the Council hut to watch what happens. We all show our sorrow and our worry for Richard. Out liberty and lives depend on the result, in addition to Richard's life. He sees there is no escape from going through with this, but I am surprised how calm he is.

The time comes and he enters the Council hut and stands straight in front of the priests. The room is crowded and there are hundreds of people all around. The chief priest explains what is to happen and although this is in their language everyone knows what it means. Then he hands Richard a large calabash. What is in it looks like water but it is not really so. Richard drinks what is not water straight down and then throws the empty calabash on to the ground. Everyone thinks they will see the result at once but this is not what happens. He is still standing firmly and he quickly goes out of the Council hut. People back off to make room for him. When outside he walks fast towards our hut, not far away.

When there he first drinks the sea water that has been brought for him and warmed up. All our presents have by now been given away, the last of them to King Adoli, but we still have the medicine box and from this he pulls out a packet with some powder in it. We have sometimes used this when somebody has had trouble in his tummy. He mixes it with some warm, salty water, and then drinks this down. Lying flat on his face he then tells me to press up and down on his back, to make him feel sick. We are all very sad and frightened, but I do what he says. Very soon he starts to be sick. 'Don't stop', he says and I carry on until he has brought up all that is in his tummy. This takes a minute or two, then he says, 'I thank God, I am going to be all right' and soon afterwards, 'I feel a little dizzy, but I am all right. I will sit down now.' At this all of us, our two wives, Jaudi and I, cry out with delight and start to dance around the room. Up to now people outside probably think he is dead, as we are round him and they cannot see. It is only when he stands up and goes outside that the people there can see he is still alive. Nobody comes to us, but one by one they go quietly away. Most of them seem pleased by the result. For us there is great rejoicing and happiness. We are happy for him and we too can feel safer and out of immediate danger from the slavers.

Of course everyone thinks it must be their gods who have kept Richard alive because they see he is innocent, and Richard is specially favoured by these gods. Earlier nobody would speak to us and they would turn away if we came near, now they all look at us as if Richard is a god himself. King Adoli has changed his ways and he is good to us again, very good. The only people who are not like this are the Portuguese. They failed to get Richard killed by the poison ordeal, but they still want to see him prevented from going away from Badagry and calling the Navy to come here. The king warns him he is still in danger from them, and he tells him to be very careful of them and always to be armed when going out. This does not mean that the king is careful of *all* his people. Last night there was a bad noise when he had two of his wives killed just near where we are living. We heard women screaming and we saw in the moonlight how they were struggling to escape from men holding them. Their arms were tied up by these men, then their legs, their heads were pulled back by the hair and then the men stuck knives into their throats, saying this was punishment for saying things that offended the king. The screams died away into gurgling, then they dragged the bodies away. We saw them the next morning hung up on the Fetish Tree as they call it. There is a Fetish House near the king's house with skulls all round the inside of the walls. Blood from animals, sometimes men, is spread over them.

Many slaves are sold in Badagry. They are brought from all the country around, as it is a main market for them. Now that the British do not buy them, and some other countries are the same, the main buyers are Portuguese or from Brazil. I hear that is now a separate country but still they are Portuguese people there. Sometimes the ships do not come for a long time. Selling slaves is the trade of the Badagrians, but keeping slaves and feeding them is a cost to them Then the king and the slave owners take out the old, sick or weak ones, tie them up and take them in their canoes with rocks tied to them, and throw them into the river to drown. I hear this is done something like once a month if no ships come for them. They also get rid of criminals, enemies captured in a war, and others, making sacrifices to their gods. The way of doing this is to hit them hard behind their heads and then they cut off the heads and the priests cut out their hearts. The bodies or parts of bodies are tied to the main Fetish Tree, where the vultures come and eat them. The big sacrifice is held each year. In this way they think they please their gods and at the same time save the cost of keeping these people alive. This is done quite openly.

When we had been a month here we were desperate to find some way to escape, but no ships came. Nobody would take our messages along the coast. Even a Portuguese ship might be best for us if nothing else would come. The Portuguese traders in the town did not have any, but we heard there was one some miles east of Badagry. I was very uncertain about this, but I agreed with Richard we should go and see it. He started with Jaudi and me early morning when the sun rose, but it was a long way.

As we walked on there were many different paths. Not having a guide, we took a path that led us some way inland. The air started to get heavy with a bad smell. This grew stronger and stronger until it was very hard for us to bear. We put cloths round our noses and mouths but this would not keep out this horrible smell. Suddenly this path burst out into a large space in the bush and we found we were looking at a terrible sight. There was a large tree, which must be the town's main Fetish Tree, a very large one. Its branches were covered from bottom up to the top in bodies or cut off parts of bodies, without heads. They must have been there since the time of the last big sacrifice. The priests please their gods in this way. As we came nearer there was a great noise as many, many vultures flew off a short way, where they landed and with their sharp noses looked back at us. The smell here is so bad that Richard fainted into the arms of Jaudi and me, and we could hardly avoid being sick and falling down. I have never seen anything like this. Certainly in our Hausa country only somebody who has broken the law and this is proved against them is executed. I have never heard of such a thing anywhere else either. This gift to the gods saves the people of Badagry money, by killing all these people. Of course we hurried to get out from there and go looking for the Portuguese ship.

In the end, when the sun had climbed right up and was starting to come down again, we saw the ship at anchor. The sight of the crew who were moving about made me fear. They were heavily armed men, clearly from Portugal or Brazil, with dark faces and long black beards. I think Richard was very worried too, but when he met the captain, Don Pedro, he spoke politely and gave us grog and food in his cabin. He said he would take us to Cape Coast, and Richard arranged with him and shook hands. Then we went back to Badagry, being careful not to go near the Fetish Tree, but we could not avoid all of the smell. We got back to town when it was starting to get dark.

Next day Richard spoke to people in the town including some of the Portuguese who were less hostile. They laughed at the suggestion we should go with Don Pedro. It was clear that even they did not like him at all. They said he had been a pirate causing trouble for years, even to Portuguese ships. If we went with him we should soon be dead, perhaps by walking the plank. All he wanted of us was to get us and our things and slaves on to his ship;. Those of us not kept as slaves would be killed. This agreed with my feelings and I told Richard that I would rather die here if nobody else came for us than set foot on Don Pedro's vessel. King Adoli confirmed what we had heard. This is why, when Don Pedro came two days later to complete the arrangements, Richard told him why we had decided to refuse to go with him. Don Pedro spoke loudly about the bad character of the other Portuguese who had said these things about him, and departed in anger.

I was glad to see this pirate go away and to have avoided slavery or death at his hands, but we had still the same problem as before. This continued for weeks yet. We saw no ship, and no hope of getting to safety. We heard that there was an English ship trading at Whydah, not a slave ship, but we had no way of getting word to it. The Portuguese still showed their hatred, and we never went out without a weapon visible on us, ready for use if necessary.

Then one day a man ran from the direction of the sea and came over the creek in a canoe to Richard, and gave him a letter. Just as we had heard of an English ship at Whydah, the captain of that ship heard of an Englishman at Badagry. He could only guess that it might be someone from Captain Clapperton's party, and he came to offer help Of course Richard at once wrote a letter to say we would come and sent the man to take it to the beach. He called us and told us that at last freedom and happiness were here. We should bring all our few remaining loads, some with the late Captain's things in them, and come down to the beach. Then he went to tell King Adoli and thank him, his wives and chiefs, and say goodbye. This was the end of two months we had been kept in Badagry. Most of the time they had been kind to us but we could only be happy to get away from there. When we got to the beach we found yes, it is true, there is a ship flying the British ensign A boat came over for us and as we boarded the brig *Maria* all the crew shouted a greeting. Captain Laing welcomed us aboard. All our fears and troubles fell away from us and I have never been happier in my life.

Only ten days along the coast brought us to Cape Coast Castle. Richard, by then with a long beard and his clothes in a bad state, was received by the Governor, Colonel Lumley. He was able to sleep in the castle on a bed after two years on mats on the ground. My bed, the one the Captain gave me from Captain Pearce's things when he died, had broken to pieces long ago, but I was comfortable still sleeping on a mat in the room I was given with Miriamu. Richard told the Governor all about our journey and the things that had happened to us, how the Captain had died of dysentery, and also how he needed help as he had nothing left.

Very soon Richard brought Abuda, his wife, my wife Miriamu and Jaudi, who had always served him well, before the Governor. There he gave them all freedom as he had promised, and the Governor wrote them papers saying that they were free. Of course I was free already, as a British seaman, and did not need a letter like this. The Governor later arranged with the chief of the village outside the Castle to give us enough ground to build our houses and to start farming. He also gave us some money so that we could buy necessary things.

We were over two months at Cape Coast before a ship came that could take us to England. I say 'us' as Richard wanted me to go with him and help him on the way. He told Jaudi, Abuda and Miriamu that he could not take them also. He did not have a home over there, they would have no suitable clothes and how could they get money to keep themselves? It would be best for them to stay at Cape Coast, plant seeds and look after our farm. They were very sorry to be left behind and they cried about this. In the end he made them understand and he promised that I would come back to join them. He hoped he would be able to come and see them again after two months.

Before we left we built huts to live in and we planted seeds in our farm. The rains were beginning that would enable us to feed ourselves. I said goodbye to the others when Richard and I sailed in HM Sloop *Esk*. Richard had by now some new clothes but he kept his beard. He was unable to sleep comfortably in a hammock and the crew put up a cover over the deck where he could sleep on a mat. I got used again to sleeping in a hammock. First we sailed east to Fernando Po. I heard that Richard met there Major Denham, who had gone over the desert with our Captain, and he was sorry to learn of his death. Then we sailed to the west to St. Helena where Napoleon, the man who fought against us for so long, was taken when he was captured. Richard and some of the crew went to see his grave on the island. From there we went to Ascension Island and we got some of the big turtles that live there, but they all died on the voyage to England. It was only about ten weeks after we left Cape Coast that we finally landed at Portsmouth. The fever had come again on Richard by then, and I had to help him. Then we took the coach up to London. He saw the Captain's agent at his office, and then went to the Colonial Office, where Richard gave them the Captain's journal and the goods of his we had brought home. It was by then almost three years since I was engaged by Captain Pearce as his cook and we prepared to sail to Africa.

Richard worked much of the time on his journal saying how his travels had been. I was living in London much as I had done in the past between ships. The Captain's agent paid me the balance of my wages for the time we were away. Soon Richard told me the Colonial Office had agreed to help me to go back to Cape Coast. I had to go to the Office and they paid me a few pounds. I thanked Richard and said, 'I will now go back to Cape Coast where I expect to live in peace with my wife Miriamu. There is one thing more I will ask of you, Mr. Lander. Also in Cape Coast is Abuda, your wife that you had from Zaria. I like her and I believe she likes me too. She needs a man to look after her. I hope, Mr. Lander, that you will agree that I can marry her as my second wife. You know that it is usual in Africa for a man to have more than one wife. I am sure she can live happily with me and Miriamu. They like each other and I will treat them alike. What one has the other will also have. It will be fair and equal between them. I hope you will find a good wife for yourself and that it will not worry you to think of Abuda as my wife now.' We talked about this for some time, and he agreed to what I asked. With this I could leave him happy, but I still hoped we could see him again.

Part Two

Chapter 13 — A New Start

<u>March - July 1830</u>

It is two years now we have been at Cape Coast, living in huts we built on land in the village outside the castle walls. The Governor, Colonel Lumley, who has since died, kindly arranged this place for us .My wives are with me and we are happy together and Jaudi is with us too. Our crops have been good. Living near us are two men from Bornu, Ibrahim and Mina. Mina is about my age. He was once a slave to a white doctor but then freed. Ibrahim was rescued from slavery. Both lived for some time in Sierra Leone, and they know something of how the white men live.

    Before Richard sailed with me to England he said he hoped to come back within two months. At the time I thought he was saying this because the wives were very unhappy about his going away. Perhaps he really intended to come back, I do not know. Probably he has married in England and settled there. We talk about him much but we had heard nothing from him – until today!

I did not notice when I heard that a ship called the *Alert* was coming with the new Governor Mr. Maclean to begin his second tour and some merchants. Then somebody told me that a man was asking to see me at the castle When I got there I could hardly believe my eyes, for there was Richard who I thought had left us for good. I am very excited to see him again and I sent a man to the village to call Jaudi, Miriamu and Abuda to come quickly to see him. When Richard and I had greeted each other in our Hausa way he said, 'I want you to meet my companion. This man, who looks like me, is my junior brother John Lander. This is his first time in Africa but he wants to see everything and to keep me company.' So I said, 'Mr. John, we are happy to see you here with your brother. I hope it will be a pleasure for you.' When the others came from the village they were excited also and they joined in making the greetings. Ibrahim and Mina came too and met the brothers.

Then Richard told me they had come to complete the travels we had made with our late Captain, and to find out where the River Kwara or Niger ends. He said he hoped I could travel with them, as I had shown I could be a good interpreter. If any others of our party would wish to join with them, this would be a good thing. When I explained this to the others there was no hesitation. They all said yes, yes, they wanted to come! So our party included Miriamu who had been my wife from Kano, and Jaudi who had been with us from Zaria. They had been set free by Richard when we got here. Richard was particularly glad to have Ibrahim and Mina join us as they speak English as well as Hausa. He said he hopes it would take less time than when we went with the Captain. He looks forward to going home to his wife Anne and his small daughter Harriet. Abuda, who had been Richard's wife from Zaria and was now my wife, stayed behind to look after our farm and house.

We arranged with the village chief that everything will be looked after for us until we get back Some reliable men and women will help farm the land and they can keep half the food they produce for themselves, They will give the land back to us when we return. All this is confirmed by the Governor. Soon everything had been made ready and after a week we sailed first to Accra. From there we were taken on HM Sloop *Clinker*. While on this ship we were joined by a young man, Antonio, who wants to come with us inland and then go down the Niger to Bonny where his father is king. At Badagry we all landed, getting wet in the surf as usual. After landing, the Lander brothers put on the Turkish dress that both our Captain and Richard had worn before, with big gowns and turbans, larger than those we have in Hausa land. People at Badagry go almost naked and they laughed very much at this strange dress as they followed us right into the town.

The next day when we greeted King Adoli he did not seem pleased to see us again. We soon heard that he had had troubles since we left. There had been fighting with Lagos, in which some of his chief men were killed. His house had been burnt down in a fire that destroyed his things, including some of the presents he had from our Captain. Some people tell us that his troubles were caused by his having let the Captain go through his country and the gods were unhappy with him. When Richard gave him a present he did not like it, saying it was too small. I can see that Richard and his brother have less to give as presents than Captain had before to give as presents to anyone. All the leading men of Badagry came one after the other to greet us, and of course they all expect to be given presents. I could see that Mr. John became more and more worried as the line of them coming to us went on and on.

Richard must have told him how, on his previous visit, not only the Captain but also Captain Pearce, Dr. Morrison, Dr. Dickson and the seaman George Dawson had all died, so Mr. John must have understood that he was risking his life in coming to Africa. I expect Richard had also told him how lots of people would keep coming around and making much noise, and that even without people coming to us there is noise from babies, animals and all sorts of things, so that it can be difficult for others to rest quietly. I can see that Mr.

John finds it hard to get used to the way men live in Africa, but he always keeps cheerful and his aim is to keep his brother good company

The Portuguese who gave us so much trouble before have gone away, perhaps to Whydah where they came from. But I think the chiefs here still deal in slaves and there is talk of a big ceremony coming up in which many slaves will be sacrificed. This is still their main trade, but you might say the second one is to get as much in the way of presents as is possible from visiting white men! We want to get away as quickly as we can, but you may say the second trade is to get all they can of presents from white visitors! We have to wait for a Muslim festival to pass by before we can leave. After that we had difficulty getting King Adoli to promise us a good canoe to take us up the creek from here. When we have been able to start we have been taken on a route different from the one we followed before, because the rains are starting and some of the road is bad. One day I was having difficulty keeping up on foot with the brothers on horses, as we did not have enough horses for all of us and I have one leg shorter than the other, but the next day an additional horse was sent to us from Badagry. Some people had made fun of me before that, but when I was on a horse I told them to be sensible. At the same time my liking for Mr. John increased when I heard him say to Richard that my experience and knowledge were proving very useful to them.

Soon we came to Ijana, where I married Yetunde long ago, the foolish woman who left me and went away with my things at Katanga. At Ijana who should we see but Yetunde?

Really she came right to us. She pushed towards me a baby a few months old saying, 'Hey, Pascoe, here is your baby. You must look after it now.' She had some Hausa women with her and they loudly said the same thing with their screeching noise until Richard told them to be quiet and go away. I said, 'It is more than three years since you were with me, before you ran away. How can this young child have anything to do with me?' Richard joined me in saying it was clearly not my child, so Yetunde should go to its real father who should look after it. At last she saw she could not succeed in getting me to take care of the child so she went away. I am glad to say that we saw no more of her. She was silly to leave me once, so why should I want to have anything more to do with her?

Further on we passed some naked boys being taken the other way. We heard they are slaves being taken to Badagry to be sold. Then, after going through the hills and rocks of Shaki, we came to Katanga. On the way people gave us food and places to stay but we did not have large crowds coming to look at us as had happened when we came with the Captain. They are less interested to see white visitors than at first. After we reached Katanga we rested that night at the house of our old 'friend' Fat Ebo, now a big counsellor of the state. Then we went to greet the Alafiin at this palace. He should know by now how white men greet each other, but it seems he forgot and expected them to get down on the ground like other men do here. When Richard and his brother came forward and bowed and held out their hands to him he thought it very funny and laughed a long time with all his people. Then Richard gave him a present and he gave one back,. but I could see that they were small. One extra thing the Alafin got from this meeting was Richard's bugle-horn, and he made Richard show him how to blow notes on it, which pleased him very much. Then we went back to our lodging with Fat Ebo. This was a good place and he kept away many people from coming to worry us, as he had been told to do. People obeyed him as one of his duties now is to be the head executioner!

I heard Mr. John say to Richard one day that he had expected Katanga to be a bigger and stronger city. Parts of the city walls are falling down. We hear that Ilorin is now larger than here and they seem to be pushing into this country. It does not look as if the Alafin here or his people are doing much to protect their city. I did not hear any word about Richard coming to help as Prime Minister or War Chief. Even before, when the Captain failed to do anything to help them I think they had no more real hope of the white men doing anything for them. Out stay this time has been just one week, unlike the month we stayed before and the .Alafin made no attempt to stop us going. He did not suggest we could go through Ilorin or Nupe so it had to be by Borgu Our final visit to the Alafin was polite but short. He and his wives and the other women there talked some time and then collected a small amount in cowries to give to the brothers to pay those who had brought them from Badagry. Then the Alafin wished them well and put a final present of one cola nut in the hand of each of them and they said good bye. Even getting five carriers to help with our loads was difficult.

From Katanga we had to go back some distance to the west until we could cross the river Moshi, to the village where I had had to steal some yams so that we could have good food. Once across, we went northwards to Kaiama. We were greeted by King Yaro, now looking much older than when we last saw him. The place we were given to stay was good except that it was very hot, and we got plenty of food. It seemed odd that Yaro got angry when Richard spoke about our going on through Wawa, but he said the chief of Wawa had kept three slaves who took our late Captain's loads there and they were no longer friends. Another complaint he had was that his niece, the Widow Zuma, had had to flee to Bussa after a quarrel with the chief of Wawa We would therefore have to go another way.

When we come to Kaiama we always seem to find a Muslim festival, and this was as usual. Yaro says he is a Muslim, although he still has idols or carved figures around his house rather as some of our Hausa chiefs have, to the annoyance of the Muslims. People went to the praying ground and then sacrificed sheep and goats as they always do. All the men and boys are brightly dressed, on horses with bells and coloured tapes, even small boys who had to be held on the backs of their horses. The girls are still naked except for strings of shells round their middles. In the afternoon there was horse racing as before, except that Yaro did not enter the races himself but sat watching. We left Kaiama after a week there.

As we travel along, of course Richard and Mr. John are together most of the time. I live with my wifee Miriamu. Jaudi stays with Ibrahim, Mina and Antonio I have little chance to talk with Mr. John. Most of my talking with Richard in the past was after the Captain died. I do like Mr. John: I can see he finds it difficult to get used to African living, but he is always cheerful and sensible about things. So far he has not been sick either.

From Kaiama we went with Yaro's eldest son who will show us the new way which will not take us through Wawa. This is through a forest with few men in it but many wild animals. We could hear hyenas and jackals going round at night and we stayed close together for safety There are many elephants and people some times kill them for their meat. Sometimes they can sell the elephant teeth, but there is little trade for them One place we passed is said to be where some Fulani sent from Sokoto had gone on south to make a raid but when they were coming back they found themselves starving as the people around would not sell them any food. It is said that they saved food by killing twenty slaves who were with them. I did not realise it would be so difficult and I had bought only one day's food to take with us, but Richard blamed me for not having three days' food, although I have shot a guinea fowl. To make things worse, Mr. John became very ill with fever. Richard sent me ahead to find our carriers who had our medicine chest. Next day I saved the party by finding the carriers, bringing back the medicine chest and also much food that I had been able to buy. As is usual with fever, it comes and goes, and some days Mr. John seemed better, then the fever starts up again. It did become very bad and, although we did not say so to each other, I could see that Richard was very anxious, like me, that this could be as bad as when the Captain had been so ill. Fortunately, things got much better after that. We managed to reach Kubli, a town with a steep hill beside it, and we rested there.

It needed only two days from there to Bussa. I had not been there before, but Richard went there alone once when he wanted to find the Captain and we were having trouble about the Widow Zuma with the Chief Mohamed. When I was on the way back from Sokoto with him he tried to take me there from Wawa but the road was so bad that we could not make it. He remembered how good the king and his wife were to him before, and they were so again.

I specially wanted to see the Widow Zuma because of something I forgot to mention before. This happened when she was trying to get either the Captain or Richard as her husband to help her defeat the Chief. . She thought I could help her, and I did some business with her then I wanted to buy a wife, one of the most attractive of her slaves. This was separate from her giving me a slave woman, not one of her best. We had agreed on this and on the price, and I had paid her part of the money. Then the whole problem came, when Chief Mohammed objected to what she was doing, and everything went wrong. She rushed off with all her servants to follow the Captain and when she came back she was in disgrace and had to stay quiet, and the next day the Captain started on his way to cross the Niger and go towards Kano. In all the rush I was unable to complete my business with the Widow and I had recovered only part of my money from her. I had to leave Wawa without the wife I was buying but with some of my money still in the Widow's hands. When we saw her this time in Bussa she was plainly dressed and full of troubles, although talking quietly. She said she had done nothing wrong but the Chief had been so angry she had had to get over the city wall in the night and run off to Bussa on foot with nothing. This cannot have been easy for her as she is so big! The Chief had then taken away much of her property and many of her slaves, including the one I wanted to marry, so she said she was unable to pay me or do anything for me. She has not lost any weight in all this; indeed she is even bigger than before. Only with difficulty could she squeeze through the wide doorway into Richard's hut. I have been so angry about this loss of money but the king of Bussa would not judge the case for me. Then I said the king had better take my place and get the money from her, but he says that since it is her money this would be quite wrong and he could not think of doing such a bad thing. So I am the loser – no wife, no money. It is not made better for me by the story going round in Bussa that her son did some stealing in Wawa, something she knew about, and this was why Chief Mohammed punished her. I do not see what I can do, so I can only stay away from her. Bitter honey indeed!

Richard and Mr.John have tried to find out about the death of that man Mr. Mungo Park that the late Captain had been asking about. The king showed them a rich gown that the previous king had bought after Park died. It is like the outside gown that one of our own chiefs would use at important times, very heavy with ornaments and hot to wear. As he did not want to keep it he later sent it to Richard as a present. I was sent to the king to ask for any of Mr. Park's books that he had, but he said it had all happened long ago and he did not have any books. A drummer who works for the king told us to ask again, as he believes there is at least one book in Bussa, and Richard at once sent him to ask the king again. He said he would ask around. If this is the time of year when Mr. Park came you can see how he might have struck the rocks. Although the rain is now on and we have storms at night the water in the river is low. What comes from up river is not here yet, and you can see rocks everywhere.

The next day the king came with a man who had a book wrapped in cloth under his arm. Richard was excited but his face fell when he found it was a printed book such as a seaman might use when sailing. It was not one written by Mr. Park at all, although it had some loose papers from him. Everybody was sorry that it was not useful and they did not take it.

We stayed only a few days at Bussa. The King and his Queen were very kind to us and made no effort to detain us. As before, they were most worried that we should not eat food cooked by other people and risk being poisoned. The worst thing at Bussa is the mosquitoes at night, but everyone says it has always been like this. I managed to sleep in my cloth but I do not think Richard and his brother slept well. The king sent us off in a canoe, while our horses were taken over the river and then by foot. We went in three days, stopping at small islands where they speak a different language and live by fishing. We sent word ahead and were met at a village near Yauri by the Prime Minister, who is an old Arab. He said this is where Mr. Park came and stayed in his boat. His guide was paid off and left there to go back up river to his home.

The Arab took us to the large city of Yauri with a very big wall. The kingdom is not under Sokoto. It has a problem of a revolt in Ngaski to its south. This has now been put down with some soldiers killed. We heard much talk about trouble in Nupe too, including Kulfo where we stayed twice before. When in Katanga our Captain had doubted whether Nupe had any war, and he thought the king or Alafin was saying this to stop us going there. Later we heard that two brothers were fighting in Nupe over who should rule there. The Fulani from Sokoto were helping one of them who seemed to be winning. Later the Fulani tried to get all power for themselves and supported first one, then the other, of the brothers. Fighting there still seems to be bad, which made Richard change his mind. He had thought of going to Kulfo and then to Funda that we did not reach before, but now he and Mr. John gave up this idea. They decided it would be better to go back to Bussa and they sent a messenger to see the king, and asking him to help provide a canoe to go down the river.

Then something happened that caused us to doubt whether we could go that way. The Widow Zuma's son, whose stealing in Wawa had led to her being driven out to Bussa, had fled across the river into Nupe. From there he had made a raid to seize cattle from near Wawa. Probably she had been behind this action, and as she is afraid of what may happen to her she has also fled across the river to Ngaski. However, the chief there did not want her and he has sent her back to Bussa. What will now happen to this troublesome woman I do not know. But the end of this affair improves our chances of getting back to Bussa and then Wawa.

The mosquitoes are bad here too and Mr. John tells me that he and his brother cannot sleep at night but either talk together or read by lamplight. They would like to sleep in the daytime when they have little to do but the king's daughters, some of whom are not so young, come and visit them every day and chatter, always trying to get presents. I can sleep all right and if it is a fine day I go out and shoot pigeons or other birds. This helps us a lot as the amount of food sent to us has decreased much from how it began The last harvest is months ago and the new harvest has not yet come.

The king sometimes gives things to us generously but most of the time he seems to want to get as much given to him as possible. People here say he has a way of taking money from people as a loan or he buys things and then he makes them prisoners by them having to wait to be repaid their loan or paid for what they have sold. He gives them promises and excuses but does not keep his word. It is said that some visiting Arabs have waited for years. With us, he 'bought' some things from Richard but never pays for them. In the end he has said that he is too poor to pay and he has offered Richard a slave girl instead! Richard did not want her but felt he could not refuse, wanting to get away and not be more delayed. So he has taken the girl and given her to me as my third wife. This is a Kambari girl and I do not like her much. We saw Kambaris before, and I know the people here think they are only good as slaves, not good people like us. I said, 'Mr. Lander, I have two wives and I do not need a third one' He said to me with a smile, 'At least she can help you with your garden at Cape Coast Castle!' so I agreed and she came to me but will not live with me and my wives Abuda and Miriamu.

In the same way the king long refused to answer questions about any books from Mr. Mungo Park, although he earlier wrote to our late Captain to visit him to receive his books. I have taken my part in asking him about books, without success. In the end he said he had nothing to do with Mr. Park's death at Bussa and he had never had any of his books.

As time passed and we could not get the king to settle matters or give us permission to go away we wondered if we would ever be able to go. This might have continued but fortunately the king of Bussa sent a messenger to ask why we did not come to him and to say that we should be allowed to go at once. The last thing that helped to start us on our way was when Richard and Mr. John answered one of the many requests for medicines by giving the king, all his family and the Arab Prime Minster a strong dose of what will keep them active and busy the whole day! After a month in Yauri we left at last, the only benefit to any of us being my new wife!

Chapter 14 —
Farewell to Bussa and Wawa

<u>August – September 1830.</u>

Only one or two miles from Yauri we entered canoes to take us to Bussa while the horses were taken by road. Each night we stayed at a Kambari village. The African way of providing food to all visitors has served us well but here, before the harvest, there is little they can give us or sell to us. I shot some birds to feed our people. When we arrived at Bussa and had rested a little, the king and queen welcomed us warmly, as before.

The king said again what he told us earlier through his messenger, that he would sell us a canoe large enough for all of us and our loads. The canoes that Chief Mohammed of Wawa has are larger than his own and the king will therefore arrange to get one from him to sell to us. I could see that Richard and Mr. John were very heppy about this. I was with them when they took a special present to give the king which they had kept for a good occasion. It was a large medal with a chain attached, shining brightly as it is in silver. They pointed to a head showing on the medal and told the king this is the king, George III, before the present king, and there are words also on the medal. The king and the queen, who was with him, tried hard to say how pleased they are with this lovely thing, but they could only manage a few words and then they burst into tears of joy. When they could speak again they thanked Richard very much. Later they told him we should go to see the queen's brother, the Chief of Wawa, as he had been having trouble with Kaiama on account of us, and the king agreed with her.

Richard explained to them that he and his brother have decided that the way we must go is on the river, not on land. The king said that he understood but he is worried about the Fulani on both sides of the river to his south, especially in Nupe. He will go to the river himself and ask the spirit of the water whether we will be safe on the river. I think this is like saying that the British are too weak to control the water. Thinking of my long time with the Navy, I feel angry about this, and I said strongly, 'King, you do not understand. These white men are like gods on the water Why, I have worked with them for many years on the waters and I have seen how strong they are. Their boats are many times bigger than yours, and the waters they sail on are much, much stronger than any you have ever seen, even when storms come. In your canoes you can only have ten or twenty men at most, but ships I have sailed on have many times that number of men. Our ships have beaten the French many times, and other countries too. They travel all over the world and they are masters of the sea. What is more, while your canoes can only move against the waters if men in them use their paddles and the strength of their bodies and arms, the white men's ships can control the water and the winds. They even make the winds move their ships. I tell you they are like gods on the waters, whatever your river god may say.' Perhaps I said more than is right in speaking to a king, but I feel strongly about this. The king listened and thought, but then all he said was, 'I wanted to be sure they are safe, so I will go tomorrow to speak with the river. Then I can be sure.'

The next morning we saw the king again, looking very happy. He said he had been to the river with his Chief Imam to speak to the spirit of the water. The spirit told him all will be well for Richard and Mr. John. This confirmed what I had said, and we need not be worried.

As I have said, food is not easy at this time before the harvest. At first the king and queen sent us much food but each day the amount was less. There are eight of us now, apart from Richard and Mr. John, and we became very hungry. I helped by shooting guinea fowl, but we do not have much shot and powder left. The king said to me one day that he and his wife are also short of food and have had no meat for weeks. I therefore shot two extra birds and gave them to Richard to give to the king. He said I had mentioned this to him, but the king was embarrassed, saying he had not meant this seriously. It was best for me to say no more, but I was pleased that the king had realised that I could do things without having an order to do them. The brothers were then anxious to get on, and they needed to go to Wawa to see about the canoe, especially as the water of the river is now becoming full.

After a few days at Bussa we went to Wawa, taking two days as the road was bad with the rains. The Chief's head drummer, an important man at Wawa, talked to us and told us there is a big river that joins the Niger near Funda. This is news to us as we had thought, from what other people have said, that a river went the other way to Lake Chad. We also heard from the Chief that any rocks in the river end before we will come to Komi, the place where we crossed the river when we were with our late Captain. After that we will be able to go all the way down the river to the sea. The Chief sent a messenger to Komi to look for a canoe large enough for us, as that is where the big boats are kept for the ferry. Later he sent another messenger to follow this one. While we were waiting for a reply Richard began to feel fever coming on and set off to go back to Bussa, as our medicine chest has been left there, leaving Mr. John to settle things about the canoe.

Many people here are not Muslim but follow their own religion. Some of them made a noisy procession which passed by Mr. John. and then they came back to talk with him. He asked them about what they believe and do in their religion. They said they make sacrifices of cows, sheep or other animals but not of any man or woman, which they would think very bad. Some of their ideas seem to agree with those of the Muslims. They say that at the start of the world there was one man and one woman. The man they call Adam and the woman Aminatu, a Hausa name rather like that of my wife Miriamu.

Two days after Richard went back to Bussa he sent word to tell Mr. John that he is now much better. He also said that the queen there said she would settle the cost of the canoe with her brother Mohammed of Wawa. That means it is no longer necessary for Mr. John to stay in Wawa, but he did stay partly because he is not feeling well. Also the Chief asked him to stay and wait for his messenger to come back from Komi. In addition, he was waiting for a man to come back to Wawa from another place, who he heard did have some books of that Mr. Park. When he did come, he said yes, he did have some books from the boat, but when our late Captain did not ask for them, he lost interest and later they dropped to pieces. Poor Mr. John, who had had such strong hopes, was very sad to hear this. He had been helped in this search for anything connected with Mr. Park by a young man who is nearly blind, who is a son of that woman, the Widow Zuma. This is not the same son as caused his mother to run away to Bussa, then went to the Nupe side of the river and later made a raid from there for cattle near Wawa. This is another son, who does not agree at all with what his mother does, and is allowed to live here in Wawa peacefully.

To help Mr. John with his Hausa, as he can speak little of it yet, I was with him when he went to say goodbye to the Chief,. who kept him a long time as the Chief wanted to talk with him. He asked about England and what it is like there. Mr. John told him how it is large, with many people, rich and strong. He pointed out to the Chief how they had been able to send first our Captain, then Richard and himself, to this country far away from their own, and how they trade with all parts of the world. The Chief found it hard to see how these things could be, and he thought about it, muttering to himself and making sounds such as our people do in their throats when they hear surprising news, like 'tchk, tchk.' In the end he turned to me and said, 'Can you tell me, Pascoe, is all this quite true?' I replied, 'Yes, I know it to be true. I have been there myself and I have seen with my own eyes. I have seen their big cities like London, as they call the capital, the people, their dresses, their carriages that carry them about, and everything. You may be surprised at a black man like me going there, and think that black men only go across the seas as slaves, but I am a free man and I have been to England. No man can be a slave there – their law will not allow it. I saw other black men there too, and I can see that they come and go freely. I expect that many of our people, and other people too, will go there and live together with the English people.' This is a big speech for me but I feel better for saying all of it. The Chief replied that he is very happy that men from England have come and visited him, and he hopes more will come.

Then we said goodbye and Mr. John and I rode back towards Bussa. We stayed that night in a village of Nupe people who came across the river from Nupe some years ago in order to get away from the wars in their country. Some of their talk at night was in Hausa and we could understand it. They seem to believe that white men eat the flesh and drink the blood of black men, although they could see Mr. John as a peaceful man and they showed no fear of him. We tried to tell them the truth, but I do not think we were successful

Back in Bussa Richard confirmed that the queen will settle the payment for a canoe with Chief Mohammed. Richard and Mr. John will sell her their two good horses which they got after their previous horses fell sick and died. If there is a difference in price between the canoe and the horses, this will be adjusted one way or the other between them. Richard thought we had already given one horse as a present to the king, but found that the king had got the wrong idea and not understood me. In fact they still have both horses to sell.

Ibrahim, one of the Bornu men with us, has been sent to Kulfo to sell an ass and some needles in order to obtain some money. The king here has also sent a messenger over to the Nupe side of the river to ask them to send to all towns and villages to tell them to let us go down the river past them peacefully. This should be spread as far as Raba, a Fulani town I remember our late Captain sent to about any books of Mr. Park. It is now the Fulani's main town, with Mallam Dendo, a cousin of Sultan Bello of Sokoto, as their ruler. They say the Chief of Wawa will send a messenger to do the same on this side of the river.

Ibrahim has come back from Kulfo but Mr. John is disappointed at how little money he has brought. He claims a lot of money was stolen from him, but how can we know? We will have to wait for the other messengers to come back. The Chief of Wawa has sent a canoe but it is far too small to take all of us, so more delay is likely. This onc could not possibly take the eight of us, Richard and Mr. John, and all our loads. They say there are larger canoes at Leaba, down the river some way, and it seems we shall have to go there to get one.

Richard and Mr. John are very angry about this. They think the queen and her brother at Wawa have deliberately tricked and failed them. But I have seen how much they have tried to help us, and I do not think they are trying to cheat us. The reason may be, as I see it, that unlike the position on board ship, they do not know clearly enough what to do and when to do it. When I entered the navy, in two days I learnt that if the lieutenant or the boson tells you to do something, he does not mean that you think about it and then do it some time later. He means you must do it this minute and do it well. I realised this when I saw a man punished at the grill with a lash because he did not move quickly enough to carry out an order. I was not punished then, as a new man, but they said it might happen if I failed another time. Since then, I always act immediately when I receive an order, and I have kept out of trouble. Chiefs here do not have a good idea of dealing with things quickly and completely.

Part of the time we have been waiting has gone brightly, with a Muslim feast.

The king first goes through the Muslim rites and then goes out of the town to a place where there is an old fetish, where he performs the rites of the people's religion. That is what he really believes. After that there come celebrations with everyone in their best clothes, horse racing and dancing. The king is the best dancer in this country, and when he performs everyone watches and applauds it. I saw this myself.

Then, just after the celebrations and dancing, something happened that made all the people cry out with fear. We all saw how the moon went dark and the night became black, not because of any clouds but because the light disappeared.

For myself, I had not seen this before and I was terrified. I ran into the hut where Richard and Mr. John were, crying out in alarm. Some were saying the sun has stolen the moon. Others, especially strong Muslims, say it is a punishment for men's sins. I did not know what to think. To my surprise Richard and Mr. John remained quiet and said they had a book which told them this would happen that very night. They had not thought it necessary to tell the king beforehand, but they can tell him now when it will end. Meanwhile outside all are beating drums and irons and are crying out with loud voices, thinking they can drive away the darkness and bring the moon back. This goes on until at length the moon does turn bright again, like the brothers have said, and the night becomes less dark. Then most people go to bed, but not me, I cannot sleep after all this.

Mr. John is always asking questions to try to understand the people and places we visit. As his Hausa is still poor, he needs my help. Nearly all the people here can speak Hausa, although it is not their own language. He has been asking about slavery, having seen that more than half the people are slaves. What does it mean to them? And do they not want to run away? They tell him that what it means is that you have to do work for your master, but for much of the time you can farm or do other things for yourself and family. Some have become slaves by capture in war; some have committed crimes or are in debt, some are born slaves because their fathers were slaves. Some work as servants in their masters' houses, and they are usually regarded as members of the family but with a low position. Most slaves accept how things are and do not run away. In fact, they are often sent by their masters to do things away from home and come back. If a slave does run away his punishment will not usually be any beating, but later they may be sold. Mr. John says how different this sounds from the slavery in America or the West Indies. It sounds, he says, like how many men used to be treated in England if you go back since, since, since. The name he used sounds like a 'villain', but I thought that means an evil person who does very bad things.

At last the king of Bussa's messenger that he sent to Nupe and the Fulani at Raba has come back, saying he has been well received. Everyone looks forward to our visit and they promise to give us their help. The Magia, one of the claimants to be king of Nupe, has sent his own son and another man to be our guides. The king of Bussa is very happy at this news so that he has been running about like a boy and even weeping with joy. He says that now we shall be all right, and he knows that he has done everything for the safety of our party that he could do, just as a king should do. Now he can let us go on our journey safely. We have prepared a stock of corn, beans and other things to eat. The king and queen have added rice, honey, and vegetables. To add to our loads we have some elephant teeth given to us by the king of Bussa and

Chief Mohammed, which we hope we can sell somewhere to raise more money. We had been worried as to when we could get away, but now our stay of six or seven weeks has come to an end. It is with the thanks that they deserve that the king and queen receive our goodbyes. As we go to the waterside to get into the canoes provided for us by Bussa to begin our journey, all the people line the way to say goodbye, often with tears and on their knees.

We had two canoes and the king's boatmen, who guided us between rocks, going quite fast. Our boats are heavily laden, sitting low in the water, and we soon found they need some repair. This was quickly done at a small island. Then we passed Komi, the ferry place across the Niger. It is on a large island called Patashi, fifteen or twenty leagues from Bussa, that we landed, with another island nearby called Teah. It seems a rich island with a very pleasant Chief. It is not far from Wawa, and we expect to get the large canoe we are buying sent from there. The Magia's son says if we do not get a good canoe from there, we should ask for our horses back and then he can use them to get us a large canoe in his country.

A messenger has come from Wawa, saying Chief Mohammed is displeased we did not visit him again, and asking that at least Richard go to see him. He says a large canoe is ready for us at Leaba to our south, but if Richard wants to have the horses back, he can have them. I hear Richard explain to Mr. John he is uncertain what will be the best things to do. The king of Bussa has arranged for us to visit the Magia in Nupe and go to the Fulani at Raba, but the Chief of Wawa is against our going to the Nupe or Fulani at all. Which should we do?

We had to wait four days for Richard to go to Wawa and come back. He was angry when he came back as Chief Mohammed told him he had not yet got a canoe ready for us. As I said before, the Chiefs do not prepare things well in good time. While we have been waiting, there have been many visitors. It is the first time any white man has come to Patashi and everyone wants to come and see them Those who have come have always been quiet and if Mr. John makes any move towards them they back away if not run off as the women or children mostly do They have also provided plenty of food, as their farms on this island are good. The Magia's son is going away to see his father, but he hopes to see us at Raba. The Bussa boatmen have left us to go back to Bussa, but messengers from there and Wawa will still be with us. We have boatmen from Patashi to take us to Leaba. It is a good thing they will take us, as we find to our surprise that there are still rocks in the river, although we thought they would have ended before now. The worst has been at a place called Awuru, very rocky and with a narrow channel The boat went very fast through this place. After that, things became easier and we were glad to see Leaba soon beyond. There we hope finally to find our good canoe, as promised.

Chapter 15 —
Going with the Stream

<u>October – November 1830</u>

I am glad we have left Leaba. There is no law there. We hoped to find the promised canoe, big enough to take all of us, but there was nothing for us. We nearly lost what we had. The Chief of Patashi sent us there in his own two canoes, with his own paddlers, who naturally wanted to go home. It was only the three messengers from Wawa and one from Bussa who said no, as there was nothing else we must keep these canoes, and the Chief of Wawa would pay for them So all the messengers and the canoe men went off, while we kept the canoes. Richard and Mr. John did not like this, as the chief of Patashi had been very good to us, but what else could we do? Leaba is under Wawa but they have no people of their own there now. They are Nupe people there, from across the river, who supplied us with food as they would do with any other strangers. The trouble lies in other parties from the Nupe side of the river who keep coming – we saw some of them while we were there- who only want to rob the people.

One help to us was a man called Duku, a Bornu man. He says he has power from the Nupe rulers across the river, and people seem ready to obey him out of fear. He welcomed us and helped us to get accommodation and food. He also made sure we could keep the boats, even having them pulled out of the water and guarded. Once he took them without asking us, to send one party of Nupe back, but he returned the boats to us. Even when men came from Teah, the island near to Patashi, though not under Wawa, and said they, not Patashi, really owned the canoes. Richard nearly gave in and agreed to them taking them away, but Duku prevented them doing so. A second thing that helped us is that we had muskets and pistols. This scared the Nupes, who may be strong at robbing, but are cowards. This is why they wanted to go back across the river, to get away from us.

Duku gave us some trouble, however. For one thing, he wanted to talk and talk for hours: One thing he claimed to know all about was what happened to Mr. Mungo Park. Worse, he tried to make us stay longer then we wanted, and even claimed it was up to him to say when we could go. Richard and Mr. John got so angry that they went to him with their pistols drawn, threatening to shoot him. Only then did Duku see that he had better let us go, and he helped us put everything in the canoes and start out on our journey. This gave us relief.

After that we found we could go down the river quite fast. It is several miles wide, with no rocks in it, and with a good current. We had to stop at some places to change canoe men, and when we spent any night Richard made us go out and take paddles from canoes on the river banks, and hide them in the bottom of our canoes. If we have to paddle ourselves some time, with no boatmen with us, we will need paddles, and we could not find anybody either to give us any or to sell them to us. You can call this stealing, but I think it is necessity.

In this way we got along the river easily, with hills on either side, in a southerly direction. Just where the river turns towards the south-east, we passed a very tall narrow rocky hill, which stands up straight from the river. It is called Mount Kesa, and it is believed by the people around it to house good spirits. This may be fifty miles from Leaba, as I judge distance on the water, and we had done this in two days. At one time we had a friendly race with another canoe. Our canoe men worked hard when women in the other canoe sang and played a guitar.

On the Nupe side of the river we passed a number of islands with fishermen living there, until we stopped at one island. In the evening the Magia's son, Mohammed, who we last saw at Bussa, came to see us, saying he had been expecting us. A young messenger came with him, sent by Malam Dendo, the Fulani ruler of Raba ahead of us. They said both Malam Dendo and the Magia would welcome us and try to help us.

The next morning we were told we would meet the *Sarkin Bakin Ruwa*, the King of the Dark Water. He is a Nuipe under Malam Dendo who rules the islands and river banks. He is a big man, tall and rather old. He came to us in a large canoe, leading a small one, both with flags and ornaments. The large canoe was paddled by twenty men, and with him were six wives, musicians and boy pages, all very neatly dressed. To greet him Richard and Mr. John, who have since ceased wearing their Turkish robes, dressed to look smart Richard put on a naval lieutenant's coat which he has been keeping, and Mr. John wore fine clothes. As Richard had instructed us, Jaudi, Ibrahim, the others in our party and I all put on clean white gowns. A sheet was fixed above our canoe, with a Union Jack flying above it, such as you might see at sea. We really looked very smart, as if on parade, to greet *Sarkin Bakin Ruwa* There was some delay so that the chief could talk with his people, then we went off in convoy until we came to two large towns facing each other across the river.

To out left hand is Raba which we have heard of before, on a rising slope going beyond our view. This is where Malam Dendo, cousin of Sultan Bello, lives as Fulani ruler. They say he is now old and is arranging for his son to take over from him. It seems he is now the real ruler of Nupe, and the Magia can only do what he allows. The Magia's brother has given up his claim to be king of the Nupes and most of his soldiers have joined Malam Dendo. On out right is Zagozhi, a large flat island so low that in the wet season, like now, much of it is covered in water. This is where the *Sarkin Ruwa* lives, and he takes us himself to find a place not too much in the water where we will stay. He is worried when Richard and Mr. John fire muskets, until they explain to him this is done as an honour like a king. We have been told that Malam Dendo thinks it will be best for us to stay in Zagozhi rather then among the many people at Raba, and we agree to that.

Presents brought to us from Malam Dendo and others include three sheep and other food. It will not be easy for Richard to find enough to give back as presents, but he prepares things to give to their messengers. These seem pleased when they are shown what is prepared. We are short of money and, as Raba has a large market, Ibrahim and Jaudi are sent to sell needles. Unfortunately they cannot find buyers for the elephants' teeth we have brought from Bussa and Wawa. We receive presents too from the Magia's son and Malam Dendo's messenger. They advise we should give a little money to *Sarkin Ruwa* to make him ready to let us have a canoe. I go with them to make sure the money gets to him.

I hear that the Fulani under Malam Dendo are getting ready to attack Katanga and then to go beyond there to the sea, but they do not always win in battles. A short time ago they were ashamed when defeated by Kambaris, people who everybody thinks are too weak and low down to do anything like that. Then Malam Dendo sent a force against Funda down the Niger, but they fled back, saying there were a large number of white men opposing them. I had to go and see Malam Dendo about something and he told me about this. 'Do you think, Abubakar,' (as I am known to him),'there are really white men fighting for Funda?' I replied, 'No, Sir, I am sure I would have heard if there were white soldiers anywhere in this country. I am sure the only white men are the two peaceful men you have as guests here.' He seems to accept this from me. I think he knows I only speak the truth and he can easily speak with me, as a Hausa man who knows the customs as well as the language of the people.

Not everybody here speaks the truth. The other day two Arabs came up to Richard as if to greet him like old friends. The older of the two took him in his arms, with a smile all over his face, saying how good it was to see him after this long time. Richard was taken by surprise and did not at first recognise the man. Then Richard's face went dark as he realised who it was. How could this man come to him as an old friend? It was the man who had cheated the late Captain and was sacked. Richard took him on again as we were going to leave Kano and wanted to go to Funda. I knew him well enough: this is the man who failed to bring our tent poles, and I had to go back to Kano to get them. He disappeared and we had never seen him again, until now. He is a rogue, not a good man at all, and it is strange that he can expect any welcome from those who know him. Richard reminded him of what he had done and told him he wanted nothing to do with him. He seemed surprised and would not accept this. I had to join in telling him strongly to go away and we had almost to drive him out by force. The younger man with him looked downcast to hear his companion spoken to like this, but he seems a quiet, decent man, and Richard gave him a few needles before he left us.

From the time that we were at Badagry I could see that Richard and Mr. John did not have a large amount to give away as presents. I have heard them talking to each other from time to time about how difficult this is for them So many chiefs and those who thought of themselves as chiefs have come expecting a present in return for any help, however small, they have given us This is the custom here. One may be generous in giving help but one does expect a return As we have travelled on, one thing has been finished, then another thing, and we have little in our boxes now. Richard has sometimes given only a small present, or none at all, where he would have given more in the past. I did not see what he is sending to Malam Dendo, but I know it cannot be large.

I was worried when Malam Dendo sent for me by name, not for Richard or Mr. John. I had to go urgently to him. When I reached him I had to wait some time for him to see me, and then he spoke strongly to me. He held up one thing after another that they had sent to him, and said of each one that it was not good, or he could buy something better in the market. He expected that when he welcomed these white men they could give him something much better. The only thing they had given him that was any good was a large looking glass in a frame. The rest was fit only for children I could not argue with him, of course, but I would tell the brothers what he had said. I did say that I knew they had made many presents and did not have much left, but I hoped they could satisfy him.

Richard and Mr. John could see from my face when I got back that I did not have good news. I told them what had been said and how I had tried to explain, but he insisted they must try to do better. They looked in their few remaining boxes and at each piece there, and they talked and talked together. Malam Dendo had said that if they had nothing else they must give him their guns but they rejected this idea. They would then have no means of defending themselves in any future trouble. They could see no way out of their difficulty.

I let my eyes move over the few boxes we still had, until they stopped were we kept Mr. Mungo Park's. gown, that the king of Bussa had given them. I said nothing. Then Mr. John said to his brother, 'What about Mr. Park's gown? We never think of it as ours. We want to take it back to England to give to the Colonial Office or to the Park family, if they want it. But if it is the only thing to keep us safe in completing our mission, could we use it?' There was silence again for some minutes. Then Richard spoke in a low voice, as if sick, 'I do not like the idea. It is the only thing of Mr. Park's that we have been able to keep until now to take home with us. But I think you are right, brother, this is the only thing we can do. Let us hope it will be enough to satisfy this Fulani usurper.' Here he showed his real feelings about Malam Dendo. At once he called Ibrahim to take the gown to Malam Dendo and tell him this is the best we can do. Also tell him we cannot go to see either the Magia or Sultan Bello, as we have nothing suitable to give them.

The sun was rising high when Ibrahim went and we were surprised to see him come back to Zagozhi .by canoe from Raba soon after midday with a broad smile on his face. 'Malam Dendo,' he said, 'went far beyond just accepting the gift. It was wonderful, he said, fit for a king. Keep it secret, and it will make my neighbours praise me and see my power when I appear in it before them. It is worth too much to accept it as a present and I will pay for it. What will the white men accept as the price of it?' Ibrahim of course said he would have to ask when he returned.

Ibrahim repeated all of this to the brothers. Then they said to me that I know our position well, and they rely on me to convince Malam Dendo to repay us by getting a large canoe that will hold us all and enable us to reach the sea, replacing the Patashi canoes. We know that *Sarkin Ruwa* wants paying to let us have a canoe and we hope Malam Dendo can arrange this. As a small thing, we hope he can also help us with some gowns, mats, and sandals, as ours are worn out. I found Malam Dendo still so full of pleasure with the gown that he agreed entirely and said he would settle about the canoe. Showing he was serious, he at once bought and gave us some fine mats that they make at Raba. To me, for my own use, he gave a good gown and a cap and 1,000 cowries. I was given two bags of rice and some plantains to bring back, and he said he would send some gowns for Richard and Mr. John.

Just then a messenger came from the Magia. He had promised to help us but he now told Malam Dendo that he did not believe Richard and Mr. John are poor, and they ought to give him a large present. We should all be detained and our baggage searched. It was Malam Dendo himself who told me this, as he was so pleased at the gift to him. He also told me the answer given to the messenger to give to the Magia. He completely rejected the Magia's suggestion. The white men travelled far and wore out their clothes and shoes on the way. They had put themselves under his protection and made fine presents. Should they be treated like robbers or even like dogs? They had been well treated by Katanga, Yauri,

Bussa and Wawa. How would his neighbours, or even his enemies, see him if he was to behave as the Magia suggested? Of course, after that, we have not been given any Nupe guide to help us!

I was still there with Malam Dendo when some traders came with fine horses to sell. They are Hausa but they spoke to Malam Dendo in his own language, that of the Fulani. In Sokoto I often heard people speak in that language, but it is useful to keep quiet about my knowing it. I could therefore follow what the traders said. They spoke very well of our late Captain, and recalled the good presents he had made to Sultan Bello. Malam Dendo fully agreed with their feelings, saying that as a Fulani he shared the white man's skin and blood. All of this I was able to tell Richard and Mr. John when I got back to them.

With all our affairs settled, except getting the canoe, we prepared to end our two weeks' stay in Zagozhi. A messenger came from Malam Dendo to settle matters with the *Sarkin Bakin Ruwa,* and afterwards told us it was now all settled. We packed everything up, ready to embark and asked *Sarkin Ruwa* where our canoe is, but he laughed and said, 'How can I give you a canoe simply on the promise of Malam Dendo to pay? I need to see some money.' He regarded our own canoes from Patashi as a security for any arrangement with us and wanted to keep them. How often do we find this kind of problem? Promises are not payment, and those who should receive the payment know that promises are often not kept. Sometimes they promise too many things, and when they have to spend money on their families or their businesses, they cannot meet all their promises. After some argument he agreed to take ten thousand cowries and the larger Patashi canoe. Fortunately Mr John found that the sale of needles at Raba market had given us ten thousand cowries, and the bargain was made

It was a bad bargain as we soon found, as the canoe leaked and we had to keep baling out water. Although larger than our Patashi canoe, we could not all lie down to rest. With no paddlers, we had to do the work ourselves, using the paddles we had 'borrowed' from other canoes as we came. Our only guide from Zagozhi followed us, being late. This, at least, was some good for us, as it let us decide when and where we would stop, instead of leaving it to messengers or paddlers to decide where they wanted to stop. But for a long, long way we could not find anywhere good to stop because of the swamps along the sides of the river

There are many crocodiles to be seen, and this has also prevented us trying to land on the banks, as crocodiles may be hiding in the swamps. Out in the river we are also frightened by river horses, or hippos, as Mr. John calls them We have all heard how they can turn canoes over and throw everybody into the waters. There are so many of them it seems we cannot escape them. .Fortunately, Ibrahim and Mina, being from

Bornu, say they have seen these on Lake Chad, and they usually keep away from boats and people, which makes the others less worried.

We could only continue into the night, getting very tired, and sometimes it rained on us in the night. The river flowed fast, to the east, and we saw the place where the Kaduna river enters it, the river Richard and I had first seen when trying to, go to Funda, and then we saw it again when we were made to turn back to Zaria

The next big town was Eggan, with a busy market and very many people. I went as our chief messenger to announce our arrival there. Some Nupe messengers there helped us, but we learnt that their main reason for being here is to collect taxes or, if these are not paid in time, to take some people as slaves. The crowd that came to see the white men was like what we had seen between Badagry and Katanga when we first came with the late Captain. The weather being very hot, as the rains have now ended, Richard and Mr. John found it difficult to get any good air with so many people pressing in on them. Several times they found it necessary to shut people out from their hut.

We stayed three days at Eggan. They wanted us to stay longer and advised us to wait three days, when many people would go to a large market called Bokwa, which would be much safer for us. However the brothers insisted on continuing. This is the last Nupe town, and they spoke badly about the people we should meet beyond this. They say they are likely to kill us or make us slaves. I tried to show the others we should go on. Such talk about dangers was not always correct. The sea cannot be very far away, as shown by things like cloth from overseas that we have seen. Abuda and Miriamu, my wives, will of course come with us, although I can see they are frightened. Among the men, only Antonio agrees to come on. He has been good, doing his share of work, like paddling, until now and of course he wants to go back to his country of Bonny, where his late father was king. The other men, even Jaudi who was made free by Richard at Cape Coast, say they will not come. They believe what the Eggan people say, that to continue would be very dangerous. They go to Richard and demand to get their wages. If he cannot pay them he should give them a letter to take to Cape Coast and so that they can be paid there. Richard refuses completely and says 'no going ahead, then no pay.' Antonio and I continue to argue with the others, and in the end they decide to come on, as they see it as more dangerous to stay, but they are very unhappy.

Richard and Mr. John have led us through so many difficulties that I feel we must continue. When I first knew Richard I thought he was trying to be a bigger man than the servant he was. After our Captain died I started to see him as very brave and able to defeat all difficulties in his way. That is why I agreed to follow him again on this journey. He and his brother have come through so much which could have broken other men. They will not allow anything to stop them doing what they feel they must do. I now feel I am joined with them, and this is why I want to encourage the others to continue with us.

The river went sometimes east, at other times southeast. Those who had wanted to leave the boat but had stayed reluctantly did not pull well on their paddles. After talking further with them Richard and Mr. John went as far as threatening to throw overboard any who did not do better, but I doubt if they really meant to do this. As the day went on things got better and we made good time in the fast stream To prove what I had said about getting nearer the sea, we saw our first seagull and some pelicans swimming on the river. In the evening we decided to stop to rest on an island. The people there thought we must be raiders and seized arms, ready to attack us. Our calls in Hausa made no difference until a woman who knew a little of the language spoke up They put down their arms but did not agree to our staying there. They pointed to our going on to a town called Kakunda, which the people at Eggan had recommended. We were very tired but decided to do what they said. After we had pulled away they changed their minds and signalled to us to come back, but the current was too strong, so we went on to Kakunda.

This is a town not under Nupe but some people speak Hausa there. A Muslim schoolmaster welcomed us, many of his children coming from Eggan. He had heard of two Christians being in Borgu, and here they are. We stayed in his large classroom and were well supplied with food and beer, sleeping well that night. Again they spoke badly of the people down river and advised us again to wait for a large party soon going to the market at Bokwa. If we would not do that, at least we should plan to pass a big town on the way at night, for safety. We paid for our entertainment largely by writing charms for good fishing, protection against crocodiles and other wishes, of which there were many. The schoolmaster tells us that within a day we shall pass where the river Benue joins the Niger. Funda lies up that river and beyond you can go by water up to Bornu.

When Richard refused all arguments for staying longer, we prepared our muskets and pistols ready in case of the worst, and left in the afternoon. Our party was still divided in its feelings. Jaudi joined me in promising to do our best in any trouble. Antonio said he would stand with Richard and Mr. John up to the end. The others still shook with fear but they saw that they must come on with us. Thinking of the horrors they had been warned of, everyone pulled their paddles better than ever It was past midnight, completely dark, when we could tell that we were passing a large village, with sound of music, dancing and revelry on the banks of the river, but we went by without attracting attention to ourselves.

After dawn next morning we saw we were on a wide river, now going somewhat west of south, between high hills It was so wide that we thought the part we first entered might be a branch of the Niger, but the force of the water pushed us back into that river's main stream. This must be the river Benue that the schoolmaster had told us about, a river almost as big as the Niger itself. Just before coming to the junction we had passed a town called Koton Karfi, which again the schoolmaster had told us about, but we did not stop there. High hills were seen in all directions, behind us, up both rivers, and ahead. These are rocky, like the hills at Shaki in Yoruba land. The river is fast running. Some way further on we had difficulty avoiding a bad place going round a rocky hill standing on its own in the river, which nearly upset our boat.

After a full day and night coming down from Kakunda we all needed a rest, and stopped at a level place which was not covered with trees or anything else. There were signs that other people had been there recently but some of our number were surprised to wander into a village with fires going. Hoping to be able to get some food snd some embers to light our fires they approached, but all the women there took fright at seeing these strangers and ran off. They told us about this, and then I went there with Jaudi and Ibrahim, to ask for yams and embers, but again people ran off. Soon we saw men running towards us, in large numbers carrying arms, ready to attack us. We all gathered together and seized our weapons, but these men would have been too many for us in a fight. I am thankful that Richard and Mr. John went forward, dropped the weapons they were carrying and held out their hands to the people coming to attack us. The people on the other side had arrows in their bows, ready to fire, and it was at the last moment that one of them stopped their leader from firing his arrow. The leader then dropped on his knees and made friendly signs to Richard and Mr. John. On our side, I was ready to fire as soon as their chief man fired, if he had done so Most of our people, including Antonio, had run away as fast as they could!

A man among them spoke Hausa and acted as interpreter. He said we were strangers, they had feared our attack, but now they saw we are peaceful. Soon it was all very happy and peaceful, with them astonished to see white men visiting them. We coon learnt that this is the site of the Bokwa Market that we have been hearing about. People come to it from as far north as Eggan and Kakunda, and others from the south too, always coming in a large convoy of boats for safety. There was an evening of rejoicing after this, men firing off muskets and eating and drinking well. In gifts we received much to eat and they even brought us eight thousand cowries. Seeing white men for his first time, the chief said surely we had come from heaven, but Richard said no, no, we had come from another country on the earth After the celebrations had ended, we slept well on the area of ground where we landed. I was up early and the first thing Richard saw in the morning was me roasting yams for our breakfast. He took this opportunity to say to me how good it had been to see me stand so firmly through all our troubles

When we met the chief he said we had now passed the most dangerous place, but there were places we should avoid, as the chiefs there might try to detain us longer than we wanted. One place he mentioned is called Idah, where thee is a powerful chief called the Atta. The river took us fast from Bokwa, passing Idah up on a high cliff and going perhaps thirty miles beyond it. We had worried villagers again getting ready to attack us when we stopped to rest at a village where we sat on mats under the shade of a coconut palm, the first we had seen since leaving Katanga so long ago. When they saw us sitting down quietly the villager realised we meant them no harm. Nobody was able to speak Hausa, but Antonio found a young man who could speak a little of his language from Bonny. Soon things were peaceful between us and them, but the chief was not really friendly and he sent us only a little poor food that evening. He said we must rise early in the morning, and he would take us for a long day going down the river to where his brother is a chief

In the morning, getting ready for this journey, there was a delay while he rejected what Richard tried to give him as presents. He said they were useless things, and he wanted much more. Richard showed him the little he still had in the boxes and said there was no more, but still the chief argued. He went so far as to summon his slaves to come with muskets, but he gave in when Richard showed him how all of us were holding guns or swords, ready to use them. Then we were able to set off, with the chief following us in a smaller canoe, but in the afternoon events separated us from him. As we passed a village a man wearing an English soldier's jacket hailed us in English, calling out repeatedly,' Hallo, Englishman, you come here.' We had to obey and found ourselves in a place called Adamugu, where we also found other men in English clothes and speaking a little English. We must be getting near the coast now. The man who called to us first is said to be a messenger form Bonny, here to buy some slaves for his king. There is also a Nupe man who speaks some Hausa.

This chief is much pleasanter than the one from the last village, from whom we have become separated. He says he is very pleased to see white men for the first time, and he will do all he can to help us. All the people want to see the white men too, and they have come in such numbers that poor Richard and Mr. John have to get the chief to push them back, so that they can get some air to breathe. Remembering the trouble and scares we have had in refusing to wait for crowds to go to Bokwa Market, the brothers accept the chief's advice to stay a few days until another messenger comes from Bonny, where there are said to be several English ships.

While we are waiting there are two things in particular I am chosen to do. One is to shoot a bullock that the villagers bring in from the bush, which the chief is ready to give us for a feast if one of us will shoot it for them. Richard tells me to put two balls in a musket, and when I do this I manage to put it down with one shot. The villagers are happy and say they had not thought it possible to do that. The second thing is to plead with the chief, who is usually a kind man, when a young boy stole a cloth from him and was sentenced to death. The boy knows enough English to be able to ask Richard for us to plead for mercy. I tried my best, but the chief said that only a plea from a white man would be enough, so Mr. John took over my place and was successful. After meeting such kindness as wee have in this village all in our party have lost their fears. We had a further wait while most of the villagers went off to the Bokwa Market, but now after three days they have returned We are ready to go in our big canoe, which has been partly repaired at Adamugu, with all our heavy baggage, such as we still have, while Richard and Mr. John will get a smaller canoe from the chief to take them and a few things they want to keep near them.

Chapter 16 — Captivity… and Freedom

<u>November 1830</u>

I was put in charge of the large canoe, containing Jaudi, Antonio, my wives and the others, and nearly all of the baggage we still had. We had been at Adamugu for a week and the people have been so friendly that we feel no danger now. What people told us earlier about how wicked the people are down the river cannot be true. The chief, Aboko, is friendly and we have been given plenty of food. They show how much they want us to complete our journey safely Antonio can interpret what they say through his language, and we can also speak Hausa with a Muslim Malam from Nupe land who is a big man here. He has shown the chief and people of Adamugu that the white men are good people.

They have their own gods and spirits, and before we left their priests .made prayers and looked at the entrails of many chickens. Unfortunately, they said these all gave bad signs, and this continued through all their efforts. While they were busy, they gave us much palm wine and rum, making us very happy by the time we were able to leave By then it was starting to get dark in the evening. Richard and Mr. John stayed behind while the chief and his people prepared, with more fetish rituals, to say goodbye. They will follow me in a smaller canoe from Adamugu. This will only carry them, two boxes, some goats, elephant teeth and six slaves being sent as presents for the chief of Bonny, and the paddlers. It must have been fully dark when they could leave.

Other canoes came past as we went along. Just like the Bokwa Market, many were coming, a number together for safety, to the next big market at Kiri. I called out to them, to see if they had the brothers in their boats, but this was not so. Nobody tried to cause us any harm. We stopped well before reaching Kiri but Richard and Mr. John went past us, not seeing us in the dark, until they stopped nearer that place in the middle of the night. When dawn came I took our canoe on until I met them, and we waited, with many traders' canoes, until daybreak. Then Richard moved to join me in the big canoe, leaving Mr. John in the smaller one. Kiri is at a point on the river where a creek runs off to the right that goes to Benin. The market is held. on a sandbank nearby.

Before we reached Kiri what concerned those of us with Richard was that we had had no breakfast and were very hungry. He tried to cheer us into paddling hard by singing *Rule Britannia* and taking a paddle himself. What happened next was very confused and I could not see all of it clearly. There were many canoes coming to the market from all directions. Some are very large, with flags flying over them, including the British Union flag. Many men wore European clothing, except that they wore waist cloths instead of trousers, which only kings are allowed to wear. A number of big canoes came straight towards us, pointing muskets at us. They must be war canoes, with long guns in their bows. We did not have the strength to fight them. As they came up to us men in them leant over and started lifting the loads from our canoe and putting them in theirs. Richard prepared to shoot at them but three men grabbed his gun and then took off his jacket and shoes. A man took hold of my wife Miriamu and started to carry her off, but Richard and Jaudi seized her back, while I hit his head hard with a paddle and the fell in the water and was seen no more. After that there was a lot of struggle, more with our things than with us, which was very confused. Canoes crashed into other canoes and some people fell in the water. Soon we saw that all our stuff had been taken away, and we had nothing left. What had not fallen in the water was taken to the sandbank or island and piled up there.

Various people clamoured for our things, but they were in different groups. Some were shouting for us while others were against us. Those against us were coming up the river from the south. I do not know if they just wanted to steal and saw a chance to take goods from us, or if some may have had bad times with white captains and seamen at the coast, as sometimes happens, and this made them to be against us. From the north many traders had come from Funda and Kakunda directions, many of them Muslims speaking Hausa who came only to trade. They spoke for us and tried to control what the others did. Most of the women around also spoke for us, and they gave us plantains and other food to eat, the only food we had that day. The men of Kiri wanted to keep the peace of their market. Some from the south were also for us. One man spoke to Richard in English, took him into his canoe, sent three of his men to help paddle our canoe towards the market, and gave us some rum. The traders and canoe men from Adamugu were of course for peace, and were also losing some of their things to the attackers.

 It was midday before things started to settle down, by which time Richard and Mr. John had come together in one canoe. Men of the different groups were still arguing around our loads piled up on the island after being collected from different canoes. The Malams then took charge and called our party to land on the island and examine the loads lying there. Richard found some of his things, but many were missing. Nearly all of the clothes had gone after someone had cut open a bag holding them. Some books, guns and all the elephants' teeth given at Bussa and Wawa had gone. The cowries and things like needles that could be sold to obtain money were missing. Practically nothing of the goods belonging to those like me and Jaudi and the rest of our party was left. We were all sore and angry, but Richard tried to keep us cool by saying that he would make good the value of our lost things after we reached the coast.

Arguments went on around our goods in the market place for a long time. When some thieves tried to get at the goods taken back from them this nearly caused a fresh battle. Many people, including Richard, Mr. John and the rest of us ran to get into canoes again and stay out on the river away from further trouble. Eventually we were called back to the market place to be told what had been decided. The Kiri people look very fierce and they wear little clothing except animal skins round the waist, but they want to keep the peace of their market. They have put the leader of those who attacked us in irons, and sentenced him to death, as he had no authority from the chief for what he did. If he is not executed, they will not allow any canoes from his place to trade here again. The white men are declared prisoners, and tomorrow they will be taken to King Obi of the Igbos, so that he can decide what is to happen to them

Next morning we set off in our old canoe and the Adamugu canoe which was sunk in yesterday's struggles but has been raised up again. The Adamugu people have recovered the slaves they were taking to Bonny, and have been promised compensation for the clothing and elephants' teeth they lost. Six large war canoes escorted ours as we headed fast down the wide river, going south-west. Going along the river men keep their arms at hand. We spent a long time at a village where yams were bought by barter controlled by an elderly woman, no word being spoken by anyone, both parties grasping swords and other arms to prevent the other party doing them any harm. Well into the night we stopped and got a little food, the first we had eaten since leaving Adamugu, except for the small things kind women gave us during the troubles. The next morning progress was slowed by fog, and the river had branches going off it. Later we went on to the large town of Aboh with many houses.

Some large men with loud voices spoke to us there. One said his name was Mr. Gun, son of King Forday and brother of King Boy. Together with King Jacket they rule Brass town ahead of us. Mr. Gun said there is an English ship, the *Thomas,* there, trading for palm oil. Soon we were taken to see the King Obi at his palace. He is a youngish man who seems pleasant and shook hands and smiled with Richard and Mr. John. He has good clothes and wears many pieces of coral hanging from them. Mr. Gun., King Boy and the others were there. The Bonny messenger who had come with us from Adamugu told King Obi at length the whole story of our journey. After that we were happy to be given some yam and fish in palm oil. There was much talking among all the people there, and then the palaver was held over to the next day. This continued for several days. One day was mainly for the Adamugu people to tell King Obi of all their troubles and losses. Obi gave them some yams and said he would decide what else to do.

The next day the people from Bonny argued that we should be taken there, but there were more men from Brass, who said that is where we should go. We did not know of Brass before, but they say it is on the main river, while the stream to Bonny has dried up. Those from Bonny claim the Brass people want to sell us, but they could never themselves sell white men. The argument went on and on until late at night, but we could not follow properly what was said. Our interpreter Antonio was by now working with his own people from Bonny, and he did not give us a full account of what was being said by both sides. At the end King Obi said that was enough and he would give his decision tomorrow. All that was clear to me was that, whatever might be decided, there was going to be much to pay as a ransom

King Obi is always polite to Richard and Mr. John and each morning he shakes hands with them. During the arguments he does not say much. What he does not do is to send us enough food, only one chicken and a very few yams each day, and we are all very hungry. It is not a case of having a Fat Man stealing the food meant for us, as at

Katanga long ago, he just does not send us enough. We are still ten in our party. There are first Richard and Mr. John, then me, Jaudi, Ibrahim, Mina, and Sam, a seaman who has been with us throughout, then my wives Miriamu and the Kamberi girl from Yauri. Antonio is still with our party for feeding purposes. They are all complaining, and it is my job to try to keep them quiet. The other thing that worries us all is, what will happen to the black people in our party?. We are all free people now, but will King Obi try to make us slaves and sell us away?.

When the day came for Obi's decision I went with Mr. John, as Richard was not well enough. It was not easy to follow what King Obi said, as he spoke in their Igbo language, and Antonio was not being a good interpreter for us. I could make out that Obi said that the law made him the owner of us all, both white and black men, but he only asked that he should be paid in English goods up to the value of twenty slaves. He had heard that this could be done through the English ships at either Brass or Bonny. We will have to wait here until this is arranged. He also said that he would try to get back the things taken from us at Kiri, but doing this through another king with whom he is friendly will take time. He will compensate the people of Adamugu for what they have lost by giving them one or two slaves.

Mr. John had expected something better, that as we had not come to do them any harm, we should be allowed to go on without trouble, and he felt very low after this decision. He did not see that it would be possible to get such a large ransom from the English vessels. He tried to argue with the Obi, but he could not change his mind. When we left the palaver and went back to our place he and Richard talked together for hours. They could see no hope but in prayer to God. After such a long journey, with all the many difficulties they had overcome, now at this last step they could see no way to finish and go home. It would be not so bad if they still had cowries or needles and other things which they could use to get money and buy food for all of us, but even that had gone. We only had the good thought that at least King Obi did not speak of selling us.

These men here drink too much palm wine and rum, and each night they have wild parties outside our place, with loud noises and screams as if somebody was being attacked, but in fact they are just quarrelling amongst themselves. We do at least have some kind visits from a small, fat woman who comes in with a few friends and some slaves. They bring us some palm wine and bananas, which give us some pleasure each evening. She tries to talk with us, although she has little English. She is very kind, but this does not help us far.

The morning after King Obi had given his decision we went to his court again. We found King Boy, dressed in his best clothes and looking very pleased, talking with the Obi. What surprised me most was that there were some Bonny people there, and they were weeping. After some time King Obi told everyone in his own language what had been decided in his talk with King Boy. Everybody clapped in approval, and of course we wondered what it was all about. Then King Boy started to explain to us in as much English as he could find. He said that he, King Boy, would pay King Obi the goods demanded by him, as he expected that the captain of the brig *Thomas* then at Brass would pay him back. He would have considerable expense and trouble in taking us all to Brass and so, in addition to the value of 20 slaves to be paid to King Obi, he would also have to be paid fifteen slaves in value, and a cask of rum. If we would agree to this plan, then Richard must give him a bill on Captain Lake of the *Thomas* for the value of 35 slaves.

On hearing that they would go away from King Obi and be taken to Brass Richard and Mr. John almost danced with joy, and all the rest of us felt the world had changed for us too. They thanked King Boy many times over for his generosity and agreed to all he said. Richard at once wrote out the bill requested and gave it to King Boy but told him the captain would certainly expect to see us at his ship before he would agree to pay the bill. King Boy said he understood, and as he had the bill we could get ready to go to Brass at any time. King Obi saw how pleased everyone was, and he asked that a report on him as a good man should be made when the brothers return to England. Then we rushed back to where we were staying, prepared our few things, and took them over to King Boy's canoe, ready to set off.

Like many canoes here it is very large, with forty paddlers. By the time places had also been found for the ten of us and some people with King Boy, there must have been sixty people. In addition the canoe carries guns and cutlasses, boxes of rum, clothing and other goods and, filling all the remaining space, two thousand yams being taken for the master of a Spanish slaver at Brass. They are badly stacked and there is not enough room for everybody to lie down in any comfort. We had to wait till the next morning for King Boy to come aboard with his wife, a daughter of King Obi, who had not been at Brass up to now. Of course they got the best seats, after which Richard and Mr. John were seated, up against the stack of yams and mixed up with the legs and arms of King Boy and his wife. You can guess that it was not comfortable for the rest of us!

Like all rich women in this part King Boy's wife wears rings of elephants' teeth round her wrists and much bigger ones round her legs. It cannot be easy for them to walk around like this. She does not seem to know that putting her legs across Richard's chest, with all those big ivory rings on them, is a problem to him. Sometimes it makes it difficult for him even to breathe.

At least, we get food during this voyage, one meal in the morning and one in the evening, of yam and water. Each time King Boy and his wife eat first, having fish with their yam, and we move to allow them enough room to eat. King Boy always puts a little of the food and some drops of what they drink into the river for the spirits of the water.

We take three days on this journey from Aboh to Brass town. Before Aboh the river is two or three miles wide, with considerable banks along both sides. Above the banks are villages with fields of maize, other crops, yams and bananas and plantain. One branch of the river went off towards Benin. After Aboh further branches have gone off, either to our right or west, towards Benin, or the other way, to Bonny, and there are many small creeks too. The width of the main river has become smaller as we go on , and the side banks are lower. At some point we turned left into the creek going to Brass, and this is not wide. Instead of the banks of the river, we see swampy ground, jungle and mangrove bushes growing all along. There are hardly any fields or villages that we can see, and I think the people here live mainly on fish and on food bought from the Igbo land around Aboh. The mangrove swamps hold much mud and filth and they smell very strongly, and it is very dark going under or alongside the entangled mangrove roots and stems. As yet, we cannot see, hear or smell the sea, but there is some tide, we notice. On the third day we stop at an opening where we met canoes holding King Forday and Mr. Gun, who left Aboh a day before us.

While we had breakfast with them the tide went out and left our canoe on the mud.

After breakfast some fetish priests marked King Boy all over the body with chalk in lines, circles and other shapes A cap made of grass with long feathers was put on his head. King Forday explained, between drinking glasses of rum, that this is to keep off any bad spirits when white men have come down the river as never happened before. In the other canoes too the fetish priests have been marking people with chalk and dancing about. Mr Gun, as the military king of Brass Town, has kept firing the cannon in his canoe.

Coming into a bay we saw King Forday's town on one side and King Jacket's town on the other side, eighty yards apart. Cannons were fired all round and then we stopped near an island. King Boy called out as if asking some questions of the river god and, being satisfied, he and a fetish priest landed and went into a fetish hut, where they stayed a long time. Then we went to King Forday's town, where a crowd of people greeted us as we landed at King Boy's house. The town is swampy, dirty and poor but the house is quite large, with four separate living areas in it. It is made of wood, which could have come from some ship broken up When the tide comes in the water comes up to the walls. Much of the house is used for King Boy's many wives, and part to store tobacco, liquor and European goods. Richard and Mr. John have one room. Together with the rest of our party my wives and I are on a verandah outside. When we were coming down the river we had those two meals a day but here King Boy seems to allow us only half a small yam a day, with no palm oil. He may not have seen this, but on our second day here two of his wives gave us each some rum and four yams between us. If he knew, they could be in trouble. As always in Africa, it is the women who are very kind.

When coming to King Boy's house we were surprised to see another white man. We are told this is the master of the Spanish schooner that is here looking for slaves. He finds this difficult, and he is held up by some of his crew being sick with fever. He does not act like those Portuguese captains we met before at Badagry. It seems he is leaving here now to go, with his reduced crew, nearer to the river outlet, ready to sail away.

Or course we all want to get away to return to our homes, while King Boy wants to go to the *Thomas* to receive what he is to be paid. Next morning Richard set off with King Boy in his big canoe, taking with him Mina, the Bornu man, who speaks some English. It is a long day's journey to get to the brig, and the next day as well we had to wait for Kong Boy's canoe to return with Mina, Richard having stayed at the brig., . I had to stay behind with Mr. John and the rest of our party. We did not know whether we would see that everything is settled, or be troubled that things would be bad. As the canoe arrived we could have no doubt. Mina was looking very sad, and King Boy's face spoke of thunder and storms ahead. It was late when they arrived. Mina gave Mr. John a letter from his brother but said nothing. I thought I should not speak to Mina or say anything until either Mr John or King Boy tells us how things are.

King Boy went to his wives' quarter in the house, and soon you could hear him speaking to them in an angry voice. Then he came through to where Mr John was lying down. I was not present but King Boy's voice, which is always loud, was raised very high, and you could hear him everywhere. He could hardly speak for the force of his passion, as he snarled at Mr. John and then shouted, 'You are a thief man. You told me when with King Obi that the English captain will be happy to see me and will give me plenty of beef and rum. But this English captain no will. I paid much to bring you from King Obi's slavery. I brought you in my canoe and gave you yam and fish. I felt sorry for you and gave you clothing to cover your bodies. You are no good. You are a bloody thief man. The English captain no will.' He went on and on, cursing Mr John and his brother. Mr John said nothing until King Boy had said all his say, as he knew it was too true. Then he said that his brother's letter to him showed that when all of us are taken to the brig, Captain Lake says he will arrange for payment to King Boy, but he seemed very doubtful, although he did go away for now.

When I had a chance, or course I asked Mina what had happened when Richard and King Boy got to the brig *Thomas*. He said things were very bad there. Captain Lake was in a very serious illness with fever. Half of his crew of eight had died and most of the rest were not fit to do any work aboard the ship. The captain was only concerned about getting his ship out of the river. Mina thought that the captain and King Boy hated each other and must have quarrelled previously about trade. Richard told the captain how we had come down the river, then been captured but ransomed by King Boy against his being paid on a bill for 35 slaves. To this Captain Lake replied, 'You cannot take me for a bloody fool. This man is a scoundrel, and I will not give him a monkey's fuck for his bill.' I do not think Mina liked using these words, but he had to show me how Captain Lake dealt with King Boy. Nothing that Richard could say would make the captain more willing to help us by satisfying King Boy. While they were there the pilot called Louis, who brought in the *Thomas* three months earlier, came in and demanded payment. In the same manner, Captain Lake refused to pay him anything, and drove him away.

Mina said that while they were there Richard told Captain Lake that, although his party included two women, it also had two trained seamen, Sam and me, and several other men who could help in working the ship. This made the captain much readier to have us all come aboard. At the end Richard was left there on the brig while Mina came back with an extremely angry King Boy.

The next two days King Boy did not come to us at all. Mr. John sent the Adamugu people to go to Bonny to the east, with a letter for one of the English ships there, asking the captain to give these men some things as a reward for their efforts, to be repaid by the Government. Antonio went with them so that he could return to his people. Meanwhile we got our yams each day from the wives, and something extra from the head wife, as Mr. John had helped her with some medicine. We also got some plantains from some slave boys, as they did not want a risk that we might tell on them for stealing some of King Boy's tobacco, while his wives had the same reason for giving us some rum they had taken without permission. This was just as well, as I had been unable to stop our people once going to King Forday and complaining about how we feel starving.

One day was largely taken up with King Boy running wildly round the town nearly naked, with chalk marks put on him all over by the fetish priests. He was busy condemning one of King Forday's wives for adultery. The man involved killed himself with poison, to avoid a worse death, while she bravely accepted bring tied up with a weight on her leg, to be drowned in the river. The same day but not for this reason King Forday stopped being king and made Boy the full King. They all drank much rum on that day, and King Boy was in a good temper in the evening saying that we will all leave here the next day to go the brig.

It was four days since he had previously been to the brig and come back when King Boy set off in his big canoe, taking Mr John and some of his wives with him, while I was with all our party in a smaller canoe. I believe it was sixty miles to travel, but we stopped at some villages to get food. We made our way along creeks through mangrove swamps, but as we got nearer you could feel breezes, which later became a strong wind. We could tell the water was becoming more salty. We finally stopped at midnight in the river Nun, which is the main branch of the Niger or Kwara, where we could hear the sea. We had to spend the night anchored there, in sight of the brig and Spanish ship, seen by moonlight.

After calling at the Spanish ship, the crew of which was in very bad fever, we came to the *Thomas* in the morning, and we all went aboard. Captain Lake immediately made us go to the stern, where he had made Richard load and hide a number of muskets. At the bow was the ship's gun, also loaded. King Boy clearly saw that things were going to be bad for him, and he had no fight in him at all, having seen before what the Captain was like. Richard and Mr. John were clearly very sorry that they could not give him what they had promised but they could do nothing about it now. All they could do was to tell him they would see he was paid as soon as they could arrange it. He tried several times to plead with the captain to give him what was owed, but he raised his voice again and shouted at him, 'I no will, I tell you. I would not give you a bloody flint.' Then he demanded that King Boy give him back his mate, who had been captured some days earlier by men working for the pilot Louis as he was checking the depth of water at the river's bar. Louis was calling for payment of his pilotage fee before releasing him. From what I have heard, Louis has previously deliberately brought disaster on ships crossing the bar, in order to get hold of parts of the ships after they are broken up. Wrecked sailors have had their clothing taken from them and been left to starve. Captain Lake then threatened that if his mate was not returned he would call for the navy to come and burn down the town.

Captain Lake made signs of being ready to sail. The result was that King Boy left the ship, fearing that he would be carried away. Soon afterwards the mate was sent back to the ship. Meanwhile, in the Pilots' Town near the river entrance men watched the brig and got themselves ready to seize any parts of the ship or the people on it that might be washed ashore if the ship came to disaster.

Disaster seemed very probable. Where the river and the sea meet there is a bar which is always difficult to cross. A pilot normally takes ships in or out, but we were going without one, as Louis had been sent away. We started down the river towards the place over the bar, but we stopped when the breeze dropped. ~When this happened the forward weigh was lost, and we would be in danger of drifting into the large breakers to our right, on the west side. These came pounding over that side of the bar and on to the ship's deck. The captain dropped an anchor, which prevented our drifting, but the wind strained the anchor chain. We were stopped near the Pilots' Town and we feared attack from there. Louis was walking along and looking at the brig through his glass, together with men carrying muskets. We stayed in the same place all night, keeping watch on the men on shore. A ground swell lifted the ship up and down. We were all kept busy by the captain checking and adjusting the rigging. In the morning we moved on but soon had to anchor again, after the rescued mate had sounded the water at the bar and found it not deep enough to cross over safely. He put a buoy down at the best place to cross. Next morning the buoy could not be seen: it must have been washed away. Our hope of getting across left us as the wind failed us again and we were in danger of drifting, this time east to the breakers on that side. The ebb tide was running fast and putting the anchor chain under much strain. When the ebb ended the mate checked the depths again but found them still too shallow.

To cross the bar you must have a good current, which of course changes with the tides. You must also have a breeze, enough to give you control of the vessel and in the right direction, but not too strong against the ship. If the wind changes or drops suddenly, the boat can be in danger of drifting. With us, after a bad night at anchor, the force of the wind broke the windlass, leaving the anchor cable with nothing to hold it from running out. The crew and us together fixed the cable to ring-bolts on the deck, but almost at once the bolts were pulled right out from the deck by the force of the wind. Soon after that a big sea hit the ship so hard that the cable broke and the anchor was lost. The captain at once had the small anchor or kedge lowered and it just stopped us drifting onto the breakers, but it would not hold us for long.; Some crew members called out that everything was lost, but Captain Lake stayed firm, although breakers kept on crashing against the sides of the ship. We saw men ashore signalling to us to abandon the ship, but then we could expect no mercy from them.

On the captain's orders the crew and us slackened the sails and the force of the sea became less as the ebb tide ended, but the captain decided to put everything on to getting across the bar and out to sea. He was able to lower the ship's boat and Sam and I, together with two of the crew members, manned it with oars. The kedge was raised so that we were able to row and tow the boat towards the narrow space between the breakers and across the bar. This was hard for us but we managed. Just then the breeze dropped and we were in danger of drifting into the eastern breakers on our left. It was close work, with not more than a foot to spare, but our towing and the navigation by Captain Lake took us just clear of these breakers at the last moment, and we went over the bar, with a sucking sound.

At last we were safe, and we could all give thanks in our different ways for having escaped from a horrible death. I could tell that Richard and Mr. John felt very bad about how they could not repay King Boy, who had done much for us, bringing us from King Obi's down to Brass and then to the boat. In the end, he had accepted fairly quietly his own loss of what he had hoped to get. They also saw that Captain Lake, even if he had behaved badly, had shown very good seamanship in bringing his ship and all of us safely away from Brass and the Nun River. We had been together for a year with many problems and dangers, and now we could expect to reach our homes.

INTERLUDE

Captain Lake had intended to take us only to a Cameroon island but was persuaded to take us to Fernando Po island (then British administered but later recovered by Spain, now part of 'Equatorial Guinea) where we were well received. My companions and I could then part from Richard and Mr. John Lander, heartily wishing them *Sai wata rana* – Goodbye, 'Until another day', and make our way back to Cape Coast and our homes

Surprisingly, after six weeks the *Thomas* reappeared, with Captain Lake offering the brothers a passage, but they did not wish to put themselves in his power again and declined. When he sailed again he, in their own words, '…had not got more than a mile from the anchorage ,when a large vessel with long raking sails suddenly appeared from behind part of the island, and was seen in pursuit of him. We observed this vessel fire several guns at him, which at length made him take in sail We have no doubt that this vessel was a pirate, and our suspicions were confirmed the next day by seeing the two vessels becalmed close to each other. There was no sign of them next day, and we saw nothing more of the *Thomas*.' Indeed, it was never seen or heard of again.

Instead, the Landers sailed a week later on a voyage of eight weeks to Rio de Janeiro. Another ten weeks' sail brought them to Portsmouth, more than six months since they had escaped from the Nunn River. Some news slightly anticipated their arrival.

For his considerable achievement in making this journey and solving the 'Niger problem' Richard Lander received rather tepid congratulations form the Government, probably not helped by the disdain of John Barrow, and only the £100 promised to him , John nothing However, Richard did get a better job with the Customs, which he was later able to pass on to John. Where there was praise was with the learned societies and the newly founded Geographical Society (later Royal) awarded Richard its first ever Gold Medal The brothers made £1,000 for their joint Journal, published in

1832. There was interest from the Liverpool merchants, and soon Richard was involved in plans for what became both his and Pascoe's final enterprise, a commercial one, with Richard Lander as leader.

Chapter 17 —
On the Niger with Captain Lander

October 1832 – June 1833

This time I got some warning when Richard Lander was coming. As I was hoeing my farm at Cape Coast one day a brig anchored offshore, by name the *Columbine*. When some of the crew came ashore, a young man found where I lived and told me, 'Be ready to meet Mr. Richard Lander when he arrives here in a few days' time. He has sent me to tell you he is coming on his way to the River Niger, and he wants you to join him. There are two more vessels coming, the *Quorra* and the *Alburkah*. You must be ready for a surprise; for you will see that they are not like any ships you have seen before. Mr. Lander is the commander of this expedition, and now that the way is known into the Niger, they are coming to trade with the peoples who live along that river.' I thanked the young man for his news, and I ran home to prepare everybody for this arrival. They are all looking forward to seeing Richard again. Abuda and Miriamu agree that if Richard wants me to go with him, I should go, but they wonder if any woman can go this time. Jaudi, Ibrahim and Mina are also keen to go.

Some days later the *Quorra* and the *Alburkah* arrived. I met Richard who told me all about these ships. It is too little to say that I was surprised: I was knocked over when I saw the ships. They sailed in much faster than any other ship I knew, making a loud noise and with smoke coming from big pipes standing above the decks. They have a shape nearly like that of other ships, with decks and masts, but there is a big fire inside which makes steam. The steam shoots at big paddles on each side of the ship and these make the ship move through the water But some of the time they do not make steam, and then they sail just as ships have always done. When they need to make steam they burn coal which is dug from the ground or, if they do not have coal, then they burn wood. There are some of these ships being built now, he tells me, but most of them do not travel far. The *Alburkah* is the first such ship to sail right over to America, using its sails much of the time, as it could not carry enough coal to take it the whole way. Now these two ships have come all the way from England to Cape Coast. They have a shallow draught and should be able to sail up the Niger or *Kwara*. The brig *Columbine* will wait at the mouth of the Niger, the Nunn River, to receive the elephants' teeth or other items that may be bought and brought down the river. The *Quorra* is built with a lot of wood in it, but it still has this big fire, much more than a galley fire, inside it, and it is covered in iron. The *Alburkah* is made only of iron, except the decks.

First men made sails so that the wind can move ships without anybody having to use paddles. Now they are using steam to help the winds! This must be the last and best that any man can do. What more could anybody start to do to move ships? Hearts of oak I know about, but I do not understand how steam can push a big ship. If these ships have big fires inside, how is it that the vessels do not get burnt? Iron is heavy, as you can feel, but these ships do not sink in the water. How is this? What will happen when there is a storm and lighting comes out of the sky and hits the ships? It all seems very strange to an old seaman like me. I can only leave all this to men who know more than I do, and just use the fine things that they have made.

As that young man told me, Richard is now the Captain; perhaps I should say the Commodore of the squadron. He is not now a servant to anyone, but is our top man. He and I had some troubles in the past, but now I am ready to serve him, and to say 'Aye, aye, Captain'. to him. With him is a man called Mr. Laird, who built these boats and has sailed here with Richard. Captain Harries is the master of the *Quorra* and Captain Hill of the smaller *Alburkah*. There are doctors, men who can work the engines, white officers and seamen, and black men they have brought from Sierra Leone, called Krumen, and some men recruited at Cape Coast Mr. Laird is on the *Quorra* and I am with Richard on the *Alburkah* , cooking for him. We also have a naval officer, Lieutenant William Allen, who has come to make a chart of the river.

When we reached the mouth of the Nunn River we crossed the bar. It is easier now that we have a steam boat, as there is less danger of drifting on to the breakers,. although the strength of the ebb tide still gives trouble. The *Quorra* towed the *Columbine* across the bar. What was most worrying to us was to see that some of the white men on board were already suffering from the fever, rather like it was when Captain Clapperton's followers first came out. One man on our ships has died of it, and very soon Captain Harries and the engineer of the *Quorra* died too. Mr. Laird took control of that boat himself.

Going up the river, we found the trading brig *Susan* which has been here seven months, I hear, being unable to sail out of the river as so many of her crew have died. Richard has got from her captain his own Journal which was lost at Kiri. King Boy found it and he sold it to the captain, who also paid the ransom which he had demanded and that Richard and Mr. John had promised to pay but were unable to do so. He has sent a bill to the Government in London. I am glad this has been done, so that King Boy can be a friend to us. Indeed he soon showed himself to be this, along with his father, King Forday. Mr. Laird and Richard have also made presents to them, and King Boy is now happy. Our guide up the creeks from Brass to Aboh is another person we have met before, Louis, the pilot. Mosquitoes are very bad here, as we found before, all the way along the Niger. On the way the Krumen went ashore to cut wood for our fires, having used up the coal. This has to be done often.

The creeks later widened and we could see some villages on the banks. At one village we had a fight. People shot at us and the boats fired back and some men went ashore to burn the village. None of our people was hurt but we were not sure whether any of the villagers were killed or hurt. At first we thought King Boy might have planned this, but later Richard and Mr. Laird decided this was not so. The villagers may have thought we meant to do them injury. When we met King Boy he said that there was often trouble there, and his trade canoes pass there at night. At some other villages they said it was good we had burnt that place.

Before we reached Aboh some large canoes flying flags came to greet us and take us to meet King Obi. We were also given a gift of much food and palm oil. Of course we wanted to show him we are not now the weak, almost naked and starving men we were before when captured at Kiri and brought to him. Richard wore a general's uniform with a long ostrich feather reaching low towards the ground. Several white men wore army or naval uniforms. Even the Krumen had on kilts and velvet caps that Mr. Laird had brought for them. Jaudi, Mina and I wore soldiers' jackets and caps. We were therefore ready for meeting the king. He was finely dressed with many strings of corals round his neck and body and on his cap. It was a good palaver there, all the people of this large town coming happily to see us all again. King Boy was present and, when speaking to King Obi, he always knelt down and touched the ground with his forehead, to show that he recognised Obi as the king above him.

The king later came to visit the *Alburkah* with six of his wives. As Richard's cook I prepared food for them with help from the Krumen. After the two boats left Aboh we went into the wider Niger River, passing the places where the side branches go off to Benin to the west and Bonny to the south-east. A week later fever caught everyone by surprise. We had a few men who had died earlier, beginning with Captain Harries, but this was very bad, like how the gentlemen had died after coming with Captain Clapperton. In a week thirteen white men died on the *Quorra* and two men on the *Alburkah*. Those who were left alive were very ill and were either in their hammocks or just crawling round the deck. Captain Hill had to leave us on the *Alburkah* and move to the *Quorra* for a time, as there was nobody else able to take command there. He thought that ship had a link with the disease, and was relieved to come back only a day later although that was when he also fell ill. Richard then made the *Alburkah* tow the *Quorra* up to Adamugu. Most of the crew were unable to do their work, Dr. Briggs, the first Medical Officer, appeared near death ,and Mr. Laird was kept in his hammock for weeks. Richard was one of the very few who were quite well. Some of the crew were treated with quinine but it had little effect.

Another trouble we had was with the mosquitoes. They are always bad near water, and in this lower part of the Niger they are so many there is no preventing them biting you all the time. I think many people found it impossible to rest well at nights. This is a great nuisance, but mosquito bites do not kill you, do they? It seems to be the bad air from decayed tree branches, especially in the mangrove swamps, that give us trouble and cause sickness.

When we reached Adamugu we met again their chief, Aboko. He and his people had been so good to us when we visited there with Richard and Mr. John as we came down the Niger. As we learnt at that time, he is the junior brother to the Atta at Idah, a place we passed but did not visit then. Aboko told us how their father had been very powerful, stronger than the king of Funda, and very rich. Liking to keep his money to himself, he had it all buried with him when he died. The senior brother became the Atta, but was poor. Wanting to be rich, he decided that their father's wealth was useless lying in the ground. He had it all dug up and had their father's body also dug up. Aboko assembled people who were horrified by this and raised a revolt, but they were defeated. Since then the brothers had lived apart, the Atta in Idah and Aboko in Adamugu, and they had not spoken to each other. This is what we heard when we first came. Richard wanted to bring them together and make peace between them. He took Aboko in the vessel with him to Idah to meet the Atta in his town standing high up above the river He made the two brothers stand together, put their hands together and said that they are now friends and must remain so. I saw that neither the Atta nor Aboko said anything, and they did not look properly at each other. The Atta took back his hand and sat down alone. However, the people around all clapped when they saw the brothers together.

Mr. Laird was then very ill and could not go, but Richard went to the Atta's court several times with Captain Hill and Lieutenant Allen, hoping to do some trade for elephants' teeth. Around this time there was a big palaver near Idah, and I saw Mr. Allen watching it but not taking any part in it. The Atta was not there, and his brother Aboko was the head person there. He made a long speech in their language, using many words. He also made lively signs with his body and arms, and his speech was clear and strong. A man called Malam Catab then translated this into Hausa, speaking in the same way and making the same signs with his arms and body as Aboko had done. This showed that Aboko had said that they were all friends with the white men who had come to them, and they want to do a good trade with them. After that I had to interpret it again into English so that Richard, Lieutenant Allen and Captain Hill could understand. I think I did this correctly, but I did not use the kind of language or signs of the body as the previous speakers had used. I know that Aboko is a good friend but I am not sure of the Atta, whether he is truly a friend too. Afterwards I spoke to Richard in Hausa. I do not usually do this, but I wanted to be understood by him but not by the others. I said I was not certain of the Atta's friendship, and I had heard that he has a bad name among his people for being cruel and only interested in what he can get for himself. I suggested to Richard that we leave Idah and start trading higher up the river, and then come back to Idah later. I hope nobody overheard what I said, who can speak Hausa and tell the Atta about this. I know Richard did not like him. Once the Atta had two men brought in and he ordered that their throats be cut, right there in front of us. It was difficult for Richard to persuade him not to do this. I think the Atta is probably afraid of the white men, and wants to show them his power and strength.

After that Richard prepared to leave Idah, starting the engine of the *Quorra* and taking the *Alburkah* in tow. He went into Idah again to inform the Ata we were about to leave but could not find him, which annoyed him. As Richard was actually leaving, the Atta sent an elephant's tooth to him as a present, but Richard sent it back and said he came for trade and not for presents. The Atta did not like this, and a canoe came after us with Aboko and a message from the Atta asking us to go back for trade. However, Richard decided to go on and open trade with Koton Karfi and Funda, if we could get there. The Atta tried to stop us first by sending men in canoes to make a fetish in front of our boats. We took no notice, Then the Atta sent a large number of men in war canoes, intending to attack our boats. After some time they went away, seeing the size of our boats and the guns they both have.

We had done very little trade anywhere up to then, especially in elephants' teeth, although Richard thought we should get more later. Even when they could be found, we had few men in good health to do the trading and bring the teeth. But then we found a new problem in that nobody would sell us either elephants' teeth or any foodstuffs. We learnt that the Atta had sent messengers round all his villages forbidding anyone selling us anything at all, or they would be taken straight away to Idah and have their heads cut off. This was serious, and we soon ran short of things we could eat. Richard sent a message to the Atta saying he must decide whether to be friends or to make war. If it was to be war, then we should burn their towns, though it would be difficult to do that with Idah because it is so high above the river. The Atta decided it would be best for him to be friends. He sent his messengers again to the villages and told them they could now trade with us. After that it became easier for us to get food and some elephants' teeth, but after some time things went back again, especially up where the Alburkah is. That is near where the River Benue comes into the Niger, the *Quorra* being further south of there. Richard was then moving between the two ships as nobody was well enough to take command. Mr. Allen, Captain Hill and Dr. Briggs all had times when they were very ill. Mr. Allen once looked near death, and his fever got so bad that he became mad for a time. Seizing a knife off a table he stabbed me. A Kruman took hold of him and, with my help, made him lie down on his hammock and be quiet. It was only a cut in my arm, which soon healed. When Mr. Allen recovered he told me he was very sorry for what he hd done. I knew it was not his fault, and I did not hold this against him. Mr Laird was a good friend of Dr. Briggs, so he was made very sad when Dr. Briggs died.

We had come again to the area we saw when going down the river, where there are high hills on both sides. Some places are shallow and will stay like this until when the main flood comes down the river. The *Quorra* became stuck on a sandbank, lying on its side. All our efforts to get it off were unsuccessful, and it was decided to wait for the flood to raise the level of the river. This is once a year, and it is not yet due. Once Richard tried to go up the river towards Raba but there was not enough water. With the *Quorra* beached on its sandbank and the water generally low we could not easily move very far, but Mr. Laird decided it might be good for his health and useful if he could go up the River Benue to Funda, which nobody has visited yet. He arranged for the pinnace of the *Quorra* to be fitted up so that he could go in it. It was difficult for him to get into the boat in his bad state of health but they managed it and they set off. We wonder if we will see him alive again. Since he left we have heard a little news of him but we have seen no more of him up to now.

When Mr. Laird sometimes came across from the *Quorra* to the *Alburkah* I know that he appreciated my cooking, just as Captain Clapperton used to do. He said so once, and although he does not eat much, I notice that he is always the first to take a second helping. I have heard him and Richard arguing about the poor trading position. He clearly thinks Richard has claimed too much about the amount of elephants' teeth and other things that they can buy, and he asks if it will get any better. I think he would like to command the whole expedition, or perhaps to go home, as he has talked of doing after visiting Funda. Sometimes I speak with Richard about places we have visited or that we are near, and tell him what I think of these places or their chiefs. He even asks me what I think. I believe that Mr. Laird does not like this and he thinks that as I am not an officer, it is not for me to give an opinion on these things. Richard himself seems glad to have my views. He and I know more of this river and its peoples than anybody else, and what I say can help him. In our early days together he would simply give me orders, as he was uncertain of his position. By now, he knows he can rely on me. He is more certain of his powers, even making threats of war against hostile chiefs, and ordering naval punishments with lashings for Krumen who do not do their duties properly. He has become an officer, which I am not, but I think he sees me now as a petty officer who is necessary to him.

Richard sent me in a canoe to go down the river to sort out a complaint about the *Columbine*. He had received a message from King Jacket saying that with it standing there flying the Union Jack, it is keeping traders away, by which he means of course the slave traders. I had not gone far when he called me back, as he had decided to go himself to the coast. He especially waned to take Captain Hill there, as fresh air might save his life, or he can be sent on to Fernando Po to see the doctor there. Richard himself has dysentery. He will probably bring back the second Medical Officer, Surgeon Oldfield, who has been on the *Columbine* all this time, to replace Dr. Briggs, Another reason for his going is that I know he has heard that his wife Ann is expecting a second child, to join Harriet, and he may hope to get news at the coast. Until now the *Quorra* is on a sandbank south of where the River Benue joins the Niger. The *Alburkah* is five miles to the north, near the river junction. Richard has asked Lieutenant Allen to take charge of this smaller vessel, and he left me there to be the cook and interpreter to him and the few other members of crew that remain after Mr. Laird and he have taken some away. I am pleased to be with Mr. Allen, as I know him to be a good naval officer and a pleasant man. Richard has been away nearly two months now, and I expect he will return soon. Things are quiet here and nobody is trying to cause us any trouble. The Atta is allowing people to trade with our ships. Even though Richard and Mr. Laird are both absent, I to not think the Atta will do anything bad to us

We are moored not far from a town that is under Idah. On a high bank thrown up round a bend in the river, Malam Catab has his house, and he invited me and any of the crew who would like to come to visit him. Ibrahim and three of the Krumen came with me. This is the man who translated what Aboko had said at that palaver into Hausa. I asked him if he knew the town of Zangon Katab which I had been to with Richard: that was after Captain Clapperton's death, when we were going from Kano to, as we hoped, Funda, and again when we were made to turn back and go to Zaria. 'Yes,' he said, 'that is my home town.' After that we had a good talk about all the places we had been to and the difficulties we had met on our journeys. Then he gave us some good food which we enjoyed. He asked us to visit him again before long, and we were happy to agree. The second time we went he gave us good food again, and he had managed to get some rum brought up from the coast. 'Of course I may not drink this, because of my religion, but I know how sailors depend on this drink, so go ahead and enjoy it.' That is what he told us, and once more we ate, drank and had a good time. He said to us that we are very fortunate to have such a good commander as Mr. Lander, and also to have Mr. Laird with us. He said that everyone praised them and is glad they have come. He hopes we shall have good trading with them, and a safe return home. On a third visit he made very tasty foofoo and plenty of it. I was very hungry then, and I ate a lot of it, with great pleasure. He also had more rum for us, and I must admit that I drank a lot of that too. As before, he talked like a good friend, and said things we had to agree with. After all that, I felt very heavy in my head, and all I could think of was to go over some of the journeys I had made with Richard, their troubles and joys. Just before I went to sleep I happened to remember our visit to Bussa, and how good the kind queen there had been to us. I also remembered how she had more than once warned us to be careful not to eat food cooked by people we did not know well.

DEATH OF PASCOE

Pascoe probably died shortly before 19th June 1833, when Laird arrived back from Funda and heard of the death during his absence. After eating heartily of the poisoned food, it is said that on returning on board he complained of pain in his stomach and soon expired. Ibrahim ate little and survived. Three Krumen who were with Pascoe died after showing similar symptoms, probably suffering lingering deaths. On 18th July, the day after the last death, Surgeon Oldfield, newly arrived with Lander from the coast, found the body being sewn into a shroud for burial by his fellow Krumen. The man was reported to have felt indisposed for some time, with a burning sensation in the pit of his stomach, thirst, debility and occasional involuntary stools. Some of the body was discoloured, swollen and with a ghastly, livid and appalling appearance. Oldfield saw that a dark coloured liquid was oozing from each angle of the mouth. The Krumen adamantly refused his making any *post mortem* but he managed to peel back the cloth from round his head. Oldfield 'strongly suspected that the poor fellow died from ulceration of the stomach, having swallowed something of a poisonous and deleterious nature.'

The previous day Lander challenged the Atta over a report he had heard that Pascoe and the others had been poisoned, but the Atta denied all knowledge of it. However, six months later, on 21st January 1834, the Atta told Oldfield 'that he had caused poison to be administered to poor old Pascoe.' He accused Pascoe of being the cause of the boats going up the river and giving all the best gifts to Funda and Koton Karfi, not to him. He said one of his eunuchs heard Pascoe tell Mr. Lander in Hausa to get away directly, as he (the Atta) was not good, and his heart turned particularly against Pascoe. Oldfield was quite astonished at the open avowal of all these atrocities.

On 4th May 1834 Malam Catab boarded the *Alburkah* and gave some food gifts to Surgeon Oldfield who, after referring in his account to Catab's reputation as the Atta's poisoner, said, 'In order to alarm him, I told him that I heard he was going to do me an injury by poisoning me, and threatened that if I had any reason to suspect him of putting (poison) into anything he sent to me, I would instantly shoot him. He said that no Malam in the country had (poison) which would cause death, but I replied that I knew this to be false, and instanced the death of poor Pascoe.'

The bodies of Pascoe, the three Krumen who died similar deaths, and a European sailor with an unrelated death, were buried on the lower slopes of a hill then named by the Scotsman Macgregor Laird as Stirling Hill, near the confluence of the Niger and Benue rivers.

Afterword

Pascoe must have started his naval life somewhere in Africa but how he entered the Navy remains a mystery. Admiralty Clerk John Evans said he volunteered in 1808 for a ship called the *Little Belt* which was then on its maiden voyage to Cape Coast. After a month there she returned to England, then going to Halifax in Canada. She later had a scrap with an American warship six months before war was officially declared in 1812, was damaged but sailed back to England, and then disappeared totally from the official records. Pascoe was never listed on her, and indeed on that maiden voyage nobody was added to the list outside Britain. It is possible that Evans was misled by a vague indication of date from Pascoe.

From 1811 to 1813 a squadron of four main ships and perhaps some smaller ones under Captain Irby was acting under instructions from London that a recent treaty provided for action against Portuguese slaving ships outside recognised Portuguese ports, as recorded in Hugh Thomas, *The Atlantic Slave Trade* pp.574-6. A number of Portuguese ships were seized until repeated protests from Lisbon led to the squadron being called off. The rescued slaves were sent on the captured ships with prize crews,, not their captors' ships, to Freetown. There they became 'prizes to the British Crown' and were subsequently encouraged to enlist either in the West India Regiment or the Navy, but few seem to have chosen the latter. Lander's account of Pascoe having been enslaved and then rescued seems quite plausible, as few people would admit freely to having been enslaved. Some support to his having had contact with this squadron is given by one Muster List in 1821 showing him as having been then ten years at sea, but on the other hand his place of birth was always shown as either Africa or Cape Coast, never Freetown which would have been the obvious place to enlist if this slavery- and -rescue account was correct. An officer in Irby's squadron killed in an action with a French privateer in 1813 was called Lieutenant William Pascoe, perhaps his main rescuer from the slave ship. It seems a reasonable conjecture, as shown in this book, that he was already in the navy under a different name and he changed it between voyages to the dead lieutenant's name, something not unparalleled among freed slaves in Sierra Leone.

Most of the places named are readily identifiable, but archaeologists have found little trace of old Oyo or Katanga, even its famous walls, due to rapid decay in the wet climate. On their visit there in 1830, the two brothers correctly assessed the declining society's passivity in the face of growing Fulani pressure. Dr. Samuel Johnson's 'The History of the Yorubas' (1921), though vague on dates, shows that a resounding defeat came soon afterwards. A new Oyo was built much further south. The old site is in miles of uninhabited bush. Kubli hill on the brothers' route from Kaiama to Bussa still points up but the town has vanished. A large area round it, perhaps seventy miles across, now includes the Borgu Game Reserve and is devoid of people. On the lower Niger the markets of Bokwa and Kiri, to which many people from all directions went on known market days in large numbers for protection, seem to have vanished long ago. I could find no trace of any recollection of Clapperton, Lander or the Widow Zuma in Borgu. However, the area of *rimi* trees near Zaria that Clapperton commented on still exists 180 years later, although being thinned as more land is used for farming, and I *did* once hear a saying roughly equivalent to that quoted about Zaria. Badagry, never attractive, gained a better reputation as the base for the first Christian mission in modern Nigeria.

When the Lander brothers did solve the Niger question on Richard's second journey John Barrow conceded only that they had found the conclusion of the river seen by Mungo Park, but said that it could not be the true Niger as reported by the ancient writers, as it went across Africa to join the Nile.

. One can sympathise with him earlier being, one imagines, bleary-eyed when struggling to edit Clapperton's scrawl in penny notebooks but I think he was very unfair in calling him uneducated and complaining of a lack of descriptive purple passages in his Journal. This contained only preliminary notes set down while he carried the whole administrative burden of the expedition as helpers dropped around him, being more often than not unwell himself, Clapperton was strong in his sense of duty but he does seem to have been low on imagination, for example not appreciating the Yoruba 'talking drums', which the Lander brothers did later appreciate. He was also weak on political understanding. He failed to grasp Sultan Bello's hint – masked as an alleged opinion from Bornu (unlikely at that time)– that between Clapperton's first and second visits to him he had become more suspicious of British intentions, based on information from Mecca pilgrimage sources showing how their original handful of traders in India had swarmed to become the almost total rulers there. Clapperton also failed to understand that his own pressure to be allowed to visit Bornu, which was hammering at the gates of Kano and threatening to engulf a major and prosperous part of the Sultan's domains, could have appeared to the Sultan rather as a proposal to go on a Grand Tour through Napoleon's Europe might have appeared to William Pitt and his successors in Britain.

Sultan Bello showed himself as being far-sighted Knowing that the British were powerful, able to project themselves over thousands of miles of ocean to India, and foreseeing that they might one day try to do the same in his country(as indeed happened eighty years later) he carefully avoided antagonising them. He used guile rather than the force he could have used to get Clapperton's companions and belongings brought up to Sokoto for examination. He overlooked Clapperton's abusive words towards him. Although he saw Pascoe's potential benefit to him (a capable seaman, speaking English) he reluctantly let Lander take him away, at least temporarily. He also agreed to pay Lander for goods he had exacted from him. .

Lander deserved the description 'The Indomitable Servant' in his biography by Mercedes Mackay. In his own book Lander described himself as 'the only surviving member of the expedition', but officially both he and Pascoe had throughout been personally-engaged private servants, paid by their masters. Only retrospectively did Lander become a 'member' of the expedition when the Colonial Office, pondering what should be paid to whom, and having received a letter from Clapperton when living and heard what he had said on his deathbed, decided Lander should be deemed successor to Columbus who had been officially a part of the expedition but had died very early on (see Chapter 4), and paid the balance of his rather meagre salary. Pascoe did not receive any such benefit.

Lander cannot be blamed for two deficiencies at the end of his canoe voyage down the Niger with his brother. The circumstances of their capture and subsequent escape prevented them paying King Boy the ransom promised him, but the British Government accepted the liability and paid it before Lander's final voyage. Secondly, the Journal he wrote from Badagry up to his capture was then lost. It was recovered by King Boy and returned, and it is now held by the Wellcome Library of the History of Medicine, London. It appears to have been affected by rain rather than immersion in the river. The nautical handbook of Mungo Park's that the Lander brothers saw at Bussa but did not take was also recovered later and is in the Library of the Royal Geographical Society in London. The silver medal that the Lander brothers presented to the ruler of Bussa is still held by his successor, the Emir

Richard Lander's book and that written by the two brothers jointly are full of useful information but it may be said that the extensive Hausa vocabulary printed with Richard's book after he had been using the language for a year is much inferior in quality to the efforts of Admiralty Clerk John Evans who never visited the country. Lander's spelling in English was peculiar, e.g. 'whas' for 'was', and 'hask' for 'ask'. His persistent use of a distorted form of the name 'Pascoe', with no first name ever hinted at, apparently aimed at creating a distance between them. It owed nothing to any African origin for the name, which clearly came from his time in the British Navy. Lander was familiar with the name Pascoe from his native Cornwall, including his own teacher at the school he somewhat intermittently attended.

The 1832-4 expedition involving Richard Lander, Laird and Pascoe was an almost total disaster, the only positive features being Allen's charting of the river, and the first British visits up the river Benue to Funda and beyond. It was riven at the top by dissension between a Lander possibly out of his depth and a Laird wishing he had the command himself. The steamships *Quorra* and *Alburkah* ended being beached and left to rot in Fernando Po. Any minimal commercial proceeds would have been limited to whatever Laird might have carried on the *Columbine* which he took and sailed back to Britain. Worst of all was the casualty list. Of the 47 Europeans on the two steamers only 8 survived: such was the frequency of the 'crossings of the bar', in the euphemism for death which became common in Victorian missionary circles. Richard Lander was the sole casualty in hostilities, getting a musket ball during a fracas on the lower Niger near his anus, which could not be removed, and dying in Fernando Po aged just under 30. (His son Richard, born while he was on the Niger, died almost coincidentally). Some men died from dysentery, but the majority from malarial fever. Its cause was not yet known, and oddly nobody seems to have used mosquito nets even just for comfort. The use of quinine for treatment was known, but apparently not its prophylactic use.

A few barely survived to continue active lives. Macgregor Laird started a transatlantic shipping line and sent the first ship to go to America on steam power alone. Twenty years later he financed a much more successful expedition to the Niger which established Lokoja at the confluence of the rivers Benue and Niger. William Allen, then a Commander, went with Commander Trotter up the Niger again in 1840 and survived once more in spite of a bad death toll. Surgeon Oldfield's Journal shows that exceptionally he had no serious illness at all on the river.

Losses among the *Columbine* crew and the non-European men generally were not fully detailed, but certainly some occurred, as well as Pascoe and the three Krumen being poisoned.

King Boy on the whole comes out rather well in this narrative, but it would be difficult to find any positive word about the Atta of Igala at Idah at that time, unlike his brother Aboko.

To go back to the clashes of evidence between Richard Lander and John Evans set out in Chapter 1 - first, where was he born? Katsina (as in Evans) appears correct. The deciding factor, in my judgment, is his naming King Agu Raji as king of Katsina at the time he left there, shown in a king list as ruling from 1788 to 1802, the second ruler before the Fulani jihad began in 1804. It remains quite plausible that Pascoe later moved to Gobir, with which place Lander associated him, and frequently went south on trading trips.

How old was he? If he was 16 when leaving Katsina, then from the king list that puts his birth date back to between 1772 and 1786, making him probably between 40 and a little over 50 years old when Lander first knew him in 1825-6, not 60 or more as Lander judged him to be then. . It can be difficult to judge the age of somebody of unfamiliar appearance. Clapperton and others frequently referred unspecific ally to 'old Pascoe' as did Lieutenant William Allen when he made the only known picture of Pascoe, 'The Palaver', based on an incident in 1832, in his 1840 book 'Picturesque Views of the River Niger.' Unfortunately he did not identify the persons there, but whichever he was he hardly appears as a man then 66 or more as he would have been on Lander's reckoning. I would split the difference between Lander and Evans on age at, say, 45 in 1826 or just over 50 in 1832

As regards character, it is unlikely t hat Pascoe would have claimed to be either a hero or a paragon. However, telling a preposterous story, or even obscuring something embarrassing in one's past, is not necessarily an offence. He was evidently an active womaniser, although on the second journey with the Lander brothers he seems to have been a model husband to his then wife, who stayed permanently with him. . Pascoe seems to have had a 'clean' naval record.

After fifteen years on the lower deck, he does not seem to have become like the Badagry people as John Lander found them, 'many of the inhabitants have picked up a number of English words, which children and schoolboys at home would term 'very naughty' and these are made use of at all times without any particular meaning being attached to them. It was an achievement becoming skilled in European-style cooking. As a man not registered at Greenwich a a pensioner, he was not eligible to be a ship's cook, and the opportunities for individual cooking on a warship were very limited, yet he became a personal cook to an experienced captain for three years. Both Cl;apperton and Laird later appreciated his cooking, but Lander never mentioned this. It is not the only omission on his part. . It seems inconceivable that Pascoe and the women with them would have stood passively by and not raised a finger apart from lamenting, when Lander had to undergo his poison ordeal at Badagry, as implied in Lander's writings' Lander specifically recruited him for the 1830 and 1832 expeditions, on which he was evidently found invaluable and given some responsibility. Even with no trace of his having been literate he comes through as having intelligence and sound sense 'above his station', as they might have said at that time.

  Pascoe clearly did have trouble with Richard Lander early on (never, it seems, with his brother, and in the Journal of the two brothers going down the Niger references to

Pascoe were as favourable as are shown in this book). We have only Richard Lander's account of the trouble, lacking any explanation of *why* it happened, a gap made good in this book, consistently with what Lander in fact recorded. Probably Lander's account is true in itself, and possibly 'nothing but the truth', but not the *whole* truth. When Clapperton went from Kano to Sokoto alone leaving Lander and Pascoe behind, he probably assumed (as did Lander) that Lander would be in charge but, there is no sign that he left any clear instructions. Lander, the pub landlord's son who had ever only been a servant, was probably savouring his first-ever little taste of authority, with Pascoe increasingly rebelling against what he could have seen as a fellow-servant trying to boss him about. One was the Captain's cook and the other his valet, and who was superior in a status-conscious society? Overall there seems little ground to reject the basically favourable evaluation of John Evans, even though he had only a few months' acquaintance with him.

Any doubt that Lander's Journal and book have substantial omissions should be removed by the following letter I found at a late date in the Colonial Office records:

> To W. Hay, Colonial Office –
> I suppose you are acquainted with the conduct of Pasko, who was taken by the late Captain Pearce from the *Ranger,* to proceed with him into

the interior of Africa, and after his death retained by the late Captain Clapperton as his Cook. He was to receive a seaman's pay, and provisions and grog money, during the time he should be absent from England. He was discharged by my late Master at Soccatoo for his behaviour, but retaken when I myself, being very ill, was unable to pay proper attention to his urgent and many needs. On his deathbed Captain Clapperton solemnly forgave his past conduct and promised that it should be forgotten*. It was in virtue of this declaration that Pasko continued to remain in my service and return with me to England after his lamented death, much against the wishes of Sultan Bello, who did all he could to prevent his leaving Soccatoo and would by no means have given his permission to depart, until I had first protested he should be sent back on my arrival at Kano*. On my journey to the coast I found nothing to complain of in Pasko's behaviour. He at all times rendered the most essential services, giving quick, prompt answers to the interrogations of the Kings and Chiefs who were suspicious of our motives for visiting the Fulatahs (Fulani), with whom they were at war, when the least hesitation might have been the means of having my head severed from my body.

That is not all. When desperately ill with fever and dysentery, and quite blind Pasko paid the utmost attention to me, and was the means, under Divine Providence, of my preservance from a miserable death, and of the safety of the papers committed to my care.

Under these considerations, Sir, I hope you will overlook, as my Master did, his past conduct which, from the known conduct of the African race, every allowance is to be made, and send him to Cape Coast, where he has left his wife and friends.

I remain, Sir, with the greatest respect,
Your most humble servant,
Richard Lander

- Items not carried out by Lander, as also with his further promise at Kano to return Pascoe from Kulfo.

(Note appended- Mr. Barrow agrees to give him a few pounds to sail back.)

This seems a positive letter, but it is Richard Lander who is the mystery. In his own Journal and book, mentions of Pascoe's attentions to himself when sick are low-key and do not suggest Pascoe's saving him from death. Lander's few references to only two rulers who challenged him (at Kaiama and Katanga), on the return journey from Sokoto, about their having gone to visit the Fulani ,never imply any threat at all to Lander's own safety, and Pascoe's having intervened to save him from any such danger is simply never suggested. These were major omissions indeed. Why did he subsequently recruit Pascoe twice more to go with him? Why should he, who generally wrote objectively, put on permanent record in his book such a one-sided and negative account of Pascoe? Did his publishers, even then, or somebody else, press him, in the modern term, to 'sex-up' his writings? Or could he not finally make up his own mind as to what he did think, as with his misspelling of Pascoe's name (making it either 'Pasko' or 'Paskoe'?) Or what? In my opinion belated justice should be done to Abubakar, William Pascoe, who made a good life for himself in spite of many difficulties. However, he never clearly showed that he was closely related to the rulers of Gobir and this remains an open question.

Hausa Glossary

BATURE European, white man (plural TURAWA)

BATUREN GABAS Arab or Moor (lit. White man from the East)

MALAM Learned [person (nowadays, equivalent to Mister)

SARKI King, Chief

MARMATA Eunuch

SHEGIYA Bastard (female)

KARUWA Harlot (female)

BARAUNIYA Thief (female)

YARO Boy

WAWA Fool

MAGUZAWA Non-Muslim Hausa (lit. Those who run away)

TSOPHO Old man (woman) (fem. TSOHUWA)

GULBI River

RUWA Water

DADI Pleasure or sweetness

BAKI Dark or black

BIRNI Walled town or city

KATANGA Mud wall, walled city (particularly used of Old Oyo)

RIMI Bombax tree, producing silk-cotton or kapok

KUKA Baobab tree

KOSAI Bean cake

ZUMA Honey

TUWO A staple Hausa food, resembling porridge

ALBARKA A blessing, gift from God

GYARA Benefit, improvement

HABA! Exclamation – 'come, come' or indicating doubt or rejection

SAI WATA RANA Goodbye (lit. Until another day)

BUSSANCI The language of Bussa (names of languages usually end in 'nci')

WORDS IN BUSSANCI (properly BISAGWE)

DOH One

PLA Two

PINGI All

Appendix 1 —
Unknown Report by John Evans on Hausaland in Nigeria and Pascoe in 1823

Hausa country comprises several of the northern states in Nigeria, whose main peoples speak the Hausa language. Some of these states have been known to outsiders since the time of Leo Afriicanus in the 16th century, though only under the collective name of Hausa (at first Housa or Houssa) from 1790. Unified for the first time in the *jihad* started by Usman dan Fodio in 1804 and continued by his son and successor Sultan Mohammed Bello, it was conquered by the British in the early 20th century and became a major part of the Protectorate of Northern Nigeria, some years later absorbed into a unified Nigeria.

This presents new evidence on this country in the shape of a 15 manuscript page report which the author found in the naval section of the British National Archives (formerly Public Record Office) by whose permission it is published. Written in 1823, it had lain probably unseen for over 170 years. It is reproduced here verbatim, including numbered footnotes in the original.

'A short Account of Houssa, a Kingdom in the interior of Africa, situated on the Banks of the Niger. obtained from Abou Bouker, alias William Pasco, a native of that Country and a Seaman now belonging to H.M.S Owen Glendower Commander Sir Robert Mends Capn, Coast of Africa April 1823, drawn up by John Evans Admiralty Clerk.

'Since the establishment of the Association for exploring the interior of Africa, a considerable degree of curiosity has been manifested by the Public respecting that Continent. The Abolition of the Slave Trade served further to increase this, and affected the views and interests of a great part of the Nation. By this event the accent of commerce was turned into another Channel; and our Merchants became desirous of knowing the productions, and whether any Trade could be carried on, that would indemnify them for the loss of that inhuman traffick, which for centuries had been the principal object of their speculations The Philanthropists, having overcome the greatest obstacle to the civilization of this unfortunate country, wished to become acquainted with the manners and customs of the Negro Nations in order to facilitate their conversion to Christianity, and Men of Science confidently hoped that the time was not far distant, when the great Problem in African Geography 'the course and termination of the Niger,' would be fully solved

'It is a discouraging fact that very little solid information on these points has been obtained, since the death of the adventurous Park. It is true that the Public are daily amused with a variety of fictitious Narratives and Pamphlets One, pretending to be a correct description of <u>Timbuctoo,</u> obtained of an Arab of undoubted veracity, and another despising the obstacles presented by Inland seas and rivers, Forests and Deserts, gives a minute account of a journey from Mecca across the continent to the Ocean. One author learnedly demonstrates the identity of the Nile and Niger, while another with equal modesty concludes that the termination of this celebrated river must be the Congo.

'The following Narrative is however widely different from these contemptible productions; the person from whom it was obtained is a Native of Kashni. He speaks our language sufficiently to enable him to explain his ideas with facility and the veracity of his account cannot be doubted. This alone is sufficient to claim for it the preference with those who are desirous of forming correct ideas of the state of the interior of Africa.

'Abou Boukar is apparently about 34 years of age, and was born at Bernin Kashni the capital of Houssa. (1) This city is one of the largest in the interior of Africa. He represents it as being twenty times larger than Sierra Leone. It is situated in the midst of a vast plain, about one hundred miles distant from the banks of the Niger in a Northerly direction.(2) The Waters of the River overflow over the face of the country in the last months of the periodical rains. This inundation is of the greatest benefit to the Rice, which is the chief food of the inhabitants, but it sometimes injures the plantations of Indian Corn and Yams. The houses are generally built of stone and but of one story high. The Market is held three times a week throughout the Year. It is resorted by a great number of white Men, called by his countrymen 'Tura Angubus.'(3) They wear cloths round their heads and have long beards. These Men supply the people of Houssa with Salt, which they bring from a distant country on the backs of Camels, and are paid for it with shell money, or <u>Cowries,</u> which is the circulating medium of the country. He has seen dollars with these white men, but not in the same manner as at Sierra Leone.

'The country produces Rice, Indian Corn and Yams. Their fruits are Grapes, Figs, Apples, Peaches, Lemons and Oranges. He never saw Cocoa Nuts before he came to the Sea. (4) They make no Wine but extract a strong spirit, which is their favourite liquor, from Indian Corn. Their domestic Animals are Sheep, Oxen, Camels and Horses, the latter being very numerous.

'He describes the King's palace as be(ing) as large as Sierra Leone. He who reigned when Pasco left his country, was called Agou Rag. He has a very large Army, both of Horses and Foot .Their Arms consist chiefly of Spears, Bows and Arrows, fire arms not being in general use. Elephants are used for carrying the baggage when the Army takes the field.

'Their Religion is Mahommedanism. The Priests are very numerous, and the number of Mosques in Bernin Kashni amounts to fifty. The ceremony of circumcision is of course practised on all the Males who are also marked with parallel lines from the ear to the mouth. Polygamy is permitted to the greatest extent, so that as Abou Boukar expresses it, 'More Wife one Man have, more Gentleman he be.'

'They manufacture a species of coarse narrow cotton cloth. Gold is found among the hills in small solid lumps, which they dispose of to the white men chiefly in exchange for Salt. A great number of Slaves are annually forwarded by Caravans towards the Coast, and one great Article of their Commerce is the Coola Nut (5) the use of which seems to be universal among the Negroes of Northern Africa. It is procured by the People of Kashni in a country called Gunja to the South of the River on the route towards the Coast.

'The town next in size to the capital in Houssa is Bernin Hiatawa. About one day's journey to the Westward from Kashni is situated a town called Zulimi, inhabited by white Men with beards and long hair. They are called Fullani. (6) These people he represents as very warlike but dwelling in huts constructed of Mud and the Branches of trees, and frequently shifting their place of abode. The other towns with which he is acquainted are thus situated towards the Sun setting from Kashni. Zangfara in Houssa is three days' journey, and two days' journey from this last place is Alkali, the capital of a country called Gober (7)_, which is built on each side of a large river; and has resisted all the attempts of the King of Houssa to take it. He does not seem to be acquainted with the countries to the Eastward, but states that his Grandfather (whom he represents by an expression common to the Negroes, when they want to give an idea of the power or courage of a person) as 'One Hell of a fellow' has often been to Bernin Bornou, which is fifteen days' journey from Bernin Kashni, towards the Sunrising. Doura is halfway between the two places. Bernin Bornou is considerably larger than Kashni and the people speak a different language from the people of Houssa.

'Abou Bouker left his country and his friends about the year 1805, when sixteen years of age, and joined a caravan of Merchants proceeding to the Southward. Some to procure Coola Nuts in Gunja, and others to sell Slaves to the people who carry them to the Sea Coast. The company consisted to about forty persons, the greater number of whom was mounted on Asses or Mules. Their rate of travelling did not exceed 25 Miles per day, as they rested at night time and for several hours during the greatest heat of the Sun. In the villages where they stopped for the night houses were provided for their accommodation and food brought them free of expense. They were often obliged to admit the Asses and Mules under the same roof as themselves, to protect them against the Wolves, which were very numerous.

'Four days after leaving Bernin Kashni they crossed a large River called <u>Kouara Luwan Dadi</u> , i.e. river of fresh water. (8) They passed over it in Canoes, and the breadth of it at that place is greater than that of the Gambia at St. Mary's. The water of this river is not fit for drinking being muddy and full of Insects. It flows to the right of the Sun-rising and comes from the country of Gober.

'Pursuing the route to the Southward, in five days after leaving the Kouara Luwan Dadi, they arrived on the banks of another river, deeper and broader than it, called '<u>Gulbi Gagari</u> (9) which runs through the countries of <u>Guari</u> and <u>Nouffi.</u> He is of opinion from what he has been told in his country, that these two rivers join into one stream at <u>Zugum</u> near Kaba, and that it afterwards proceeds on to Bernin <u>Bornou</u>, where it is very wide, The water has a strong saline taste, and the river abounds in Hippopotami and Alligators.

They crossed it at a place called Affo, and each person paid three cowries for this passage over

'Continuing to proceed on a Southerly direction after several days travelling they came in sight of a range of high mountains One of them called Wasony (?) (10) is much higher than the rest. The top of it is white like Marble, and in appearance it greatly resembles Fogo, one of the Cape de Verd Islands. They observed here a great number of Eagles.

"About a week after leaving these Mountains, they discovered the Sea from the summit of some high hills, and descending they crossed a small river called 'Eco' (11). They continued their route from this in the direction of the setting sun, having the Sea in sight at intervals_on the left hand, and in ten days arrived at Annambon and Cape Coast. Here Abou Bouker took the Christian name of William Pasco and entered on the Little Belt Man of War, with the determination of following the Sea, a resolution denoting no small degree of boldness in a young Man arrived from the Interior of Africa, and beholding that Element for the first time. He has since continued in His Majesty's Service, but he expresses a great desire to revisit his Native Country, especially since he has been informed by some Slaves (12) natives of Kashni captured last year by the Iphigenia, that a young woman to whom he was attached, and who had been betrothed to him, is still single, having refused several advantageous offers, firmly believing that the object of her early affections would one day return and claim her as his bride. This instance of female constancy and (sic) to which few parallels can be found in more polished regions. It must however be confessed by all those who have the pleasure of his acquaintance, that Abou Bouker, by his good qualities, is fully deserving of such an attachment and in order that his <u>Dulcinea</u> may not be disappointed he states it to be his intention, when the Ship shall have been paid off, to return to Houssa, taking the route of the Gunja Country from Cape Coast.

'The Ancient Geographers it appears were much better acquainted with the interior of Africa, north of the Equator, than we are even to this day. Herodotus and after him Ptolemy described the Niger as flowing from West to East, and Park in our tine found this to be the fact by observation, although the Arabian and the Portuguese writers had given to it a contrary direction. This adventurous Traveller ascertained the course of that celebrated River from near its source as far as Timbuctoo, and since his death the question has been as to whether the same river flows on to Kashni and Bornou, or whether it loses itself in the swamps and lakes of Wangara agreeably to the Hypothesis established by Major Rennell.

'Wangara is supposed to be situated South of the countries between Timbuctoo and Houssa. The name is totally unknown to our Informant. It has never been clearly described to any Traveller, and its existence, except as a name on the maps, is more than doubtful

'All the evidence obtained from the Moors and Negroes by Travellers, who have penetrated to the Southward from the Barbary States tends to prove that the River seen at Timbuctoo and Bornou is the same. The most authentic account on this point is that given by Hadje Hamet to Mr. Ritchie (see Note No.7). The preceding Narrative strongly corroborates it and as we have previously observed, this coincidence of information derived from quarters so opposed proves beyond a doubt the course of the Niger from Timbuctoo as far as Bornou, beyond which it is again involved in obscurity – and as nothing certain respecting its termination is known by our informant, we will not by making conjectures on the subject, add to the number of those, who, as D'Anville expresses it, 'abusent du vaste champ que l'interieur d'Afrique leur lasse ouvert (?).'

'We cannot however refrain from remarking, that in our opinion, more valuable information may be obtained from Natives of Houssa and Bornou, who have been brought into the Colony of Sierra Leone, than has been collected by all the Travellers, who have attempted to penetrate into the Interior of Africa from the Shores of the Mediterranean.

'The expedition under Major Gray, which was three years without getting further than upper Senegal, and which it is said cost Government upwards of £30,000 – proves the inutility of attempting to advance with a body of Men from that quarter. Would it not be worth the experiment to educate some of the many Natives of the Banks of the Niger who are brought young into the Colony, with a view of inducing them to travel into those unknown regions from which no white man has hitherto returned. The Narrative of Abou Bouker shows with what facility travellers may proceed from our settlements on the Gold Coast to Kashni and Bornou, and the hopes of a Moderate reward would induce them to return and communicate the result of their observations. Were an enterprise of this nature to be set on foot under the patronage of the present Governor in Chief, who has already done so much for the civilization of Africa, we should confidently anticipate, in a short time,. a greater advancement in our Geographical knowledge of that continent than has been made this last Century, and that the ultimate result would be, the discovery of the termination of the Niger.'

(Note in a different hand): 'Abou Bouker has been discharged to accompany the celebrated Belzoni on his travels towards the Niger'

'(1) Houssa is the name of the Kingdom' and not of a town as is generally supposed. Kashni is the capital and Bernin signifies 'Town' in the language of the country. Thus they say Bernin Kashni, Bernin Bornou &c

'(2) Kashni in most of the maps is represented as built on the banks of the River but its real location is four days journey from it.

'(3) The Moors.

'(4) Cocoa Nuts are however plentiful at Timbuctoo as appears from the information obtained from a Native of that City by Mr. Ritchie & from the narrative of Adams, an American Sailor who was shipwrecked on the coast of Barbary & carried as a Slave into the interior. Botanists have decided that this fruit could not (sic) thrive only in the vicinity of the Sea Coast and the circumstance of their being seen in Houssa confirms this opinion and impeaches the veracity of Adams and Mr. Ritchie's information

'. (5)Great quantities of this Nut are offered for Sale in the Market of Sierra Leone. The Mandingoes and Foulahs use it constantly, and they will travel for three or four days without any other sustenance than the juice of it, which is of a bitter taste, but not disagreeably so. '(6). These must be the Felllata Bedouins, mentioned by Burkhardt, Ritchie & other Travellers_as being very powerful in the countries on the Banks of the Niger westward of Bornou, and according to accounts given by Hadje Hamet a native of Bernin Bornou to the latter gentleman. Bello, a chief of this tribe, has lately made himself master of Kashni and subjugated all the neighbouring Countries.' (7) Hadje Hamet informed Mr. Ritchie 'that he had been at Timbuctoo when young and believed the distance from Timbuctoo to be about 28 days journey, and from Bornou about 45 days. The places are Gober, Zanfara, Nyffe, Zegzeg, Melli and Fouta, but he did not know their respective distances from each other Abou Bouker describes the three first mentioned places as being on the Gulbi, the name given to the Niger in Houssa, and the coincidence of information derived from sources so opposite places it beyond a doubt that the Joliba of Park flows on from Timbuctoo through Houssa to Bornou where we are again left to conjecture. '(8).The Kouara Luwan Dadi appears to be a branch of the Niger. '(9) This is the Main stream of the Niger, which comes from Timbuctoo through Alkali the Capital of Gober, flows through Zanfara, Nouffe & Guari to Zugum, where the Kouara Luwan Dadi joins it and proceeds to Bernin Bornou. Mr Ritchie's informant Hadje Hamet says 'five days to the

Westward of Gano is <u>Kashni </u>where the River is about one mile broad. It is here called the <u>Gulbi.</u>' Extracted from the Quarterly Review.

'(10) Probably part of the great Central Belt which Geographers have affirmed as stretching across that Continent, and called in the Maps the Kong Mountains or Mountains of the Moon.

'(11)The River Lagos of the Portuguese, from which hundreds of Abou Bouker's unfortunate Countrymen are annually shipped for the New World. '.<u> (12)</u>They were captured off Lagos in a small Portuguese vessel of 100 Tons. In the hold of this miserable coffin were crammed one hundred and eighty seven human beings, the greater part of whom were heavily chained, and all were suffering tortures from the confinement and want of air. By the prompt and humane attentions of Commodore Sir R. Mends they were released from this dreadful situation. Ninety of the Men who suffered most were immediately removed to the Iphigenia and proper regulations were adopted for ameliorating the condition of those who remained. The former became in a short time reconciled to the Ship & evinced their gratitude for the kind treatment they experienced by every means in their power. They cheerfully assisted the Seamen in their work & every evening when the weather was fine they would amuse the Officers and Ship's Company with their Songs and dances and exhibiting various feats of agility. They were chiefly Mahometans from Houssa and the adjacent countries. The names of Aladdin, Hamet, Sadi and Selim were common among them. Yet in the face of these facts the Miscreant who commanded the Esperanza had the villainy to declare before the Court of Mixed Commission at Sierra Leone that he had shipped the Slaves at Maloumba, a place six degrees Southward of the Line where not the slightest traces of Mahometanism are to be found. But this abominable perjury did not avail him, the case was too clear and the sentence of the Judges condemned his vessel and emancipated the unfortunate Captives.'

To elucidate certain points in the report, 'Kashni' was a mistaken earlier form of the name for Katsina which, before the *jihad* began in 1804, had been probably the most powerful of the several Hausa states, but there had not then been any single 'Kingdom of Hausa.' A reference in the document to 'the King of Hausa' meant the Fulani *jihad* leader, Sultan Mohammed Bello, mentioned in the text, who then dominated the Hausa states, but his rule was incomplete, as is shown by the reference to the continued struggle with Gobir (this also applied to Katsina). The Fulani in general and the Arabs with their paler skins, were regarded locally as 'white men', and the name for Arabs in Hausa is 'Turawan Gabas' meaning 'white men from the east.' As with other Hausa expressions given by Evans, although he could have had no reference books to guide him, they are all perfectly recognisable in spite of later developments in orthography, more so than the attempts of succeeding explorers up to Barth. Concerning 'Wangara', see Bovill's 'The Golden Trade of the Moors,' second edition, Chapter 14. There was a ruler of Katsina called Agu Raji, two rulers before the *jihad*. References to Sierra Leone as a place mean Freetown. The reason for the captured Portuguese slaver's argument in Footnote (12) is tat a treaty then applicable between Britain and Portugal had outlawed slave catching north but not south of the equator. Some points in Evans's account seem inaccurate, such as saying that most houses in Katsina were built of stone, but relatively little could be questioned in it. It is difficult to reconstruct the caravan route followed by Pascoe from Katsina down to Cape Coast. They seem to have avoided Katanga or Oyo, and possibly went rather westwards, then due south across Borgu to the Yoruba hills near Shaki, then down to Lagos, and finally along the coast to Cape Coast, but this is very uncertain. Cape Coast is about 350 miles west of Badagry and Freetown in Sierra

Leone is about another 900 miles west. St Mary's was the principal town on the River Gambia, later renamed Bathurst, and now Banjul.

Appendix 2 —
How the Author
Discovered Evans's Report

It does not appear that the document quoted above has previously been known. In summary, European exploration of Africa had by 1823 reached a tantalising stage where both the main questions of the day, the nature of Timbuktu and the termination of the River Niger were still unknown. The writer John Evans, Admiralty Clerk, was clearly an intelligent, well-educated man (then aged 25), but not otherwise known, sufficiently informed on this subject to be able to comment both trenchantly and sensibly on the controversies of the day. He made an excellent suggestion that young Hausas or other Africans then in Sierra Leone (as freed slaves) could be educated and induced to go back to their native countries and bring information on them, rather than sending expensive expeditions from abroad, a proposal that seems never to have been taken up

Having published a life of Mungo Park in 1979, the author was trying to find out more about the last days of the erstwhile explorer Giovanni Belzoni, who died near Benin, Nigeria, in 1823. Moving from Italy to England twenty years previously, he had been successively a hydrological engineer, then when lacking funds an actor representing Samson and Hercules (being a large and strong man) in London and elsewhere, and a pioneering Egyptologist. He had gone to Egypt in an unsuccessful attempt to interest the Khedive in machines for irrigating the banks of the Nile, and had there been enthused by the Swiss traveller Burkhardt into archaeology. Among other things he had been the first to find some Pharaohs' tombs in the Valley of the Kings, a low-level entry to the Great Pyramid of Cheops, and then a way into the great temples of Ramses II at Abu Simbel by removing most of the 3,000-year accumulation of sand across the entrances. It was known that Belzoni, taking up Burkhart's unfulfilled ambition to visit Timbuktu, tried to get there first by going over the desert from Morocco, and when an initial permission had been withdrawn, by sea to Benin, but it was not clear how he had done so.

In *The Times* of London, the author found an entry dated 26 April 1824 praising a Captain Filmore for permitting a native of Hausa then serving on his ship to be discharged in order to accompany Belzoni The help of a friend, the late Ken Breen, who had taught History at St. Mary's College, Twickenham, and had a strong interest in naval matters of that period, led to a box file "Letters from Captains F 1823", No.ADM'/1/1815 in the National Archives. It included a substantial report by Captain Filmore on his naval duties which at the end said that his vessel had conveyed the celebrated Belzoni from Tenerife to Benin. Attached were the actual letters exchanged between Belzoni and Filmore and, as an unexpected bonus, the report now cited. Almost certainly John Evans had brought Belzoni and Filmore together as he knew there was available an English- speaking Hausa man who might accompany Belzoni. Thus Pascoe (the spelling is variable) made his first trip with a European explorer. After Belzoni died, still near Benin, Pascoe went back into the navy. Filmore's report with this document was forwarded to the Admiralty in October 1823, six months after Evans had written the document in question, by which time Filmore had assumed the command after the death of Captain Sir Robert Mends, and Evans was no longer serving on the same ship. What became of him later is not known.

By October 1823, therefore, there was much information on written record about both Hausa land and Evans's chief informant, Abubakar or William Pascoe, but it was known to very few and very soon lost to sight as it was never published until now. In succeeding years much more became known as is shown in this book.

On a second journey the explorer Clapperton died at Sokoto but his valet Lander managed to get home, taking his cook Pascoe with him. Both Clapperton and Lander wrote Journals containing much information about Hausa land, and with many references to Pascoe. Lander also wrote his own book, published in 1827, in which there is a considerable account of Pascoe, depicted rather scathingly as at best a likeable rogue, saying he showed 'low cunning', with 'some evil' in him. They were certainly not on good terms when away from Clapperton, with Lander claiming that Pascoe had run away from him three times and stolen some of his goods. Clapperton and, it seems, an official local messenger with them, sided with Lander, but it is very noticeable that Lander twice subsequently deliberately recruited Pascoe to go with him on other journeys, and apparently found him to be very useful.

Evans's and Lander's accounts were written several years apart, and there is no reason to think there was any contact between them, or that they were even aware of each other. Now that the two accounts can be brought together it is very striking what astonishing discrepancies there are between them as shown in chapter 1.

There can be no doubt that these were independently expressed opinions on the same man. There is much to be said either way. The author's considered opinion is that while Lander may have spoken the truth and even perhaps nothing but truth, it was not the whole truth.